Adventures in
CARAVANASTAN

Adventures in CARAVANASTAN
Around Australia at 80ks

GREG BEARUP

A William Heinemann book
Published by Random House Australia Pty Ltd
Level 3, 100 Pacific Highway, North Sydney NSW 2060
www.randomhouse.com.au

First published by William Heinemann in 2009

Copyright © Greg Bearup 2009

The moral right of the author has been asserted.

All rights reserved. No part of this book may be reproduced or transmitted by any person or entity, including internet search engines or retailers, in any form or by any means, electronic or mechanical, including photocopying (except under the statutory exceptions provisions of the Australian *Copyright Act 1968*), recording, scanning or by any information storage and retrieval system without the prior written permission of Random House Australia.

Addresses for companies within the Random House Group can be found at
www.randomhouse.com.au/offices

National Library of Australia
Cataloguing-in-Publication Entry

 Bearup, Greg.
 Adventures in Caravanastan.

 ISBN 978 1 74166 629 8 (pbk).

 Bearup, Greg – Travel.
 Automobile trailers – Australia.
 Travel trailers – Australia.
 Australia – Description and travel – Anecdotes.

 919.4

Cover design by Design by Committee
Caravan photograph courtesy Getty Images
Caravan drawing by Michael Fitzjames
Maps by Odette Odisho
Internal design by Midland Typesetters, Australia
Typeset by Midland Typesetters, Australia
Printed and bound by Griffin Press, South Australia

Thanks to the following: the Random House Group for permission to quote from *Pobby and Dingan* by Ben Rice, published by Jonathan Cape; Les Murray for allowing me to use his poems; John Butler and Rob Hirst for allowing me to quote lyrics; and the ABC for permission to use various quotes.

Random House Australia uses papers that are natural, renewable and recyclable products and made from wood grown in sustainable forests. The logging and manufacturing processes are expected to conform to the environmental regulations of the country of origin.

10 9 8 7 6 5 4 3 2 1

To my darling Lisa,
for your passion, your integrity and your
Katharine Hepburn cheekbones.

This trip would not have been possible without the generous support of Volvo and Jayco. Thank you, in particular, to Laurissa Mirabelli and Todd Hallenbeck at Volvo and Andrew Ryan at Jayco.

Prologue

Our silver all-wheel drive is broken down in a metre of muddy water which is infested with crocodiles, probably the saltwater variety and if not, then the freshwater lot. Who can tell? We are in the outback of Western Australia, in the middle of a wide brown Kimberley creek. Water is seeping in through the floor. It is pooling, oddly, in only one spot – behind the driver's seat. Lisa is laughing that excited laugh that masks anxiety. Our 18-month-old son, Joe, is desperately trying to crawl out the window to go for a swim. He hasn't been this excited since he discovered escalators in Cairns. 'Wah-ta! Wah-ta! Wah-ta!' he shouts, as if I hadn't noticed. I am getting more and more angry and annoyed. I have no one to blame but myself.

I suggest climbing out through the window and wading to the bank. 'Are you mad?' warns Lisa, as she reads the words printed in bold at the bottom of a pamphlet she'd been given earlier. '**You are in crocodile country. No swimming unless otherwise stated.**' It is not otherwise stated so we sit and wait, and with good reason. In the past few days, the airwaves have been abuzz with news from Cooktown where 62-year-old Arthur Booker was last seen alive walking along the Endeavour River to check his crab pots. His camera and watch were eventually found next to an ominous slide mark leading into the murky waters.

So, how did we get to this?

Lisa, Joe and I have been on the road for the past eight months. We've driven 30,000 kilometres on a trip that's taken us from Tasmania to the Torres Strait, Cairns to Kununurra, all the while living in a caravan – a space no bigger than an average bathroom.

It had all seemed so romantic as we chatted with comfortable friends over comfortable dinners in our comfortable house in Sydney's inner west. We would travel around Australia for a year enjoying the time with our son, seeking out interesting people and issues to write about – putting together a collection of stories about Australia and Australians. Lisa, a broadcast journalist, would take a camera and possibly file a few stories for SBS, and Joe would be saved from childcare for another year. I had been approached by a publisher and the idea had taken on a life of its own. *Adventures in Caravanastan* was born.

As we prepared to leave, dozens of people told us they hoped to do the same trip one day. It's like the Australian Haj – a pilgrimage, a duty, to be undertaken at least once in a lifetime. Our friend Lucian, who was born in a mud hut in Tanzania, reckons he would have a hard time explaining caravanning to his friends back in Africa. 'Although, maybe the Masai would get it,' he said as he helped us pack up our furniture.

Lisa and I had both spent time living and working overseas, most recently a three-year stint in Pakistan and Afghanistan. Like many 30-something Australians, we had seen a lot of the world but not much of our own country – Australia was for later. Lisa can talk for hours about the pitfalls of propping up dictators in Pakistan or how often the Americans bombed Laos during the Secret War but, before this trip, she would have been hard pressed to point to the Kimberley on a map.

Years earlier, at a café in Dubrovnik, we had made a solemn promise to each other: we would never have a boring life together. This is part of the deal. This trip would connect us with the land of our birth but, most of all, we wanted it to be an adventure.

We found sponsors. Volvo generously – some at this point might say foolishly – loaned us a vehicle. Jayco loaned us a caravan. I took leave from my job. The year leading up to our departure had been all about getting to the point of taking off, with little thought given to what lay ahead. Like a pair of bank robbers we had planned the job meticulously but didn't know what would happen after we had jumped the counter with the cash.

We had set off in the getaway car, albeit a getaway car with airbags in every crevice and a five-star safety rating. The cops were nowhere to be seen. Joe was in the back seat gurgling with happiness, all blond hair, blue eyes and big smiles, like some Nazi experiment gone right. At the beginning, he had been a willing accomplice.

And now, here we are, stuck in a creek with reptiles that have survived an ice age lurking just the other side of the cream leather upholstery.

It was a disaster that had unfolded in slow motion.

'Do you think it's safe?' Lisa asked as we approached the water.

It was a wide creek, but it didn't look deep and we had passed through others safely. Ordinarily, I'd have taken off my shoes and walked across first, to check the depth, but with crocodiles that was not an option. Besides, if it was dangerous or too deep there would be a warning sign, surely.

'It'll be right,' I said dismissively.

I eased the car into the creek. It was a little deeper than I had expected, about knee-high. A small wave formed in front of the vehicle, and all was going well until we were a bit over halfway. Suddenly, there was an unexpected dip. I panicked, just a little, and accelerated ever so slightly.

My acceleration caused the sleek nose of the Volvo to cut into the creek, pushing a small film of water gently up the bonnet. I willed it to change direction, like a golfer urging a wayward putt, but it had a mind of its own. A ripple disappeared into the back of the diesel motor. The engine stalled. Silence.

Things were bad at this point, I later learned, but they may not have been terminal. My next move was akin to taking a wooden stake and driving it through the heart of our ailing Swedish beauty. It didn't seem so violent at the time. I didn't even have to turn a key. I just had to push the snazzy ignition button. The motor whirred hopefully and it seemed like it would start, but then ... nothing. Death came quietly. The engine simply took a last breath and then no more.

Before we set off on this trip Lisa and I had argued about the need for a satellite phone. I thought it a ridiculous waste of money – middle-class overkill. People used to do what we are doing in a Kingswood, I'd claim. Lisa thought my resistance was irresponsible, especially after my little sister, Jenny, had spooked her on the eve of our departure. Jenny loves a good medical horror story and will leave no detail out, regardless of how gory or intimate it may be; my brother-in-law's piles, the size of grapes apparently, are famous throughout northern New South Wales.

Lisa sat engrossed as Jenny told the true story of her friend who had been travelling around Australia with a little boy when he decided to do a pee in a remote creek. Some freakish tropical creature bit the poor kid on the penis and he went into convulsions. It was very serious and his life was only saved, my sister insisted, because his parents had a satellite phone and could call in the flying doctors. Lisa could not get this story out of her mind. I am sure she had nightmares of our little Joe writhing in agony with a horribly distended penis, at death's door because I was too tight to buy a satellite phone.

The phone had remained a source of tension until some kindly show people, who had invited us to camp behind their Dagwood Dog stand in central Queensland, insisted on lending us theirs for our crossing of the Tanami Desert. Sensible Lisa had won out in the end.

Today, the satellite phone, our only link to the outside world, is fully charged, ready for use and safely locked away in our caravan, 100 kilometres away in Kununurra.

And so we sit and wait . . . and wait.

There's plenty of time for contemplation, and, unlike Burke and Wills, lack of water is not an issue.

When we set off, our aim was to see the country, the 'real Australia', yet in many ways our trip has been a discovery of the un-Australians. Despite the stereotypes of outback larrikins and rugged bushmen, 90 per cent of Australians have little to do with the vast parts of the country that don't hug the coast or centre on our major cities. Your typical Australian owns a house within 30 kilometres of the beach, works in middle management and is building a nest egg for the kids' education. Clancy would be appalled. Our trip has been about meeting the other 10 per cent who choose to live out here, beyond the city limits.

The land that we have discovered is more interesting than we ever imagined; who knew that native people still feasted on dugong and turtle in the north of Australia, or that the nomadic show people, who travel with their amusements from country show to country show, trace their ancestry back to the Romany circus people of Europe?

One of the first people we met on our trip was the poet Les Murray. I wanted to talk to him about the things that have shaped his view of Australia. Les writes beautiful poetry but he has a somewhat gloomy view of the nation. He told us over lunch that the beauty of the country was often his consolation for dealing with the people.

For us it has been the opposite. The land is undoubtedly spectacular, but it is the people who have sustained us.

We've met opal miners in Lightning Ridge, octopus hunters in Torres Strait and people who dive for abalone in Tasmania. We've interviewed some fabulous characters: artists and hippies and a reclusive former brain surgeon who's now translating ancient Chinese poetry on an island off Tasmania. We've even been on the road with the ageing night club singer, Jade Hurley. The people we have met have become our consolation for living in a space six paces long and two paces wide.

These people have often drawn our attention to the two great issues facing modern Australia – the environment and the plight of Aborigines.

For the moment, though, we have more pressing problems to contemplate, like how to get out of this creek.

I try the motor again. Nothing. Our regular mobile phones blink mockingly – *no signal, no signal*.

'Wah-ta, Daddy,' says Joe. 'Wah-ta. Wah-ta. Wah-ta, Daddy.'

Suddenly, dealing with the Taliban in Pakistan and unexploded ordnance in Laos don't seem like such bad options when compared with being eaten alive by a crocodile.

'Well, darling,' says Lisa. 'It's certainly not boring.'

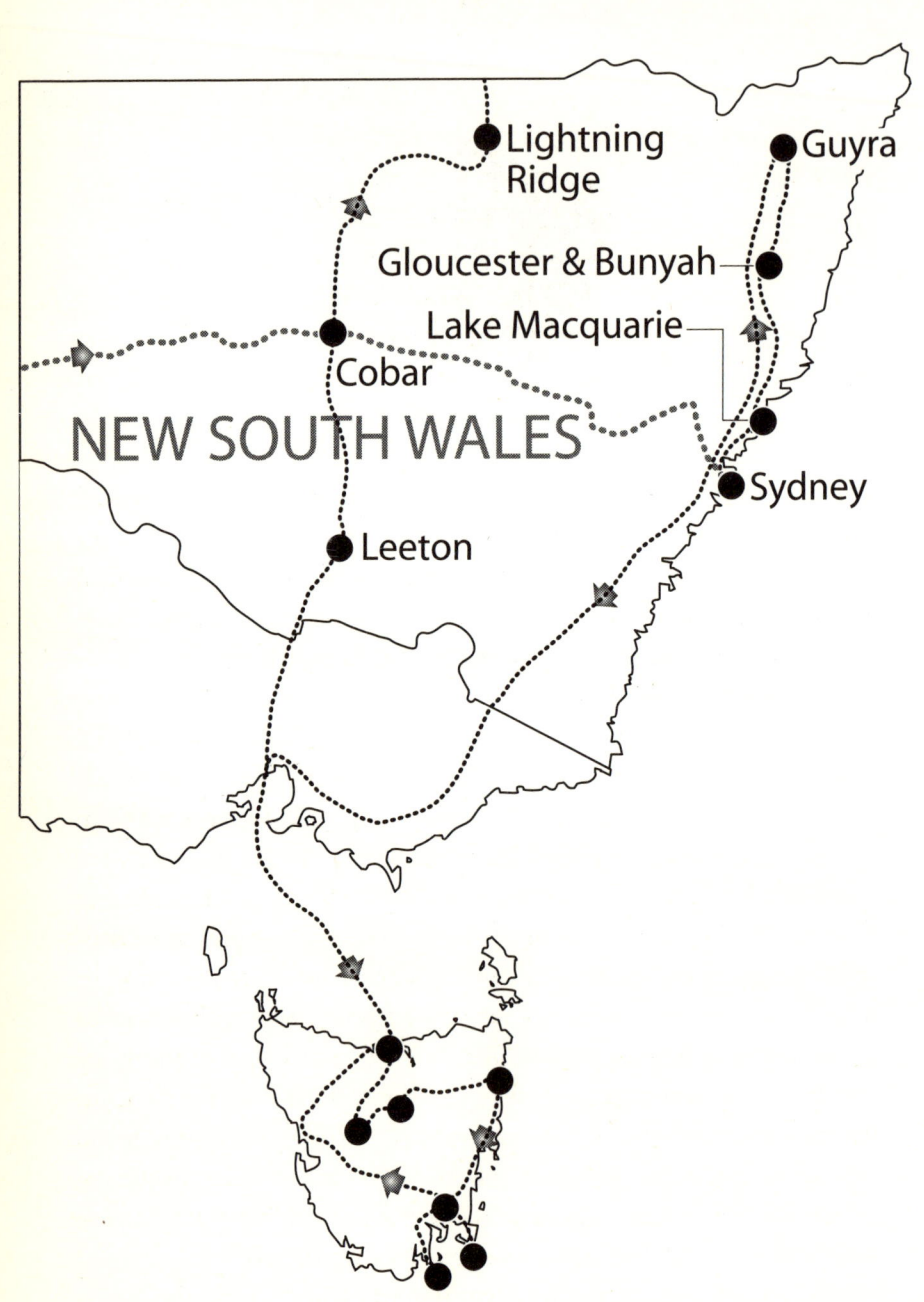

1

'Do you think we should have spent at least a weekend in a caravan before committing to living in one for a year?' Lisa asks, as we purr up the F3 freeway north of Sydney with the heady smell of new-car leather in our nostrils.

'There's not much we can do about it now.' I laugh.

Wangi Wangi, on the western shores of Lake Macquarie, is to be our gentle introduction to the world of caravanning. As we take the Morisset exit off the freeway I turn to Lisa and grin, 'How did we get away with this?' We are both deliriously happy, not even the storm clouds billowing in from the coast can dampen our enthusiasm.

It's mid afternoon when we roll into the Wangi Point Lakeside Holiday Park. The park is beautiful in the most unpretentious of ways – a good old-fashioned caravan park where people come to relax and fish. Two knobby hills of eucalypts sit at either end of a bay where small sailing boats and little motorised cruisers are anchored, or tethered to trees on the shore. These are the boats of people who love the water, unlike those who love to be seen on the water. They are owned by people who are at peace pottering about the lake; fishing, sailing and checking their crab pots for blue swimmers and the occasional jackpot of a mud crab.

A dozen or so tinnies lie scattered, upturned, along the grassy bank of this working man's paradise. It began as a campground after the Second World War for the hard men of the mines, men who dug the coal seams of the lower Hunter Valley pits at Cessnock and Kurri Kurri. Today it retains the rough feel of a coal miner's retreat. There are no other Volvos.

I collect the key from the kiosk while Lisa shoots footage of our arrival. The manager gives me the rundown of the park's features and informs me proudly that Lake Macquarie is 'the largest saltwater lake in the Southern Hemisphere'. To prove it, he pulls out a map with Sydney Harbour overlaid on the lake. The great harbour sits miserably in a corner, dwarfed by the lake. Australian country towns love a geological claim to greatness, but surely, I think, South America or Africa could throw up something to compete.

In the rundown of local attractions – the clubs, the lake and the walks – the park manager fails to mention that Wangi was also home to one of our greatest artists, William Dobell, whose old house overlooks the lake just a few bays away. 'There are very good fish gutting facilities down by the water,' he says, as I make my way out the door.

For now, I put aside all thoughts of art and fish because I have to reverse park the caravan.

A couple of weeks ago Lisa had booked us into a $425 caravan towing course with a man called Graham, who wore a fluoro shirt with 'Graham' written across it and another bloke called Gerry, who'd been involved in the 'volunteer rescue movement' for the past 33 years. They'd been pushing for years, they told us, to change the law so that people towing caravans would have to obtain a special licence. But they felt that rich and powerful forces within the caravanning industry were fighting against them, fearing it would lead to a drop in van sales.

We were the youngest participants by at least 20 years in a group which included a retired butcher, a marriage counsellor and an engineer.

Graham and Gerry regaled us with stories of the caravanning mishaps they had encountered over the years. Wheels that had fallen off, annexes that had flapped open – even a van that had come loose and passed the four-wheel drive that was towing it along a lonely desert highway. They'd seen the lot.

'You touch that clutch when the van's swayin' and you're in angel gear,' Gerry said, as we listened in like kids to a ghost yarn, 'between a wing and a prayer.'

It reminded me of the wonderful stickers that once adorned every Sandman panel van in the 1970s: 'If the van's a-rockin', don't come knockin', or 'Don't laugh, your daughter's inside'.

'Do grey nomads have an equivalent?' I joked with Lisa. 'If you hear something creakin', Albert's new hip needs a-tweakin'.'

I never got the chance to ask because the caravan horror stories kept coming.

'You can never be too careful with a caravan,' said Gerry to Graham.

'That's certainly true,' replied Graham. He then lowered his voice to a hushed tone, which drew us in: 'A caravan rolled over my father and killed him.'

We all stood shocked into silence. At first I thought there was going to be a punchline, that this was just a joke. But it was a true story.

Graham's father, an experienced caravan man, had left the safety chains off when he unhooked his van and it rolled over him and crushed him. He may also have had a stroke, but it was the van that killed him. Gerry was on duty with the rescue squad that day and was called out to find a man he had known for 30 years dead. He then had to phone his mate, Graham, with the news about his father. We all shuffled about uncomfortably, until Graham said cheerily, 'Let's break for a cuppa'.'

After tea, we moved on to reversing.

It all seemed so easy in the vast carpark at the Sydney Olympic Equestrian Centre where the course was held, but here in the Wangi caravan park, it is a different matter. The roads in the park are as narrow as a Cockney lane and each time I try 'The Method' the front of my car bumps up against the annexe of a permanent van across the road. I am in danger of becoming jack-knifed. After a couple of failed attempts, Lisa puts down her camera to help me navigate, but is confused about left-hand-down and right-hand-down and how that translates into the movement of the caravan. The tension is rising.

After five or six attempts, and with the eyes of Wangi upon us, she insists that she will drive, I will navigate and we will use the technique we were taught at Graham and Gerry's caravan school.

'But it doesn't work,' I growl.

'Just humour me then,' she says, with equal venom.

It is now raining, torrentially. On her way around the park to straighten up the van for another attempt, Lisa spies a whole heap of empty spots on the water's edge that require no reversing. In her enthusiasm to tell me she rounds a corner too sharply near the kiosk and I watch in horror as the side of the van skirts perilously close to a very large gum tree.

She spots the terror in my eyes and realises what almost happened, but is still overjoyed by her discovery. We drive onto our new patch near the water. Lisa deals with Joe while I go about the task of securing the caravan in the rain. Our van opens out like a Swiss army knife. The 'bedrooms' fold down at either end. The roof pops up. The awning rolls out and the stabilisers drop down. After a few minutes I realise that I have no idea what I am doing and wish I'd paid more attention to Graham and Gerry, or that they'd spent less time telling horror stories and more time teaching.

After half an hour a kindly man takes pity upon me and wanders over to render assistance. Thank God for Gary from Gympie. If I leave the awning as it is, he tells me, without tying it to the ground, it could end up in the lake with the next good gust of wind. We have no spare rope, so he produces some, along with a couple of spare pegs.

'The van is a bit lopsided. Have you got a spirit level?' he asks.

'What's a spirit level?' replies Lisa.

We offer Gary a beer in return for his help but it's warm because we haven't worked out how to use the fridge. He gives us cold beers but won't take warm ones in return. He heads off after showing us how to turn on the fridge.

ADVENTURES IN CARAVANASTAN

Later, with Joe in bed and the caravan secure and unpacked, Lisa and I toast our success with a glass of gin and a late dinner of Barbecue Shapes. We snuggle up in bed, as happy as kids in a new cubby house – once again congratulating each other on our great escape.

By midnight, Joe is howling with the worst case of teething he's ever had. We try everything to console him – cuddles, milk, Bonjela and lashings of paracetamol – but nothing works. At one stage I go to the toilet block and can hear his screams through the bricks, a couple of hundred metres away. I pity the poor sods in the caravans surrounding us, separated by wafer-thin sheets of aluminium.

We take the only option left and put Joe in the car, to go for a drive. At about 4 am we are scouring the streets of Newcastle looking for a McDonald's to get a coffee when Lisa breaks the silence: 'Darling, this time a year ago, exactly, Joe was born.' I drive along with a lump in my throat, tears in my eyes and a smile on my face. My son: trailer trash at one.

We spend five nights in Wangi. It is meant to be a little holiday to unwind from the pressures of packing up our lives. It is a living hell. During that time we touch upon almost the entire range of human emotion. Lisa cries, more than once; there are moments of manic laughter; we have some good loving and several fights. Huge thunderstorms punctuate the generalised heavy rain – the sort they say is the heaviest in living memory. Joe barely sleeps and nor do we. Some bastard even steals a carton of our beer. There is elation that we've left suburbia behind and dread at what lies ahead. Both of us think, at different times, that this is the worst and the best decision we have ever made. Worst is winning.

We are due to pick up a new caravan, with an enclosed annexe, in a few weeks. But for now we have to entertain Joe in the 16-foot space of the caravan we have. At home, one of his great joys is to systematically pull books off our bookshelf. In an act of innovative desperation, Lisa takes him to the local library and sets him loose in an aisle out of the librarian's sight.

On another day, we take a trip to a camping shop to pick up more equipment, including an outdoor table and chairs that we had somehow overlooked.

Along the way, Lisa turns to me and says, 'I just don't know if I can do this.'

I stay silent, eyes fixed on the road, thinking exactly the same thing. I wonder how we can make the house payments if I have to give back the book advance. They've already employed someone to fill in for me at the magazine. Well, bugger her, she can just go back to work and I'll stay home with Joe. We'll spend all day at the pool – swimming, drinking lattés and eating Paddle Pops while she goes to work, I think vindictively, as we drive to Camping World.

Our time in Wangi is like the perfect emotional storm – a new environment, a tiny space, a beer thief, torrential rain, a teething toddler, no sleep for days, a desperate man with nicotine cravings and a one-woman rock band called Menstrual as Anything. It's a wonder we make it out alive.

2

The Bucketts Way leads us west off the Pacific Highway north of Newcastle, up into some of Australia's earliest rural settlements. As we motor inland the tensions and traumas of the previous week are soothed away by the soft, green hills. We have lunch at a café in the village of Stroud and for the first time Lisa and I are able to joke about the horror week we've just endured. We are contented to know that at least our son has a future, albeit in torture, working as the CIA's Chief Sleep Depriver. In the afternoon we pull into the Gloucester Holiday Park and it feels like The Promised Land.

The park is enormous and green – 22 acres says the brochure – and in the distance I can hear the fast-flowing River Gloucester. I don't even have to reverse park the van. We pick a spot, hundreds of metres away from anyone else, and let Joe loose in the paddock as we set up camp. His teeth have stopped throbbing and he is crawling about chewing bark, fleeing some imaginary foe on all fours, then fighting it off with sticks. I keep an eye on him while attempting to master the intricacies of a pop-top caravan.

People take this route to get to the wild Barrington Tops National Park or the prosperous little grazing towns on the tablelands. Few stop to admire the small but impressive range that rises out of a cow paddock just a few kilometres away from our camp. The hills are inelegantly called The Bucketts. If they were located somewhere in the backblocks of the Northern Territory thousands of people would visit them. There'd be signs asking you not to climb them, out of respect, and you would be able to buy snow domes depicting the craggy peaks. The Bucketts are not large or imposing but I find them very beautiful.

'They are called The Bucketts because they reckon they sort of look like upturned buckets,' says the woman at the caravan park reception, unconvincingly. It is akin to naming Uluru 'The Big Dog Turd', except The Bucketts look nothing like buckets and are more like the calcified remains of a giant armour-plated dinosaur that came to rest in these otherwise soft dairy paddocks. The name, I am later told, is a bastardisation of the Aboriginal *Buccan Buccan* (pronounced book'n book'n and thought to mean big rock). There have been several attempts over the years to revert to the Aboriginal name but all have met with staunch resistance.

Buccan Buccan is so much more poetic, and it is poetry that has brought us to these hills. Gloucester is not far from the home of the country's most famous living poet. In fact, some would say he is Australia's *only* famous living poet, apart from John Laws.

Les Murray has spent his life writing poems about Australia and its people. He was asked, by former PM John Howard, to write a new preamble to the constitution. He is loathed by the left and many on the right are also wary of claiming him. He's a great poet, a great conspiracy theorist and a defender of the underdog, from Pauline Hanson to rural rednecks and the poor. He has suffered great bouts of depression after enduring a horrible childhood. He has slept rough on Sydney's streets and knows what it's like to 'fill your belly with water to keep it from feeling hungry'.

There is also something I read about him that has always intrigued me. He said he was interested in 'catching the sound of rocks knocking together in fast-flowing water'. Sometimes I have tried to put words to this image but all my attempts have been inadequate.

Also, conveniently, Les Murray happens to live on the way to Mum and Dad's place at Guyra. We figure we can pop in on the way up the mountain. I ring him to see if he will talk. He tells me to bring a teacake – they do a fine teacake in Gloucester. I explain that we come with small child. He says that's all the better.

We set off for his farm early one rainy morning. A woman from the caravan park calls me on my mobile just as we are out the gate. 'Some bloke called Leslie Murray rang,' she twangs, unaware, it seems, that the man she's talking about is perpetually in the running for the Nobel Prize for Literature and is possibly even more famous, overseas at least, than the cricketer, Doug Walters, who also grew up in the district.

'He says not to bring the caravan. The creeks are up.' We'd figured as much. We'd packed Joe's cot into the car for his midday sleep and left the van behind. Joe is dressed up for the occasion and we have selected a raspberry teacake.

At Kramback, a village where the Murrays attend Sunday mass, we stop to ask for directions. The postie says there are two Les Murrays and asks which one we are after.

'The poet. Do you know him?'

'Only met him a coupla times,' says the postie.

'Do you know any of his poems?'

'Nah. They reckon he's pretty famous, but I can't say I know his stuff.'

He's not alone. I recently asked all my friends to name just one Les Murray poem. None of them could. People just don't get pissed and recite Les Murray around a campfire or at a bar in Earls Court – Cold Chisel is the new Banjo Paterson.

The postie photocopies us a detailed local map and sends us off on the most direct route along a road that the poet says 'wriggles its hips'. The landscape on the drive to Bunyah is soft and sensual with rounded hills that even in times of drought are freshened by the odd coastal shower. Today it is lush and plump, and contented cows wallow in the misty rain. Plain little wooden farm houses, their verandahs hanging low and wide like the straw hats of beach fishermen, dot the roadside. For a bit, the bitumen ceases, and we travel along a narrow dirt track which becomes tarred again just out of Bunyah. The village consists of a sparkling new volunteer bushfire shed, a couple of timber houses, an automatic telephone exchange and the Bunyah Public Community Hall 1926. There's been no shop here since 1923.

A few kilometres out of the village we come across a small sign on a ramp – '1054 Cecil's'. The number 1054 represents the property's distance in metres from a turnoff – the new bush numbering code designed by emergency servicemen. Cecil is Les's late father. One or another of his family has owned this sad little 16 hectare plot since 1870. Les bought it for his father in 1974, from an uncle, and Les and his wife Valerie and their five children moved back to Bunyah from Sydney in 1985. Bunyah is an Aboriginal word for bark. For the Murray clan it has always translated into misery.

As we near the house, along a rutted drive, Lisa is sure we have the wrong address. The garden is lush and overgrown and the house looks like a poorly constructed kit home. The cladding is unpainted and a fog of poverty envelops it. It reminds me of a place I was dispatched to as a young reporter, on the outskirts of Newcastle, to interview the relatives of a toddler who'd been attacked by a dog. The writer, Bob Ellis, Les tells me later, described it as a 'tin humpie'. Les corrected him – 'it's a fibro humpie.'

Valerie Murray emerges from this jumble of fibro. Her greeting is warm and friendly. It's like we are old friends. She seems happy for the company. Valerie is wearing a faded red shirt and jeans and the rounded features of her central European heritage. Her family fled communist Hungary when she was a child. Les waddles out after her. He is a big man with a bald head and a couple of teeth missing. He is the antithesis of what you imagine a poet should look like. If I'd been asked to give his occupation based on looks alone, I'd have guessed he was a retiree of Gloucester Shire Council where he'd spent his entire working life behind the wheel of a grader, smoothing out the corrugations on those back roads to Bunyah.

Their faces light up at the sight of Joe. 'It's a long time since we've had a baby in the house,' says Valerie. 'When you said you were bringing a child, I thought he would be a bit older,' says Les, with delight. I wonder if anyone has ever turned up to talk to Salman Rushdie or John Updike armed with a portable cot.

Valerie takes Joe in her arms for a hug, then leads me to a spare room to set up the cot, in readiness for the 'tired signs'. I emerge a few minutes later to see my son dribbling on the leg of the man *The New Yorker* described as among the world's 'three or four leading English-language poets'.

We all settle down around a dining table. Joe weaves his way through our legs as Valerie serves up the first cake of the day with tea. The room is cluttered. On sideboards and in cabinets the detritus of life jostles for space – books, bills, children's sports trophies, porcelain dolls, hats, vases, CDs, antique bottles and video cassettes. On one wall there's a lovely Iranian carpet, which Valerie says Les bought many years ago. 'We only just paid it off this year,' she says. Near the carpet hangs a calendar from Barry Austin Mowers. A door that leads into one of the bedrooms is plastered with stickers, one is for the North Sydney Bears, a team that was long ago banished from the National Rugby League. Thin, wispy spiders' webs float from window frames and from the ceiling.

This part of the house was built for Cecil and there is another dwelling next door, built when Les and Valerie and their five kids moved from Sydney a decade later. It houses their bedroom and his study and is in better nick.

It is within a radius of a few kilometres of where we are now seated that the great events of the Murray family have been played out over the past century – a vast, unrelenting tragedy.

Les's grandfather, Allen, had always pitted his two sons against each other. One day Allen ordered Cecil to fell a tree, but Cecil refused because the tree was rotten and he deemed it too dangerous. His brother Archie was sent out instead. The tree fell on Archie and killed him and Cecil lived forever with the guilt.

Cecil then married Miriam, a nurse from Newcastle, and although they were in love they lived in bitter servitude to old Allen, waiting to inherit a miserable few hectares that even in the best of years would barely sustain a living. 'Dad was trapped,' Les says. 'If he walked off he'd be completely broke and he wouldn't have any money to buy a farm. All he could do was wait for his father to die.'

When Les was born there were complications. 'My mother, through sheer bad luck, had a series of miscarriages.' Miriam was unable to have more children. 'So between Mother's defective womb and Grandfather's unending rivalry, Dad was bloody trapped and it all turned out badly.'

Les says his mother loved him but was not affectionate, and became more bitter and angry as the years went by. 'I have a habit of craving praise. It's what I got from my mother. I didn't get hugs and kisses and things, I got praise. But she was driven to great anger and bitterness by the poverty and the miscarriages. She was one of God's frozen people.'

To cope, he lost himself in books. As a child he read obsessively 'anything that was printed. I read her eight volume encyclopaedia. That was useful. I have always wanted to know everything as a result of that because if you start off reading an encyclopaedia you get an interest in everything.'

This lonely little boy, living on a farm with embittered parents, occupied himself by reading and playing pretend army games against an invisible enemy. 'My consolation when I was growing up was the non-human part of it,' he recalls. 'The hills, the trees, the forests and the animals and all of that.'

And then, when he was 12, his mother died of complications from yet another miscarriage. The remainder of his childhood was spent 'living a perpetual funeral' alone in a house with his father who was 'marinated in grief'.

The nearest high school was at Taree and Les was sent, because there was no bus, to board during the week. He was bright but socially awkward and for the entire time he went to the school only one other child ever called him Les – 'all the rest of my names were fat names'. Today, as he recalls those events from more than 50 years ago, his voice tightens and he shifts in his chair. He carries a grudge, still, against the township of Taree, like a returned serviceman who forever hates the Japanese, as well as the cars and the crockery they produce.

'I don't trust Australian country towns in a way,' he says, with his glasses perched on his forehead like a set of frogs' eyes. 'I had one pig of a time at Taree High School. I guess I know Taree too well. There are many, many nice people in Taree but it's a hard place with a mean spirit. I tend to keep downwind of it.'

Childhood grief and torment have, of course, forged the man and his poetry. 'The key to Murray,' says *The New Yorker* critic Dan Chiasson, 'what makes him so exasperating to read one minute and thrilling the next, is not landscape, but rage. "How naturally random recording edges into contempt," Murray writes, identifying the poles of his own combustible poetic temperament.'

This combustible temperament may be a fine thing in a poet, but living with it can't have been much fun. Throughout his life Murray has suffered severe and prolonged periods of depression, often lasting years. He says he has it under control now, but the black dog never departs entirely. 'You can smell the fur, but it's not chewing on you anymore,' is how he has described it.

He and Valerie met while working on a play at Sydney University. She was doing wardrobe and he was playing Satan.

'Was he romantic?'

'He was a bit vague, he didn't make very good eye contact,' Valerie says across the table. 'Shortly after I met him, we were walking along Parramatta Road on opposite sides of the road – me going one way, he going the other – and I saw him out of the corner of my eye and he made a point of crossing the road just so he could walk past me and say hello. And I thought, "Gee that was pretty deliberate." I was pretty naïve and innocent but I knew when I was being given the eye and I just didn't like the eye. They were just after one thing and I wasn't too keen on that.'

Les says he never had the faintest idea how to give the eye. They were married six months later.

A feeling of gloom descends as we talk about current family tensions. The Murray's eldest boy, Daniel, has completely cut himself off from his parents. They haven't had any real contact with him and consequently the grandchildren for many years.

'Our younger kids are almost another family because there's a nine-year gap between the first two and the others so they're a different kettle of fish and I was much better at being a parent by the time they came along,' Les says. 'I was older, more experienced.'

Valerie tells us how she has tried to make contact with Daniel but has heard nothing back.

'It's the last thing I would have expected,' she says, the tears welling up. 'You may as well talk even if it's a bit acrimonious. I have tried. I write a few words on his birthday and at Christmas . . .'

'His handicapped brother wrote to him once,' Les says, taking over. 'Years later he got a reply but for a long time Daniel believed that we put Alexander up to it.'

A few minutes later, as if on cue, Alexander rings. It immediately brightens the tone. He has autism and lives in a share-house in Taree. He asks his father to name another word for fish. Les chortles with delight. 'Water creature with gills/fins/scales,' he replies. 'Anything else? Okay mate, bye.' Alexander calls with these sorts of questions all the time.

'I've got a bit of that,' he says, referring to his son's disability. 'If not autism then a bit of Asperger's. It didn't come from nowhere.'

Lisa tells the couple they are very open about the darker chapters in their lives.

'Trying to keep secrets did my father immense harm so I've always regarded it as being beneath me to keep secrets,' Les replies. 'The old man, the day he was trying to get an ambulance for my mother, he was going through a telephone switchboard run by the worst busybody in the district and he didn't want to say how serious things were.'

Not wanting to alert the district that his wife may be having another miscarriage he told the doctor that Miriam was just having a 'bit of a turn'. The doctor never sent an ambulance. 'That was fatal and my mother died as a result of that and the old man never forgave himself.'

I ask Les why he stays in this place that is so bound up in sadness. 'The reason I returned was that the old man was getting on and I wanted to look after him. To get back to daily contact with things in the country was important. I never felt at home anywhere else.'

'Despite the demons here?'

'That's right. Where else would you find your demons except at home?'

This persona of grief is essential to Les Murray. He wears it like a comfortable coat and would be lost without it. He mentions a girl in Taree who was sexually abused by her father. She had lost most of her hair and was teased at school for both. In one breath he talks about down-trodden blackfellas and the next of the scorn heaped on Pauline Hanson. He identifies with the teenage killers from Columbine – not their actions, but their rage. 'We're shooting back now,' he told an audience in America.

This suspicion that the world is against him is borne out in his poem, *The Mare out on the Road*. He writes about driving around a bend to find a horse across the road. He chooses to run the car into a ditch and risk his life, rather than deal with the scorn of a neighbour. The poem is written from the perspective of the persecuted. What he doesn't explore, however, is the other alternative – simply that the neighbour was at fault for leaving the gate open and letting the horse out.

> *Sliding round the corner on gravel*
> *and there was a mare across the road*
> *and a steep embankment down to the paddock.*
> *The moment was crammed with just two choices.*
> *Sliding fast, with the brakes shoaling gravel.*
> *Five metres down, and would the car capsize?*
> *The moment was crammed with just two choices.*
> *One of two accidents would have to happen.*
> *The poor horse was a beautiful innocent*
> *But her owner never let a grudge go by.*
> *No court case, just family slurs for life.*

The level of Les's paranoia is sometimes surprising. He thinks there are dark forces out to get him in the media. Newspapers are 'absolutely anti-democratic institutions in our society' and he believes that *The Sydney Morning Herald* sent a man to Stockholm to stop him being awarded the Nobel Prize – a grand conspiracy that had to involve the editor, the journalist and the judges of the prize, all out to get Les Murray.

Later he tells us he doesn't trust his computer because 'there you are, typing with one finger, as I type, and it goes "burp" and a whole lot of kiddie porn comes up on the screen and the police jump through the door and take you away.'

For this reason he prefers to write the old-fashioned way, in longhand, then types up his work on an old typewriter. In his poem, *The Instrument*, he answers the question about what drives him.

Why write poetry at all,
For the weird unemployment.
. . . For always working beyond
your own intelligence. For not needing to rise
and betray the poor to do it. For a non-devouring fame.

And even if he wanted to be devoured by fame, Les believes the tall poppy syndrome in Australia makes it impossible. 'An American put it nicely when he said, "In America, if you want to get ahead you marry a Republican. In Australia, you marry a publican." It is the compulsory egalitarianism which doesn't allow for too much fame.'

If he had moved to New York or to London, he says, he would have been infinitely better known, and better received back in Australia. 'I would have been a less good writer and I would have got away with more achievement.'

After a great deal of talking, it is time for lunch. Valerie serves up a hearty and tasty meat soup, which Les slurps up in great gulps. Afterwards the poet retires to an old couch that looks more like a mauled sheep, with tufts of stuffing poking out the side. Les says they are planning on going to 'town' for a new one this week. Lisa tucks Joe into bed, while Valerie puts a tape in the stereo and turns it on low. It is Billy Joel's 'Piano Man'.

We chat for another few hours with the occasional interlude for a piece of Gloucester raspberry teacake or to entertain the baby when he finally wakes. We talk about Les's desire to live in the bush, although he was always clear about never wanting to be a farmer. 'I found poetry was an adequate substitute because it kept me just as poor and the work was never as hard.'

Les believes that during the 1970s Australians decided to stop focusing on the romance of the bush in favour of urban living. Country people were suddenly looked down upon. 'It was impossible to imagine country folk being sophisticated but a lot of us were and I thought "I am going to prove this wrong. I am just going to make absolute confetti of this".'

Before the afternoon is out, we tackle race and politics and writing and the wonder of living on such a vast and beautiful continent. Often Les seems to have more regard for the land than he does his fellow countrymen.

'Australia itself is often the great consolation for dealing with Australians,' he says. 'If you get sick of your fellow Australians there is always the country there to reassure you, to comfort you and show you its magnificence so you don't get too cut up about it all.'

We rise to leave, thinking about all the magnificent things we will see in the year ahead. Les advises us to tell people in the city about things they're not expecting to hear. Our hosts escort us out to the car, helping us to juggle the portable cot, high chair, nappies and baby Joe. But before we leave I have one final question.

'What', I ask the big man of poetry, 'do rocks knocking together in a stream sound like?'

'Oh,' he says with a wheezy giggle. 'They chatter to each other. They say words like *colic, colic*.'

3

On the New England Highway, north of Armidale, we come to a steep incline known as the Devil's Pinch. When I was a kid it was the most treacherous stretch of the highway and every winter two or three trucks would skid off the edge in a heavy frost or on the black ice when it snowed. The call would go out and, like crows to roadkill, every policeman within a 250 kilometre radius would arrive to fill his boot with the loot, whatever it was. One year it would be car batteries and toilet paper, the next, turkeys and car seat covers. Sometimes the road would be blocked with flocks of police cars.

They have taken out the hairpin bends now but I remember, as an eight-year-old, watching two policemen trying to shove half a side of beef into the back seat of a police Kingswood after a truck from the meatworks skidded through a corner. They drove off with a hock sticking out the window of the squad car.

The Pinch also marks the imaginary line between Armidale and Guyra. People at the top of the Pinch are Guyra people – my people – and I know their stories. I haven't lived in Guyra for 20 years, but each time I reach the top of the Pinch it feels like I'm walking in the front door of home. It is a different home from the one I inhabit in the city, with a different conversation. In Sydney, people talk about issues. They talk about politics and property prices, movies and books and things they've read in the newspaper. In Guyra, people talk about these things too, but more often they tell stories. At social gatherings people sit around in a circle and someone will tell a yarn, people will laugh, and then someone else will tell a story. It is a big part of the culture.

I once worked in a shearing shed with a man widely regarded as a master storyteller, a wool roller called Dick Davidson. He told stories almost nonstop for a week and had six men – three shearers, a wool presser, a classer and me, the roustabout – completely enthralled. Occasionally a shearer would heckle him from the board but it only urged him on. It was like living a Gabriel Garcia Marquez novel. In no particular order the stories covered his childhood: growing up in the bush with nine brothers and two sisters; the tales he and his siblings brought home from the Second World War; his numerous sexual conquests; critiques of various in-laws; drinking feats; acts of courage by dogs and men; and stories of getting older, like smoking pot for the first time at 65. He thought it had no effect until he got up to walk 'and me fuckin' legs had deserted me'.

In the city, people live in enclaves determined by income; the poor and the rich generally don't mix. Suburbs are often divided by age and colour too. You don't see many black faces on Sydney's Balmoral Beach and in Newtown young people rarely come into contact with retirees. Here, in my small town, old and young, rich and poor have no choice but to mix. Everybody knows everybody and good stories are impossible to keep secret.

But small towns are also insular. In Guyra, there are very few Asian people and if anyone's gay they're not saying so. There are unwritten rules to be obeyed and for any transgression, as Les Murray says, there'll be 'no court case, just family slurs for life'. And not all the Guyra stories are funny. I remember a dreadful story about a Scottish exchange student who was badly bashed by some local thugs outside the Golf Club, for the crime of wearing a kilt to a rugby match.

After the Port Arthur massacre, when the Howard Government moved to ban semi-automatic weapons, one of the claims made by the gun lobby was that gun owners needed such weapons for self protection. Guyra was a big gun town and I came home to write a feature for *The Sydney Morning Herald*. I spoke to the local sergeant who went through all the incidents involving guns. During the previous decade no one had used a gun to protect themselves, their family or their property during a robbery or an attack. During the same time in my home town seven young men had blown off their own heads. And then there was Ross Ruming, who drove a forklift in the produce shed for New State Stores. He shot his two little kids, his wife and then himself, after suspecting her of having an affair. Some people are still not happy with me about that article, either because they were pro-gun or because it 'showed the town in a bad light'.

But today, as we head north, I look at the land and I remember the funny stories.

Gilbert White, who was the Shire President for 26 years, owned a farm just up on top of the Pinch, not far past the Black Mountain truck stop. His wife, Mabel, used to mind us kids if Mum had appointments in Armidale.

Gilbert bragged to me one day about the size of his penis – he reckoned he had a whopper. I can't recall the circumstances that led us to discuss the size of the presidential penis, but somehow it came up.

'When I was a young bloke I would lie on my back and put a walnut in my belly button. I'd pull my horn back and let her go. It'd crack the walnut.'

They just don't make civic leaders like that anymore.

We continue towards town. At the Gun Club Hill, out past the cemetery, I remember the yarn of Ronnie Mason who was pulled over by the police for not using his blinker. Ronnie drove an old 2-tonne Bedford and would cart around small loads of stock. They call him Tongue and Groove because he has an odd habit of poking out his tongue and licking his lips, lizard-like, between words.

A few years ago, Ronnie was heading south with a load of culled ewes. He had just been to Boydy Stanley's bakery to pick up a pie and a Coke for the trip. He had the pie in one hand and the can in the other, but still managed to pull off to the side of the road to let the line of cars banked up behind him go past. He was a skilled operator. Unfortunately for Ronnie one of the cars was a police car.

'That was very considerate of you to pull over,' said the copper as he poked his head into the vehicle. 'But you failed to indicate.'

Ronnie looked at him, still with the pie in one hand and the Coke in the other.

'What do ya think I am,' he said, his tongue darting in overdrive, 'a fuckin' octopus?'

We reach town. 'Guyra', the sign says. 'Pop 2200. Elv 1233m.' A few years back they replaced the old wooden sign, which was in feet, with a new aluminium one in metres. The population remained unchanged.

I have come to Guyra because, for me, this is the start. My view of the world and Australia begins here. It is my anchor point. It is also home to Australia's Highest Caravan Park and is therefore the logical place to start a caravan journey around the nation. We drive straight past Australia's Highest Caravan Park and into the comfort of Mum and Dad's big backyard.

The journey here had not been uneventful. At Gloucester, Lisa was driving when we pulled into a service station to get some diesel. She forgot that she was towing the van. The sound of a paper dispenser scraping up the side of an aluminium caravan was like a chorus of fingernails down a blackboard. Lisa jumped out of the car and announced it was my fault. I'd distracted her, she said, by asking her which side of the car the petrol cap was on.

After that little mishap, the trip up the side of the mountain was a joy. The pastures were green, the cows were fat, the creeks were flowing fast and it was an historic day. It was Sorry Day. Something truly amazing was happening. Kevin Rudd, the Prime Minister, was being articulate. The radio faded in and out as we wound around the hills, but we caught most of the speech.

'Today we honour the Indigenous peoples of this land, the oldest continuing cultures in human history,' he said over the radio from parliament.

'We reflect on their past mistreatment. We reflect, in particular, on the mistreatment of those who were stolen generations — this blemished chapter in our nation's history. The time has now come for the nation to turn a new page in Australia's history by righting the wrongs of the past and so moving forward with confidence to the future. We apologise for the laws and policies of successive parliaments and governments that have inflicted profound grief, suffering and loss on these our fellow Australians . . .'

The speech was as beautiful as the day. Somehow Kevin Rudd, whom my colleague at Fairfax, Annabel Crabb, once dubbed 'the jargon hunter', was able to summon up the words that needed to be said.

Unlike the majority of Australians, Lisa and I both knew black people. We went to school with Aboriginal kids and played sport with them. In high school one of my good mates was Aboriginal, the irrepressible Wayne 'Wang Dang Malang' McEwan. We'd had our fights too. Black kids all knew how to fight.

Lisa's after-school job, as a 16-year-old in Cowra, was at a bookshop. One of the first things she was told when she started was to keep an eye on the Aboriginal kids to make sure they didn't steal anything. The directive was both racist and pragmatic.

I learned a bit of Aboriginal history at school, about rainbow serpents and the Dreamtime, but somehow it never related to the black kids — Morris Blair, Lisa Kennedy, Mathew Walker and the Gerard boys — who were sitting in the desks near mine. I was never aware that the farms where my white friends lived, on some of the most expensive and sought after grazing land in the country, were once black hunting grounds.

The Aborigines lived in two grim clumps of public housing in Guyra — referred to as the Vegemite Valleys. They spoke with a bit of a funny accent and I had no idea that their people may have spoken another language before English. What we did know was that Lisa Kennedy was so good at sport that at school carnivals she raced against the boys, and won. No one wanted to fight her.

In my childhood world, there were good Aborigines and bad

Aborigines. The good ones had jobs on the council, or worked picking spuds and peas, or in the shearing sheds. The bad ones lived on welfare and got on the piss all day.

The Prime Minister's speech, earlier in the day, feels historic and has me thinking that perhaps we've turned a corner in black–white relations. After we've unpacked the van, Dad and I drive out to Tingha, a small town 40 minutes to the west with a large Aboriginal population – the home town of the great Aboriginal rugby league players Preston Campbell and Nathan Blacklock. I want to see how Kevin Rudd's speech has been received. I want to be part of this day.

In the main street I run into an old friend called Craigie Connors. The year after I left school I played league for the Guyra Super Spuds and Craigie was our star half back. He had soft hands, a deadly step and could land a 30-metre pass on the chest of a winger in the clear.

Craigie and I shake hands and chat for a bit about his family and mine – some of his kids have finished school. I tell him mine has just turned one. He shakes his head. He has the car loaded up and is about to go fishing out at Copeton Dam. He tells me he heard bits of Rudd's speech on the radio, but that he hadn't paid too much attention.

'It was good hey, I suppose,' Craigie says, without any great passion. 'Do you reckon it'll make any difference?' he asks.

I say that I hope so.

We wander down the street and into the pub. There are three blackfellas having a drink and a punt. None of them heard or saw the speech. Their eyes are glued to the racing channel.

'No cunt was stolen around here,' one of them tells me.

Around at the Mrangalli Aboriginal Centre we come across Douglas Kirk who is furling the Aboriginal flag. There had been a little ceremony to mark the occasion and a dozen or so community leaders had turned up to watch the speech on TV.

'I had a lump in me throat and a tear in me eye,' Doug says, proudly. 'I never thought you fellas would say sorry. I hope we can end up living equally as one – blackfellas and whitefellas.'

A shy black woman, Geraldine Sines, the Mrangalli secretary, tells us her sad story. Her parents were alcoholics, she says, and she and her siblings were removed from their care by the authorities. They spent their youth being bounced between state-run homes and relatives. 'I don't see myself as stolen,' she says. 'It was just a pretty sad way to grow up.' She doesn't know if Rudd's apology is a good thing.

Dad and I return to the Tingha pub for a beer and a chat with some more locals before driving home. There's no clear consensus about what the apology means and a few of the Aboriginal people are clearly indifferent. I also talk to a few white men who question why we should say sorry at all. I know that nicely crafted words on their own aren't enough, but I believe symbolism is important. I chew over all these thoughts driving home.

Back in Guyra, we turn on the TV to watch the commercial news followed by the ABC. The Prime Minister's speech is just as compelling the second time around and the reaction of Aborigines in and out of parliament is moving. There is certainly no hint of the ambiguity that Dad and I witnessed this afternoon. I had gone to Tingha wanting to share in what I imagined would be a feeling of euphoria, but witnessed something more complicated.

I guess that's what this year is all about: looking more deeply at my own country; searching for the shades of grey and seeing things with fresh eyes. We have one plan, which is to meet an artist and writer called Kim Mahood who is going to be in a remote Aboriginal community in seven months. Other than that we have no idea where we'll be staying or who we'll meet. Tasmania is our first destination, after Guyra.

We stay at home for a couple of days, learning to operate the van. Annie and Geoff Thrift, who looked after me when I was a baby, help us out with some niggling electrical problems. Ray Sweeney, the panel beater, arrives to buff the ding on the van and by the time he's finished it looks brand new. He'll take no money but is happy with a carton of beer.

Friends come to say hello and goodbye and inspect our new home. The general view is that we will never make it, that Lisa and

I will kill each other, or that Joe will kill us. We did an interview with ABC radio before we left Sydney and Lisa was asked what she wanted out of the trip.

'I just hope that at the end of it we all still love each other,' she said.

I say to an old friend, Nick, that the year ahead will be tough, travelling with a baby and trying to write a book. Nick tells me to get over myself. He reckons there's only one better job, chief nipple buffer at *Playboy*. He also reminds me that I'm not shearing sheep for a living.

It is finally time to leave. Joe has had time with his cousins. Mum has unpacked and repacked the van. We've slept in a real bed for the last time. And I've enjoyed the warm embrace of my old town.

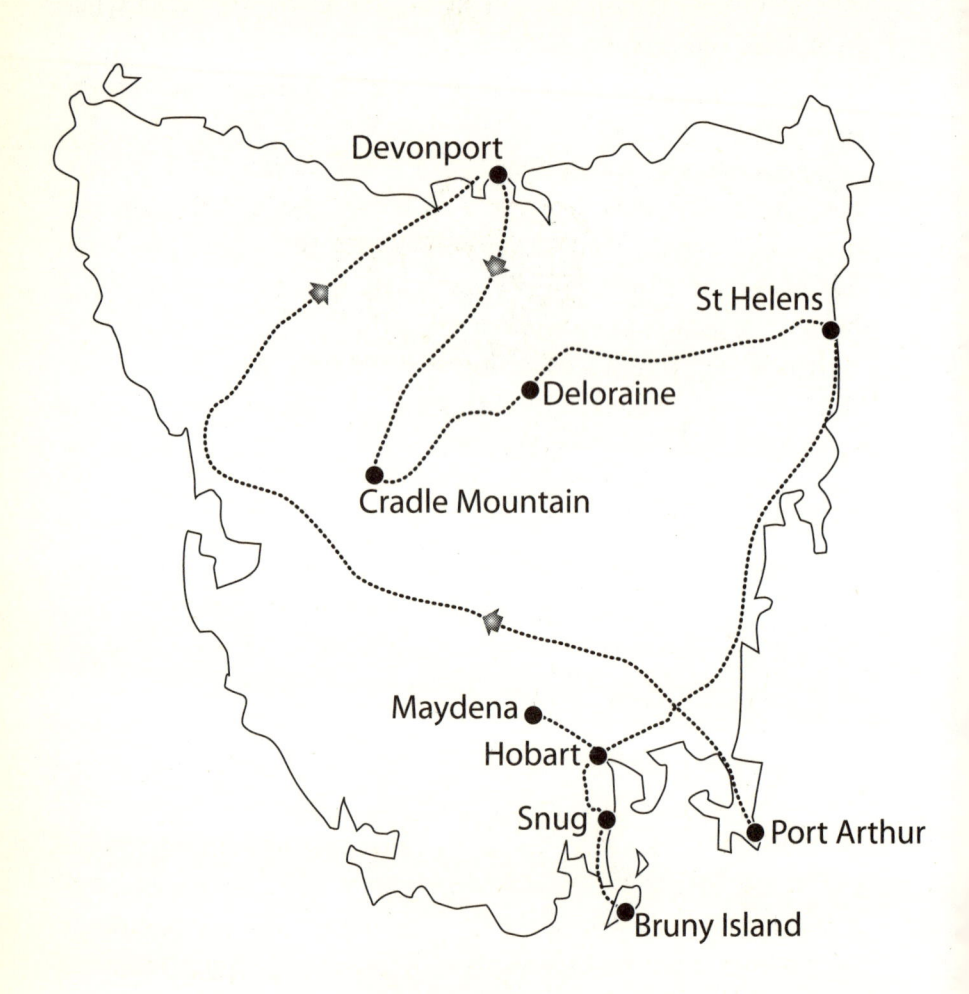

TASMANIA

4

As soon as we roll off the *Spirit of Tasmania* we are fleeced of everything remotely organic by a friendly team of quarantine officers. The replacement of foodstuffs confiscated from the vans and cars of visiting mainlanders is a vital sector of the Tasmanian economy. I am surprised to get through with leather shoes.

We drive out of the bio-security area and into Devonport. The renovation frenzy that swept the mainland appears to have been halted as effectively as fruit fly and apple blight at Bass Strait. 'It's like the 1950s,' says Lisa. Stern little brick and fibro houses remain, just as the government's public housing architects intended: work hard, save and move somewhere else, they say. The Mersey River, which divides the city, glows with the lights of a container wharf on one side and an oil storage facility on the other. I take an instant shine to the place.

We find our way to the caravan park, The Cosy Cabins, which has sweeping views of the ocean, the river and the carpet factory out the back. It is getting late. At the check-in I ask the woman if there's a good Thai or Vietnamese restaurant in town that does takeaway.

'I dunno about Thai or the other one,' she says, 'but there's a good Chow.'

'Lisa's not big on Chinese.'

'KFC?'

'No.'

'Macca's?'

'Not in this lifetime,' I tell her.

'Ah,' she says, with a shake of her head. 'Got yourself a fussy one there.'

I thank the woman. We set up the camp and tuck into baked beans on toast.

It feels good to have arrived in Devonport and to know we can stay as long as we need. Lisa and I rarely fight but these first few weeks have tested us. Life on the road has been frenzied and our nerves are frayed. Every other young family that we've met on the road says the first month is the hardest. Stick it out and you'll love it they urge, as if this gypsy apprenticeship is akin to your first pair of school shoes; with time the blisters will heal and the leather will soften.

On the journey south we've struggled with tap fittings and gas connections and have nearly come to blows reversing the caravan. We've been adjusting to living in a cupboard.

'What's it like?' asks a friend who phones from Sydney. 'A caravan is like a boxing ring,' I reply. 'There's nowhere to hide.' Then there has been the ongoing battle with Telstra, a dark empire protected by an impenetrable moat of electronic prompts.

We've been lost several times and it's been my fault. Once I said 'turn left' when I should have, in fact, said 'turn right'. A relatively minor error you may think, but Lisa was towing the van through peak-hour traffic in Melbourne on a hot Friday afternoon. We'd been on the road since early morning. Joe hadn't eaten and was tired. Whimpers turned to screams. We ended up in the country near a place called Bacchus Marsh, instead of a caravan park in the city. It cost us two hours. In a slightly animated manner, Lisa verbalised her fears that my defective genes had been passed on to Joe. It became known among friends as 'the Bacchus Marsh Incident'.

Something had to give. And it did. My diary entry for the second morning in Devonport reads:

Got drunk last night with truck driver from Queensland and Dutch wife. Their van was parked next to ours. He produced a bottle of rum. I know that I am in trouble for breaking and having a cigarette. I have a terrible hangover but I have to act like I don't. Lisa and Joe are asleep. I am not looking forward to today.

I stumble out of the van with the sun searing into my brain. Why did I drink rum? I hate rum. Besides, the guy was a bully who spoke horribly to his wife. Why did I insist on staying up drinking with him? And, I'd been going so well with the smokes . . .

I figure I will atone for my sins by putting up our brand new canvas annexe. It'll be salvation through renovation, I reckon through a Bundaberg haze. Lisa will be so excited she'll probably forget I had a minor relapse on the nicotine front. Joe will love the extra space.

I lay out all the canvas, metal clamps and pegs on the ground and stare at them, hoping an answer will come. I fiddle hopelessly and then, after a few pathetic attempts, I hear the crunch of boots on gravel and look up to see a tall man with sensible glasses and workingman's forearms strolling across the road to see me. He has a couple of kids in tow. I pick him for a Christian before he even speaks. Or an Amway salesman. Or both.

'This looks like your first time,' says the stranger. 'Would you like a hand?'

My resistance is low. I figure I'll buy whatever he's selling – soap powder, salvation, whatever – to get this thing up.

'Thanks mate. Any help would be appreciated.' I invite him and his boys into our space.

'Warren Ruhle,' he says, thrusting his big paw forward. 'These are my twin boys, Charlie and David.'

Within 10 minutes Warren and the boys have the annexe up and Warren has revealed snippets of his life. He is a farmer from the Darling Downs in Queensland but has sold his farm and is on the road with his family – his wife, Kate, and their *five* children aged from 16 down to 11 – Lucy, Annie, Charlie, David and Isabella.

'The local doctor said he would never perform a vasectomy on anyone under 30,' says Warren. 'He made an exception for me.'

Kate is home-schooling the children and Warren is picking up work where he can. At the moment he is driving trucks for the onion harvest. They plan to be on the road for two years. I am intrigued. They are like the Waltons in a caravan. How do they cope with *five* kids? I thank Warren for his help and offer him a cup of tea. He thanks me but says he has to go.

Lisa and Joe emerge when he is gone. She is indeed impressed by the annexe, but not much by me. We had been waiting for this annexe for weeks so that Joe would have somewhere safe to play. The van is too small and we need to contain him, otherwise we'll spend the next year following him around caravan parks. The annexe is the answer. Joe crawls around his new surrounds, happy, it seems. As we are admiring the canvas he makes a move. He's worked out how to undo the zipper. In a rapid dash on knees and palms he's off down the road at full speed with Lisa in pursuit. We'll spend the next 12 months pursuing him around caravan parks.

Later in the day one of the Waltons, Isabella Ruhle, is standing at the flap of the annexe. 'Mum wants to know if you would like to have dinner with us in the camp kitchen later on?' she asks. We thank her and agree to join them.

I've just been shopping and am working on a big pot of seafood soup from my bible, Stephanie Alexander's *The Cook's Companion*. I say I'll bring the chowder along.

'Great,' she says. 'I'll tell Mum.'

After dusk we tuck Joe into his cot and wander off to the nearby camp kitchen with our pot of chowder. We can see the van from where we sit and can hear Joe chatting happily to himself. Warren is cooking steak, sausages and homemade chips.

The kids sit at one table and we join Kate and Warren at another.

'So, how long have you two been married?' Warren asks, to start things off. We both hesitate, like we do with young kids who ask how the baby came before the wedding.

'We're not married,' I say.

Warren brushes it aside. 'Ah, that's okay. Kate's brother lives with his partner and has done so for years. And they've got kids.'

We run down a few more dead ends and there's the odd awkward silence before the conversation starts to flow. When it does, it doesn't stop.

'Heck,' says Kate when she learns I'm writing a book. 'Have we got a story for you.' Over the next few hours and days, the Ruhles share their experiences with us. They are on a journey that has taken them to China and back.

Warren Ruhle was born into a life that never really suited him – the eldest son of a farming family in the middle of Queensland's bible belt, near Oakey. He took to God, but not really to farming, and would spend hours on his tractor thinking about the meaning of his life. The soils of the Darling Downs are rich and fertile and he ran a competent and profitable operation but always wanted something more.

He first spied Kate across the pews, when her family moved to town. After years of drifting with the army, her father had decided it was time for the family to settle down. He got a job with the local fire brigade. One day Warren caught Kate's eye after church and they started chatting. They were soon going out. Six weeks later they decided to marry. He was 20 and she was 18. Was it love at first sight? 'No, it was lust at first sight,' she says, over a spoonful of chowder.

Lucy, now 16, was born a year after their first wedding anniversary. The four others followed in quick succession. By the age of 23, Kate had five kids at home. 'It was madness,' she says. 'Warren and I would shower together just so that we could get some time to talk, away from the kids.'

She never felt accepted by Warren's family and, constantly exhausted from caring for so many children, Kate became depressed and withdrawn.

'Warren worked long hours on the farm and I looked after the kids and did the book work. Each Sunday we went to church. That was our life.'

The marriage was not really working and both of them felt like leaving, but neither was the leaving kind.

One day Warren climbed onto the raised wall of his irrigation dam. Across the flats he could see over all of his boundary fences.

'I stood there and thought, "Maybe there's something else out there beyond those fences for me".'

It was afterwards, through prayer, that he came to the realisation he wanted to be a missionary. The calling was very specific — he was needed in China.

Despite great family opposition, he sold the farm and moved to Brisbane for bible studies at the Queensland Baptist College of Ministries. He also became aware of a US-based Christian group doing work on a farm in south-west China. On the surface, its goal was to highlight innovative western farming practices for the benefit of rural Chinese. Its other aim was to fly beneath the radar of the communist Chinese authorities and spread the gospel — at least that's what they told the church folk in the US and Australia who sent money to support them.

It was an extremely difficult two years. The Ruhles' accommodation was very basic. Two of the children became depressed and Kate struggled to cope with their new life. Warren loved Chinese culture. He had a gift for the language. However, the project was not what it seemed. The farm was high in the mountains and had poor soils. The people who ran it were no experts and it provided few benefits to the community, apart from giving jobs to a handful of locals. It existed, as far as Warren could see, to provide a lifestyle and a career for the Americans who ran it. It was, in effect, a scam.

Over dinner Warren asks about our time in Pakistan and Afghanistan and how we found living in a Muslim country. We discuss modern missionaries. Warren says his view has changed since working in China.

'The role of missionaries should be to do good work and conversion should flow from that,' he says. 'You should let people know your motivation, but they should come to you because of your deeds. "The tree will be known by its fruit."'

They'd planned to be in China for four years but their time had been cut short. It was the perfect opportunity, they figured, to see more of Australia.

'It was as simple as that,' says Warren. 'We were at a loose end after China, the kids were being home-schooled and we thought, "This is a great time to do something together as a family and to see the country".'

It is getting late and Joe has been waking at five. We thank them, say goodnight and wander back to our van with our pot and plates.

'There's another reason why Kate and Warren came home from China,' says Lisa as we're getting ready for bed. 'Warren had a fling with a Chinese woman. Kate told me about it while you were talking to Warren. She was really open about it.'

Over the next few days, both Warren and Kate mention the infidelity. Talking seems to be part of the recovery strategy.

The woman was a prostitute, Kate says. 'He was away. It was our anniversary. He was going for maximum shame.'

Warren was flattered by the attention of a beautiful young woman and one day he just gave into that temptation. He later confessed to Kate. 'I knew that it could have cost me everything – my wife, my family. She deserved a lot better than not knowing.'

But when they raised the matter with the leaders of the mission in China, to get some counselling and support, they were shunned. There was no Christian spirit of forgiveness. It was another reason to leave the project.

'We have accountability now,' says Kate. 'He has gone from someone who was never romantic to someone who is now very attentive and considerate.'

'Has it strengthened the relationship?'

'Oh heck yeah,' she says. 'Heck yeah. I could have left, but I didn't really want to. Instead of pushing him away, I wanted to be held. It shook us and we needed a good shake. It got us back on track.'

After the upheavals of the past few years, this trip around Australia is part of the process of strengthening the marriage and the family, they say.

'We told the two eldest kids about it,' says Kate. 'They had a right to know.'

Kate was able to draw on her own life experience when Lucy, her eldest, suffered a crisis of faith. 'I told her how I had experienced God's peace and love through dealing with Warren's unfaithfulness. I talked about the strength I gained through forgiveness.'

The trip is about simpler things as well, seeing the country and having fun. 'There's no point getting to old age and saying "Wow, I've got all this money, but I haven't done anything and I'm not happy",' says Kate.

But the trip was yet another decision that put them offside with Warren's relatives. Kate says her parents were fine, but her in-laws were not.

'Hokey smoke, it just hit the fan one night,' she tells me one day as we sit at our aluminium camp table sipping coffee. 'We had been living with them. Warren's Mum just said the family had got together and decided that Warren was a bludger – hadn't worked in four years – was a disgrace to the family and that this travelling thing was a joke. Our kids were going to be uneducated nothings. So, they kicked us out of the house, just like that. I thought, "Oh cripes." Warren just said, "I don't care. I am still doing it. I'm not living to please my parents anymore".'

There were other dilemmas too. The Ruhles couldn't find a caravan on the market for seven people. They initially thought they would get an old bus and convert it, but were told buses were not allowed in some caravan parks. With the help of Kate's brother, a coach maker, they built their own 25-foot caravan. Warren and Kate's bedroom is at one end while the five kids sleep in bunks at the other. The older girls have insisted on curtains for privacy. There's a kitchen with a breakfast bar in the middle. They have an annexe outside the van that becomes a classroom. Eleven-year-old Isabella has never been to a conventional school.

Kate has had no tertiary education and no training as a teacher but has devised the curriculum for her five children. When she first began home-schooling, she used a government-approved syllabus provided by their Christian school in Queensland. But now she has devised her own, taking quite a bit from the US Christian modules that she finds on the internet.

One morning I wander over to see 'school' in progress. The three younger kids, Charlie, David and Isabella, sit outside the van in the large annexe. Their textbooks and a copy of the Bible are on the table. Isabella is doing scripture.

'It's about the man who fell on the road and three people passed him and then one took pity on him,' Isabella tells me.

'The Good Samaritan,' her mum says.

'Yeah, that's it.'

The two older girls work inside the van. Annie is sitting in front of a DVD player. There is an American accent blaring out of the machine, delivering a maths lesson. 'This guy tells the worst jokes,' she says.

'With home-schooling there are some pretty weird ones out there,' Kate tells me while the kids are hunched over their work. 'You meet them through the church. A lot of them are really, really fundamentalist Christians. My kids always joke that we are not as bad as this one family we know who have to sew their own underpants.'

'The thing that blows me away is that we have been out of the school system for seven years and no one has *ever* checked up on us. I get the family payment from the government so they know I've got kids. It's not a great system because I know there are a lot of people out there teaching some pretty weird stuff.'

'What do you teach about the history of the world?' I ask.

'On matters of faith, I teach creationism. I let them read whatever they like, so they read millions-of-years-things, but based on what they know and have read they would still believe in creation.'

She says she takes her children's education very seriously. Despite having no formal qualifications she believes she is doing the right thing. 'I think they're getting equally as good an education as they would in any school system,' she says. 'If anything, they have had a lot more world experience than kids of their age.'

But it is something that plays on her mind. Several times she asks us what we think about her teaching the children. We struggle to give an honest answer without hurting her feelings.

Is it a good thing or not? They are a close-knit family with solid values and lots of love, but are their children being limited? What about the spirit of competition? What of socialising with kids your own age and of making mistakes and sorting them out, without your parents knowing? What about a little expert oversight? Lucy has a boyfriend back on the Darling Downs and wants to marry him when she returns. Annie wants to be a hairdresser. There is nothing wrong with either of these life choices but have they just been given a limited number of options?

Annie and I are talking one day and I ask her about the role of religion in her life.

'It plays a pretty big part. Well, especially forgiveness and all that stuff. It would be hard, without faith, I reckon, to forgive a lot of the stuff that has happened in our family.' She says she enjoys being home-schooled. When she went to a regular school she was bullied. 'We never had much money. I never had the right dolls to fit in.'

We have enjoyed our time with the Waltons. We don't know it yet but we're about to meet a number of committed Christian families on our trip around the country. They're not the sort of people we'd come across in our Sydney lives, but you don't travel to re-create the life you have at home.

The day before we are to leave, we are walking past a book shop in Devonport and I think of the Ruhles' boy David, who told us how much he loves to read. We duck into the shop and buy him *To Kill a Mockingbird*. The following day we hook up our van and say goodbye. We reckon we'll be in Western Australia at the same time as the Ruhles and promise to meet again. I give the book to David. He's thrilled. Kate has a book for us.

'Don't think we are bible bashers or anything, but we thought you might be interested in this.' It is *The Case for Faith*.

Driving out of Devonport, flicking through the book, we wonder if there really are lots of families out there home-schooling their kids in 'weird stuff'. And do they really sew their own undies?

5

The entrance to Cradle Mountain National Park is a field guide to the political landscape of Tasmania. The 'Welcome to Cradle Mountain' sign sits just outside the World Heritage park on a portion of land controlled by the loggers. The land is denuded apart from a few woody bones that somehow escaped the loggers' trucks and the subsequent firestorm. There's been no attempt to rehabilitate this land, or even to tart it up, even though this is the gateway to Tasmania's major tourist attraction and 200,000 people pass this point each year. In fact, the stumps of two giant trees have been deliberately pushed up behind the welcome sign by a bulldozer and the stunted roots wave menacingly, like a pair of Medusas. 'Fuck You, Greenies,' the dead stumps seem to suggest.

Tasmania is the frontline in the battle for the environment. Nowhere in Australia is the fighting as intense and the nerves so raw. Families have splintered because someone's sister took a secretarial job with a winery that is a subsidiary of Gunns, the logging giant that many believe has a stranglehold on the state, or because a logger's kid, at university in Hobart, is spotted on the news at a Wilderness Society rally.

On one side of the divide, people drive around in Subaru Foresters and Nissan minivans with stickers saying 'They Shot the Wrong Lennon', in reference to the soon-to-be-deposed pro-logging Premier Paul Lennon, or 'Tasmania – Explore the Corruption', a play on the state's motto exhorting people to explore the opportunities. On the back of Toyota Hiluxes and old battered Pajeros the message is blunt: 'GREENS TELL LIES', 'Our Jobs Our Future'.

I can't believe that up until now Cradle Mountain had somehow passed me by. It is just so beautiful. I knew nothing about it but it seems everyone else was in on the secret. 'Ah, Cradle Mountain,' people say. 'Yeah, we went there years ago. Amazing, isn't it?' It is like my discovery of *Seinfeld* when the series had almost ended.

The national park is, to date, our most expensive campground at 40 bucks for a powered site, but is worth every cent. On our second day, I decide to climb the mountain while Lisa minds Joe. She will climb it the next day.

I rise early to catch the first shuttle bus. There are two tracks around either side of Dove Lake and I choose the more difficult one, to the left. I have it all to myself and for the rest of the ascent I feel as if I am alone on the mountain.

The lake below is usually a deep, deep black like the eyes of a brooding Irishman. The water is fresh and clean to drink but has been stained by the tannins of button grass and tea trees. Today, though, its mood has lifted and there's an occasional sparkle. It is early autumn and the Tasmanian beech, Australia's only deciduous tree, has just started to turn. Dotted between the greens and greys of the celery tops, king billy pines and leatherwoods, the beech flashes shades of yellow.

The track leads high above the lake and there is an immense silence. Soon the air thins and the trees become stunted and gnarled. Some of these trees, not much taller than me, are thought to be a thousand years old.

The craggy mountain looms ahead as I pass a couple more alpine lakes which were carved out in the last ice age. That ice age finished just 10,000 years ago and, when the ice melted, Tasmania was cut adrift from the mainland.

At some point, the trees and the heath stop and the mosses begin. It seems as though the land beneath me is one giant sponge. The sun is beating down, but there's a chill in the air. Below I can see over all three lakes. I make my way across the mossy plateau to the base of the mountain peak and from here, it is a hard, rocky slog to the top.

Three hours after leaving the carpark, I am alone on the summit. I sit for half an hour and think about nothing and everything, peering out over all of Tasmania.

The following day it is Lisa's turn. I head down to the nearby resort with Joe in the pram. We check out a photo exhibition and then he tucks into a babycino. Afterwards, we find a deserted lounge area. For at least two hours we play hide and seek between the chubby club lounges. At one point an employee comes to investigate. He smiles when he sees a boy and a man, both crawling on all fours. He returns with chocolates.

Rejuvenated after mountain air and good chocolate, we head off the following day with plans to travel down Tasmania's east coast.

In Deloraine, not far from Launceston, we find good coffee at the local deli. The owner, an engaging host, is wearing the regulation uniform of the Sydney/Melbourne escapee – black t-shirt, earring and a trendy tattoo. The place is packed with locals and tourists and apart from great food and coffee, it also sells good produce from all over Tasmania. We start chatting to the owner and when we tell him I am writing a book he says there are plenty of interesting locals.

'Can you introduce us to any of them?'

Within 10 minutes we are sitting with Lynn Hayward. The owner tells me that Lynn is identified as a 'greenie'. He has to be careful because half the town hates greenies and if he is labelled as one, it could be bad for business. It seems to me that he could walk around with a chainsaw on a necklace and a Pauline Hanson t-shirt and the locals would still think he was a greenie.

Lynn Hayward is one of those people every local community needs. She serves on boards, runs committees and gets things done. She was behind the formation of the local community bank, which is now going strong and is shovelling half its profits back into the community. Lynne used to work in university administration in Adelaide and her husband, John, was a teacher. They moved from South Australia 14 years ago for the quiet life — it just never turned out that way.

Like so many mainlanders who move south they became politicised. They bought a beautiful but rundown slice of farmland that fronts the Mersey River and is surrounded by paddocks of tall, elegant eucalypts. It is 20 minutes' drive out of Deloraine. They have spent years rehabilitating it and the rest of their time fighting battles for the environment.

'Why don't you come out and stay tonight and have a look?' she says, within 10 minutes of meeting. 'We have plenty of room.'

We jump at the opportunity but insist on staying in the van. If Joe wakes early you don't want him in the next room, we explain.

That afternoon after exploring Deloraine, we follow Lynn's instructions: drive out of town and cross the Mersey at an old wooden bridge.

The property is as beautiful as Lynn described. The house is built in the valley on the high side of the river flat. It looks across the flat to the river which has cut into a hill. The hill is covered in a stand of tall and proud white-bodied eucalypts.

Soon after arriving, we are introduced to John and walk across the paddock for a swim in the river. A pet emu follows. Joe is fascinated by it and its deep-throated call — 'callummp, callummp' — like the sound of a round rock dropping into a lake from a great height. John says he often sees platypus, but with Joe's imitation callumping there's no chance of that today.

And then after a late afternoon tea, John announces that it is time to feed the Tasmanian devils. He fetches a leg from a wallaby that he'd found dead beside the road the previous day and we wander over to the devil enclosure. He tells us to keep a distance. 'They can get quite excited if we all arrive at once,' he says.

For the past four years, he and Lynn have been involved in a program trying to save the species from the rampant contagious cancer, Devil Facial Tumour Disease. It has wiped out more than half the species in just a few years.

Cancers are not normally contagious and if I were injected with the cancer cells of another person, my body would (hopefully) recognise these cells as foreign and kill them. But devils come from a slender gene pool, almost as if they are all identical twins. The cancer is transmitted when they bite each other on the face fighting or mating or chewing on the same piece of carcass. The infected animals develop hideous tumours on the face and in their mouths. They die an agonising death.

(Later, in Hobart, we meet some of the scientists who are working on saving the devils. They are excited because they think they have found some animals with a natural resistance to the cancer. One of the devils is called Cedric. We follow Cedric's progress via Radio National – he's a bit of a star on AM. One day, as we near the end of the trip, we hear that Cedric too has developed a tumour.)

'Hello, Levi,' says John tenderly, as he steps into the enclosure with the wallaby leg. 'Hello, Bronski.' John is sometimes slightly awkward with people and I suspect that he prefers the company of animals.

After a few minutes the devils appear, snorting and grunting. They run with an odd gait, like a dog with three legs. They jump into John's lap and pull on his shirt and he talks to them like a doting parent. 'Ohhh, my little babies,' he croons.

He has had them since they were tiny, weighing just 80 grams, and now they are almost a year old. Their mothers, both diseased, were trapped by wildlife officers and put down. Levi and Bronski, who are free of the cancer, will soon be sent to a captive breeding program.

Back at the house, Joe is loving the space and all afternoon as we chat one of us has to follow him as he makes another ascent of the stairs.

Over dinner, Lynn and John tell us more about the various programs – from scientific research, to isolating swathes of wilderness that are disease free – designed to save the devils. But they don't think there's enough political will to do the job. It is just another symptom, they say, of the political corruption in Tasmania. Both Labor and Liberal parties are effectively under the control of the island's main timber company, Gunns, they tell us.

John was born in the United States and his father was a wealthy businessman. He has inherited a substantial amount of money and used it to fight several court cases to stop logging operations in old growth forests on private land. It began with a change to zoning regulations when blocks like his and his neighbours' – that had been zoned rural residential – were no longer exempt from logging.

'The rules just changed,' he mutters, 'without any community discussion. They want to take every last tree on this island.'

While John has won some court cases, he has lost others and now believes the only way to save wilderness is to buy it. He has so far purchased about 80 hectares of wooded country and has put covenants on it so it can never be logged.

'Are you prepared to spend all your inheritance saving this land?' I ask.

'Is there anything more important really?' he says, as we sip coffee after dinner. 'If you really want to save the natural world, if you really love the natural world, what else can you do? It is under grave threat, especially in Tasmania where we have the fastest rate of native forest destruction in the developed world. So much of what is being done is illegal and the system is certainly corrupt.'

As we are talking there is a strange noise at the door and we all turn to see what it is. Squeezing through a cat flap is the head of an enormous wombat. It waddles straight up to John and nudges his leg.

'Hello, Nora,' he says.

This is Nora Chomsky, a wombat they have cared for since she was a baby. She lives outside but comes back for cuddles and late-night snacks. We sit mesmerised as Nora tucks into a bowl of rolled oats and sweet potato, snorting through her nose as she eats.

The next morning, Lisa films John and the devils for a story she is compiling for SBS. Lynn and I are chatting in the kitchen when she tells me that John is very ill. He has cancer and has already had three bouts of surgery to remove tumours from his brain. There are more operations to come. He is 62 and appears very healthy. I am shocked. 'He will,' she says, 'spend the rest of his life fighting for environmental causes. He wants to leave a legacy to the environment.'

6

'Caravanning is like lawn bowls,' I say to Lisa. 'Its participants are mainly old and almost exclusively Anglo-Saxon.' We never encounter any Chinese Australians or Tanzanians who need a hand with a jockey wheel. This is a white man's sport.

I make this observation as we are trawling through the caravan parks around St Helens, a quaint little port town on the north-east coast of Tasmania, looking for a spot to camp. The town sits at the bottom of Georges Bay, a busy fishing port and a short drive from the spectacular Bay of Fires with its long white sandy beaches and unusual orange-coloured granite rocks.

It is Easter and we have forgotten to book. Finally we find a place. It is in a mown paddock, on a hill at the back of a caravan park, with a view out over the bay. Perfect.

I need to chock the wheels of the van because of the slope. As I am searching about for things to use, our neighbour, in a van slightly down the hill, points me in the direction of some pavers that I can borrow tucked up beneath the balcony of a permanent van.

The helpful guy's name is Dennis. He looks as though he was a sportsman in his youth, a rugby league centre perhaps. He still likes to keep in shape. Joe, who's supposed to be at a clingy age, crawls right over to him and up his leg. Dennis is delighted. He misses his grandkids, he says. He plays with Joe for half an hour while we set up.

Dennis is joined by his wife Trish and in between banging tent pegs, we chat about the travellers' trifecta: how long have you been on the road? where have you been? where are you going?

Dennis had a small business but sold out a few years ago, doing very well out of it. The Howard years were good to people like Dennis and Trish.

'Where are you from?' I ask.

'Young in central NSW,' says Dennis. 'Cherry country.'

In 2002 I spent a week in Young, researching a story for Fairfax's *Good Weekend*. The town had been bitterly divided by the arrival of 80 Afghan refugees, who had been encouraged to work at the abattoir to fill a severe labour shortage.

Soon after they arrived, town meetings were called to expel them. Pamphlets, written by the extreme-right group, Australia First, had begun turning up in letterboxes and on car windscreens:

> *What's in store for Young, very soon? Rape-gangs, shootings of police officers, drugs, muggings, housebreakings, murders and unemployment. It starts with contract labour at Burrangong Meat Processors. Some will call it multiculturalism. Ordinary people know it's the takeover of our towns, our country!*

This was the town that gave birth to the White Australia Policy when rioters savaged Chinese miners at Lambing Flat in the 1860s. It seemed like it might happen again.

But then, from others in Young, there was great compassion. A group of volunteers, farmers' wives and teachers, gave up several nights each week to help the Afghans with English lessons. A couple coached an Afghan soccer team, which played in a local competition, while another group helped with the tricky process of visas.

A burly meatworker told me how he was moved to tears after hearing one co-worker's story of survival. The Afghan had lifted his shirt and shown the meatworker the tiny hole where a bullet had entered his chest and then the hole, the size of a fist, where it exited through his back. 'You wouldn't have thought he could have lived.' He believed the Afghans should be given a fair go.

The Afghans of Young were all Hazaras, a minority within Afghanistan who have been persecuted by all sides, particularly the Taliban. In the crude politics of the War on Terror, these are the good guys.

I casually mention to our caravan park neighbours the Afghans in Young, and then wish I hadn't.

'Don't talk to us about Afghans and Muslims,' Trish says with a viciousness that takes us by surprise. 'None of them stayed. Took off as soon as they got their visas. They are not interested in work . . .'

She rants on a bit longer and when she's spent we stand there, awkwardly, until Lisa defuses the situation and asks what they've enjoyed most about Tasmania. Dennis is silent and we think he may have been embarrassed by his wife's outburst.

We end the conversation politely, and thank them for playing with Joe, but resolve to steer clear. It just doesn't turn out that way.

Over the next couple of days, I chase up a story idea about wombats that are supposed to have been blinded by chemicals, sprayed, of course, by the evil timber giant, Gunns. It goes nowhere.

Joe continues to crawl over to Trish and Dennis's annexe and they strike up a friendship, independent of us. Trish also pops over with trays of hot cross buns that he devours with glee. She's probably appalled that the Easter Bunny failed to make an appearance in our van.

One afternoon, there is a howling gale which threatens to blow our annexe out of the park and into the Bay of Fires. It pops the pathetically small pegs that came with the annexe. Dennis arrives with rope, cyclone-proof pegs and a steel mallet and we bang everything into place. To thank him, I invite him over for a beer. It becomes dinner.

Trish and Dennis arrive at 6 pm, each with a camp chair. Dennis has a bottle of Bundaberg rum and offers me some of his

'Queensland sunshine'. I tell him I'll stick to beer – still haunted by the sunshine that baked my brain as dry as a summer clay pan back in Devonport. Joe crawls around in the annexe, while Dennis and Trish talk about their children and grandchildren. One of their kids is overseas and they tell us about the amazing holiday they had when they visited him. It is a cold night and we are all rugged up. A little electric blow heater whirrs away against the chill.

Trish departs for a bit, to fry some chicken pieces. I have cooked a Thai prawn curry and the rice is bubbling away on a barbecue that slides out from the side of the caravan. Dennis gives me a fatherly lecture about the importance of shares and investing and quizzes me about my portfolio. He can't believe I don't have one. Trish returns with the fried chicken and we all kiss Joe off to bed.

Dennis says he picked up some nice wine, down south. He fetches a bottle. It's good. He gets another. Over dinner we talk about travelling.

The conversation also skirts around some talkback favourites. Trish insists there are teenagers in Young who are falling pregnant, just to get the baby bonus.

'Really?' I say.

'Yes, really,' she replies. 'I could take you to them.'

They talk about the 'Aboriginal industry' and say Kevin Rudd should never have said sorry.

We talk about our time in Pakistan and Afghanistan. The wine continues to flow. I pull out my computer to show them photos of the mountains around Bamyan, in central Afghanistan, where I lived in 2005. This was where the Taliban blew up the magnificent Buddha statues that had sat serenely in the mountainside for almost 1500 years.

Bamyan is also home to the Hazara people. Most of the people who escaped to Young came from Bamyan. I had seen what the Taliban had done to these people and their homes.

But as I'm talking, I notice that Dennis is getting more and more agitated. Finally he explodes. 'Look, I don't care. I am sorry, I am not racist, but I just hate them. I just hate all Muslims.' He is shaking and his face is red with rage.

'What, all Muslims?' I ask.

'Yes, all Muslims.'

We square off on our respective sides.

The source of this rage seems to be that Dennis's mother was once spat on by a Muslim man in Sydney and that the suburb he grew up in had been overrun with Lebanese.

Dennis says Young used to be a place with no 'towel heads' but then the Lebanese started moving onto some of the small-acre fruit blocks out of town. Then the Afghans came as well. Trish adds that she and Dennis have only ever had one complaint made about them to a government agency. 'It was by a Muslim.'

We bat on for another half an hour, trying to convince them that they can't possibly hate a quarter of the world's population.

'Some of our dearest friends are Muslims,' Lisa says.

Joe's middle name is Batoor, she tells them, which is Pashto for 'brave and valiant'. He was named by our Pakistani friend, Aurangzaib, as valiant a man as I've ever met.

We explain that our friends in Pakistan hate the extremists because they destabilise their country and give it a terrible name abroad.

In the end, we get one concession. Dennis agrees there may be some good Muslims 'over there' but that none have made it to these shores.

They retreat to their van and we to ours.

'I wonder what's being said in their van,' Lisa says, before we drift off to sleep, uneasily, with the wind howling outside.

7

The historian, James Boyce, argues in his terrific book, *Van Diemen's Land*, that much of what we think about the early convict days in Tasmania is the result of Marcus Clarke's novel, *For the Term of His Natural Life*. It was a place where 'nature and Empire were to work together to crush the human spirit'. Robert Hughes kicked the idea along in *The Fatal Shore*. The penal settlement at Port Arthur was undoubtedly a hell on earth and both Hughes and Clarke used it to portray the depravity of life, in general, on Van Diemen's Land.

However, as Boyce points out, few of the 72,000 convicts transported to Van Diemen's Land spent their life in chains and only a fraction ended up at Port Arthur. 'From the commencement of the settlement in 1803, the British had fresh meat in abundance and the health of the population was far superior to that of the labouring classes in England.' Conditions were certainly much better than in Ireland, then 'the most primitive country in Europe' from where many had come and where a million people were starving.

Van Diemen's Land, he says, was a 'veritable Eden'. The wallabies were easy to hunt and plentiful. There were shellfish. Water was fresh and in good supply and the climate wasn't too hot. And this bounty was accessible to the majority of convicts. The Empire's poor, in other words, had rarely had it so good.

If you have a poke around the bookshelves of your most learned friend, I bet you will find a copy of *The Fatal Shore* and *For the Term of His Natural Life*, but not much else about Tasmania. These are still the most popular books about the island and they have influenced not only what we think about convict days, but also what we think about present day Tasmania.

The prevailing view on the mainland is that modern Tassie is the little brother who had potential but never quite made it. It's not his fault, he had a harsh upbringing, we think.

Successive federal treasurers have certainly been convinced and proportionally Tasmania receives more money than any other state. Lots more.

They've been conning us for years, the buggers.

Tasmania is still a *veritable Eden*. You just need to substitute 'labouring classes in England' with 'taxpayers on the mainland'. They may be a bit poorer and wages are on average lower, but the poor bastards are eating freshly netted crayfish three nights a week. And on the off nights, it's abalone or juicy Tasmanian lamb.

Real estate is cheap, so cheap that everyone in Tasmania, it seems, has not just a home but a holiday house too, or at least access to one. They call them 'shacks' so that people from the mainland won't cotton on to this grand lurk. Each weekend half of Hobart clears out to their shacks which are at an absolute maximum two hours' drive away. I know people who commute further than that each day.

People can, and do, grow vegetables all year round. No wonder the state's economy is not buoyant. Hands don't reach into wallets. It seems the only people who buy vegetables in any great quantity are mainlanders like us, who've been fleeced at Devonport.

People barter: a load of firewood for a weekend away in the shack at Easter or maths tuition for a year's supply of abalone. It is a modern day subsistence economy where cash is optional. You might use it to buy tennis racquets for the kids or to fill the car with petrol, but it's not necessary for anything that actually sustains life, like food. The first home buyers' grant just about covers the cost of shelter.

Tasmanians will forever have to endure jokes from mainlanders about their convict history and their supposed backwardness – having two heads and shagging their siblings. It is a small price to pay to live in this nirvana.

I have been formulating this theory as we meander down the stunning east coast of Tasmania, stopping here and there and reading Boyce. It becomes set in concrete when we arrive on Bruny Island, which sits at the mouth of the Derwent River. The ferry to paradise is just half an hour's drive from Hobart's CBD.

Bruny is actually two islands joined by a long, narrow and sandy isthmus – home to a penguin colony. It is more than 40 kilometres from top to bottom. The north, where there are substantial sheep stations, is quite dry, while South Bruny, where we are camped, is lush and forested. Our caravan park is on the shores of Adventure Bay.

Adventure Bay is a 7-Eleven of nautical history. Abel Tasman popped in for supplies in 1642, as did James Cook, who took time out to chat with the locals and hand out some specially minted coins in 1777. In 1788 William Bligh stayed for a fortnight to cut timber and replenish water supplies. He also planted seven apple trees that survived for many years.

One afternoon, not long after we have arrived on the island, Lisa returns from a walk with Joe. 'Greg, there's a place up here that you'll love,' she insists. We walk along the sandy beach and, apart from the houses dotted along the shoreline, it looks pretty much as Cook would have seen it.

At the end of the beach we take a road up a hill. Halfway up on a big block, sits a house. It consists of two modern Nissen huts, half cylinders, sitting side by side and joined by a circular hall. The verandahs and front walls are finished in timber. It's been built with love and care. There are great banks of solar panels on the roof and a small sign out the front says it has been designed to meet the highest environmental and energy efficiency standards. It is a clever and clean design.

And there, on one side of the house, is an enormous living work of art. In neat and weeded rows and on carefully pruned trees are apples, beetroot, tomatoes, herbs, berries, spinach, spuds, citrus, stone fruit, cabbage, grapes, lettuce, kiwi fruit, bok choy, almonds, avocados, limes, carrots . . . in Tasmania this is a bank. These guys are loaded.

Other vegetables are blooming in the greenhouse and there is a big chook pen down the back. A pet pig wanders in and out of its cubbyhouse. And there, right in the middle and on full public display, is a lush and succulent marijuana crop. 'Look at this,' I say to Lisa. 'It's a classic camouflage technique. They've tried to hide the pot next to the tomatoes.'

We are standing there admiring the house, the garden and the crop when the owner walks out with two beautiful little girls. He's got a beard and long hair. I figure he's come out to warn me off his dope. But he is friendly and says g'day. We get chatting and after a few minutes he invites us inside for a cup of tea. Peter Bowd is his name. Inside we meet Ericka, his wife. Joe plays with their twin daughters. They have two older kids who are not at home.

The Bowds tell us they escaped to Tasmania seven years ago. She had been a real estate agent in Taree, NSW, and he was a horticulturalist who ran a big landscaping business. They moved over to Bruny Island 18 months ago, and love it. Contentment oozes from them. Peter retrained as a builder and now builds houses and does handyman work in between the big jobs. Ericka does the books and looks after the kids. Within half an hour of our meeting, we've scored a dinner invitation for the following night.

On the way back to the caravan park, we buy supplies and a copy of the local paper. There's a short story inside *The Bruny News* that takes my eye. The local policeman is warning Bruny's motorists to wash their number plates, or else! He's issued numerous warnings about the grave offence of muddy number plates and says from now on he's going to start booking people. I ring him to see if he'll meet me so I can get the dirt on island crime. No worries, he says.

The police station is located on the other side of South Bruny, near the pub, and I arrive at the allotted time. Senior Constable Andrew MacKenzie is sitting at his desk beneath a poster of *Fishes of Tasmania* and is dressed in a faded Tasmanian Police t-shirt. He is a big balding man in his early fifties with a boyish face and menacingly large arms.

'You've got to be switched on,' he says, 'to be a policeman on Bruny, and a jack of all trades.' His job is made all the harder because people are 'basically stupid'. He has to warn the locals to lock their houses and not to leave their keys in their cars, not that any cars have ever been stolen. 'These people are still living in the '60s.'

The holiday-makers also make Senior Constable MacKenzie's life difficult. They're generally good people he reckons, but they come over from the mainland and 'leave their brains behind'. They do things they wouldn't do at home – loud parties, speeding... et cetera, et cetera.

Drink driving is a problem too, although he offers a fair degree of leniency. 'So the locals know it's okay to have a few beers and toddle home nice and quietly. But it's not okay to sit in the pub from four o'clock in the afternoon until nine o'clock at night and then try and dodge the policeman.'

But when it comes to dirty number plates there is to be no more Mr Good Cop. It's zero tolerance. He's had enough. 'Some of the Bruny people think, "Beauty! I can drive around Bruny for months on end, clog up my number plate so it's unreadable and when I go to Hobart the speed camera can't get me."' For the past few weeks he's been writing $110 tickets for dirty plates. 'They soon get the message.'

'What other police work is there?' I ask.

There's the odd domestic to attend, 'mainly just one shit-bag family', and sometimes a fight at the pub.

He spends a lot of time on the water, looking for poachers and enforcing bag limits for crays and scallops. He booked six people, just last weekend, all 'mainlanders' who'd taken too many scallops. The islanders rarely get caught exceeding the bag limits because they don't want to see their waters over-fished.

One of the worst crimes is to pull up someone else's craypot. It's called ratting. In the old days ratters would be run off the island. Now no one talks to them. 'It is the cardinal sin. You'd be the scourge of the island.'

By and large the 800 people who live scattered around the island are pretty law abiding, he says.

The island has some famous residents too. 'You know the guy who used to play Mr Fischer on *Home and Away*? Norman . . . what's his name? I can't think of his proper name.'

We chat about Constable MacKenzie's past and how he came to Bruny. He tells me he trained as an 'old school policeman' when the job was about 'the rule of the fist'. But things turned 'to shit' a few years ago when he hit a man and 'opened him up like a watermelon'. The constable was charged with assault but wasn't sacked. He was given a desk job and then a posting in the scrub before moving to Bruny Island.

I thank him for his time and get up to leave, promising to keep my number plates clean. If I have a few drinks, I'll take it steady.

That night we arrive at the Bowds' for dinner, with wine and a portable cot. I inspect their sparkling number plates. Peter had read the constable's warning and now diligently polishes his plates each time he traverses the dirt track up to the north.

'How do you get away with the pot?' I enquire. We have an odd conversation for a few minutes because he thinks I am talking about craypots. Finally, he bursts out laughing and takes me out into the garden.

'They are lupins,' he chortles, pulling up a bunch of hand-like leaves. 'Very high in nitrogen and I dig them into the garden. It's all organic.'

Earlier in the day Peter had been out diving for fresh abalone and scallops. And so, over an entrée of lightly battered abalone and a main of curried scallops, we chat about life on Bruny Island. 'I used to drive the latest BMW,' Ericka says. 'And we would take an overseas holiday each year, but I have never been as happy as I have been here.'

They don't need to earn much because they don't spend much. The solar panels on the roof provide 70 per cent of their power. They trap their own rabbits to eat — humanely in possum traps. They swap vegetables for a leg of lamb or a wallaby — an island favourite. 'My best barter ever was with a guy who works at the fish farm,' Ericka says. 'I swapped a couple of punnets of organic raspberries for two great big Atlantic salmon.'

We have come from a city obsessed with the price of real estate, but here dinner party conversations centre on something very different. 'On Bruny people are completely obsessed with crays,' Peter tells me. 'In cray season, whenever people gather, the talk always turns to the best spot to set your pots.'

I am more than a little jealous.

We toddle home, nice and quietly.

8

The southern stump of Bruny Island has been beaten into submission by Antarctic winds which torment it ceaselessly for weeks at a stretch. In the forests just a few kilometres to the north, near Adventure Bay, we saw local stringy bark and white gums that had grown to an enormous size, 40 metres or more in height and a couple of metres wide. Here the same species are stunted into shrubs, bonsai-ed by the buffeting. I pass an acacia that looks like a Rastafarian, with its face – the bent trunk – squinting out to sea while its dreadlocked hair – the branches and leaves – trails behind in a matted plume.

I have come here to meet a man called Ian Johnston. I had been told about him by a friend in Sydney, who had been to university with one of his children. I was fascinated by what she told me. Ian had been one of Sydney's leading neurosurgeons, a mentor to the flamboyant and sometimes controversial surgeon, Charlie Teo. And then ten years ago when he was at the height of his career, aged 59, he had given it all away. He had moved from Sydney to this remote part of Bruny Island to live as a hermit, I was told, translating poetry from ancient Greek, Chinese and Latin texts. Why, I wonder, did he leave medicine for ancient poetry? Why did he choose this place at the end of the world?

Ian Johnston is among a wave of treechangers and seachangers, like the Bowds and Lynn and John Hayward, who've moved from the mainland to Tasmania for a quieter life and for its natural beauty. The demographer, Bernard Salt, says these new migrants are moving because they like the idea of living on an island that is seen as pristine, 'looking for an alternative lifestyle without being Nimbin-ish.'

I stop at a gate, as arranged, and can see a man walking methodically across a paddock of bracken fern and waxy shrubs. An enormous dog trails languidly at his heel. The man is stooped like the trees and while one arm moves freely, the other is slightly bent out to the side, moving stiffly like a penguin's flipper. The dog, a Great Pyrenees, is more bear than dog and is a good 20 or 30 kilos heavier than its owner.

'Hello,' the man says in a clipped and friendly tone as he reaches over the fence to shake my hand.

'I am Ian. And this is Reg. Say hello, Reg.' Reg peers at me with a look of indifference – dopey and jowly.

As we are walking back to the house he tells me that he bought these 20 hectares of sea frontage for just $50,000 a bit over a decade ago. It used to be a degraded sheep paddock and he has planted thousands of native trees in the sandy soils, in an attempt to rehabilitate the land. He rattles off the scientific names but is unsure of the common ones.

The house sits at the top of the dunes, a couple of hundred metres back from the beach and was designed by the celebrated Sydney architect, Rick Leplastrier, who wrote:

> *The site looks straight into the teeth of the Roaring Forties and the next stop south is Antarctica. To build here is to look for the lee, and this small house, which was built as a retreat for study and meditation, has definite vessel qualities. The forms are inspired by the wind-sheared landscape. The sitting is as low to the ground as possible and the roof form resembles the spray dodger of an ocean-going yacht. The house is like an oyster: rough and tough on the outside, but smooth and polished on the inside.*

It is a small, simple three-roomed timber house with an enclosed courtyard. It is exquisite.

I glimpse the ocean over the dunes and through the tortured trees and shrubs. Outside there is no barrier between the bush and the house and the only thing remotely ostentatious is a lap pool that runs along the top of the ridge.

Inside, Ian and I sit across from each other on leather lounges while Reg slumps to the floor. Ian speaks eloquently, in grammatically correct sentences. It's clear he's exceptionally bright but there's not a hint of arrogance. He asks me questions about myself and our journey.

I tell him about meeting Les Murray, and that Lisa has a story on SBS news tonight about efforts to save the Tasmanian Devils.

'From what?' he asks. He hasn't heard of Devil Facial Tumour Disease, one of the biggest news stories in Tasmania, because he doesn't watch, listen to or read any news and hasn't for many years. He says he'll tune in tonight, though, for Lisa's story.

Settled with a cup of tea, we begin a long conversation that will last for a number of days.

Ian was born in 1939 at Collaroy on Sydney's northern beaches, the son of a British dentist, a man about whom he says 'I have no good things to say'. His father was violent and abusive towards his mother and then, when she left, towards his stepmother, who eventually left as well.

He was seven when his mother departed and, unusually for those times, he went to live with his father.

'The story is my mother had an alcohol problem, perhaps a mental illness, but as people have said, anyone trying to put up with him would have had an alcohol problem.'

He saw his mother once more, when he was 10, and then he and his father and younger sister moved back to England. When he was 15, his mother died of breast cancer and he knows nothing about the last years of her life.

His father made money, squandered it, moved on and left debts.

'A sort of Toad of Toad Hall character?' I suggest.

'That's not a bad description.'

Ian won a scholarship to go to the establishment school Harrow, but because they had moved house again, to avoid creditors, the letter of acceptance was never received and he went to a local grammar school, for which he was glad. 'Who knows what injuries Harrow may have inflicted?'

His father, he says, just never liked him and he never understood why. 'What effect did your father's lovelessness and the early death of your mother have on you?' I ask.

'This is a fairly major claim, but I think I might have been a fairly normal boy, outwardly,' he says. 'My love of books and study wasn't to get away from people, I was just naturally curious. I had good friends at school and was good at sport. I was the class clown and was well liked. In retrospect, in some ways, it all helped me. I resolved not to do those things to my children that were done to me. I have a good relationship with my children and now with my grandchildren.'

His eldest grandson, who is 10, comes to visit regularly. 'The boy is coming down to see me next week,' he says enthusiastically. 'He loves it – he absolutely loves it. We chat, we play a bit of cricket and football, particularly if my partner Susie is here. She can't catch. She is a particularly bad thrower. She is not much good at all with the bat, but enthusiastic. Last time, though, I did drop a critical catch that lost us the match.'

My initial information was not entirely complete. Ian doesn't live here as a hermit, as I had been told. His partner, Susie Collis, has been with him here, ever since he moved from Sydney. Before that, she had been his theatre nurse.

'I suppose in the ordinary parlance . . . she was – what would you call her – a mistress, although I don't like that term . . . I mean she was really, anyway, we won't get into nomenclature, but so . . .' It is the only time his sentences become muddled, talking about difficult aspects of his personal life.

Susie works four days a week in Hobart as a nurse, and stays with him on Bruny Island the rest of the time. They've been lovers for more than 20 years and are still very much in love.

The entire wall behind where Ian sits contains shelving packed with leather-bound Chinese books in red and blue, many hundreds of them. On another wall is the most pointy-headed book collection I have ever seen. The three books that are sitting on the heater with markers poking from them, half-read, are *A History of Greek Mathematics*, *An Introduction to Philosophical Analysis* and, for some light reading, *War and Peace*.

The man in the chair opposite me is small and often displays a slightly surprised look, like a possum. Susie tells me later that people often remark that he resembles the actor, Anthony Hopkins. He looks older than his 68 years, the result of a form of arthritis, called ankylosing spondylitis, that has afflicted him all his adult life. It affects the large joints, particularly those in his spine, and is the cause of his stoop. He was in almost constant agony and could only sleep a few hours at a time until he began a new treatment three years ago which has, amazingly, stopped the pain.

Over the years, he developed a pattern of coping which involved coming home from work, having dinner and going to bed at 8.30 pm. He would sleep for two or three hours. Ian would then work or study until 4.30 am, before returning to bed until 7 am. He was constantly sleep deprived, often falling asleep whenever he sat down.

Fortunately for the surgeon, the condition never affected the dexterity of his arms and hands and he was able to perform thousands of delicate brain operations, mainly on children, throughout his career. And he has always exercised daily, which has helped.

Here on Bruny Island, he and Reg walk for two hours each day, to the beach and back. Today I join them.

This walk, and the isolation it offers, is why Ian moved to Tasmania – and this remote part of the world is about as isolated as you can get. The cool climate allows him to think and to study, he says. He also feels at home with the howling winds and the spray peeling off the top of the waves. It had to be here or Northern Scotland.

He can go weeks at a time without seeing anyone other than Reg or Susie. He despises dinner parties and only leaves the island occasionally. Sometimes Susie will drag him to a restaurant with her friends, but he goes under sufferance. Food is not a great interest and often she will cook a big pot of soup, or a leg of lamb, and he will feed from it all week.

The walk today is like a stroll into a time before European settlement. There is scant evidence of human occupation, apart from a couple of fences. We skirt an enormous coastal lagoon to a beach which can only be reached by foot.

Ian sees strangers on this beach only a handful of times each year. It is wild and windswept and large waves are crashing into the shore where big, plump Pacific gulls and pied oystercatchers scratch for pipis in the sand. We walk from one end of the long beach to the other and back, chatting about brain surgery.

There is, he tells me, more art and instinct in medicine than most doctors would like to admit.

'There's so much uncertainty,' he says. 'So much medicine is art although it masquerades as a science. So much of it is an art based on experience.'

He says the fear that something may go wrong can paralyse a surgeon. 'I saw it happen to a surgeon in Scotland. He could almost persuade patients not to go ahead with an operation by making it seem so terrible that they didn't want to take the risk,' he says. 'That happens to everybody to some extent.'

He retired before his sixtieth birthday. The weight of witnessing so much death and suffering in children simply became too much. 'The sadness is a cumulative thing,' he says, as Reg mopes along behind. 'A lot of things that you do are good and you know you have done a good thing. But they don't carry the same weight in the memory as things that don't go well and the tragedies that you see, particularly with children.' He needed to get away to extract himself 'from the general milieu of suffering'.

When we reach the end of the beach, he strips off to his swimmers and pulls a rubber balaclava over his head and swims strongly out into the surf. He was a top water polo player at university and he makes easy work of the wild conditions. When Susie is away in Hobart, he does this swim alone and there is no one to save him if he gets into trouble. Only Reg.

After his swim he towels off and dresses in his warm clothes.

'I hope you don't mind but this is a bit of a ritual between Reg and me,' he says. And with that, he and Reg begin their dance. Ian weaves about on the beach, jumping from side to side, while Reg lunges at him in jest, a bull to his master's matador. For three or four minutes the old man and the big dog play this game and for that time they are a little boy and a puppy.

We walk back to the house and after lunch, a soup from the fridge, I leave him for the afternoon.

That night, at the Adventure Bay Community Hall, there is a performance. The hall is run by an enthusiastic committee which holds regular concerts and film nights. Tonight they are hosting Kieran Halpin, a well-known Irish folk singer. Halpin is travelling with his wife and two daughters for a year and playing at venues around the country. Fifty or 60 people have come to hear him sing.

It is a lovely atmosphere. Local oysters, freshly shucked, are washed down with cans of Guinness. Lisa watches the first half of the concert, while I stay in the van transcribing interviews and minding Joe. We swap at interval. Halpin has a good folksy voice and is an excellent guitarist.

His disc, *A Box of Words and Tunes*, becomes one of the sound tracks of our journey. Even for an Irishman, he's wonderfully maudlin and the scope of his angst is breathtaking. In just one song he moves from being touched up by Brother Brendan in the back of a transit van at the age of 15, to the tsunami in Asia and then to 'madmen in the White House' bombing Baghdad. We love it. His earnestness reminds us of a friend of ours, a lapsed lesbian, who summed up every lesbian performance she'd ever attended with this one song: *Chernobyl* – strum – *Chernobyl* – strum *Why? Why? Why?*

After the show I return to the caravan and Lisa is continuing with the transcriptions. 'I think I could fall in love with this man,' she says of Ian Johnston. That cad, Barack Obama, has yet to arrive on the scene.

★

The woman who did steal Ian Johnston's heart bursts into Bruny's Hothouse Café, high on a hill overlooking fields rolling down to the sea. Susie Collis has caught the ferry over from Hobart. She is a tall, handsome woman of 58 with a great cackling laugh. After ordering a coffee, she wants to set the record straight about her cricketing abilities. 'Can I point out it was he who dropped the catch that lost the last match,' she says. 'It was a sitter. I'll leave it at that.'

The pair first met, across an open scalp, in the early 1970s. He was the surgeon and she was the nurse. There was 'instant zing' but he was married and she was about to get married, which she did. She and her new husband moved to England. Her marriage fell apart. In 1987 she returned to Australia and began working again at the same hospital as Ian.

'We started seeing each other,' she says. 'He said he was not going to let the opportunity go again.'

Ian is careful not to say anything that will hurt his ex-wife, the mother of his three children. They are still on friendly terms and he visits when he is in Sydney. She is also a doctor and they met and married at university in Scotland. Their marriage was never bad and they never fought. It was 'pretty harmonious, obviously with a few problems at the end, but I don't know, how do you categorise a good marriage? I would, without going deeply into the meaning of the term "good" in this context, I'd say yes it was a good marriage. But often things diverge. In any situation where there are children, those years that you're embarking on are so child-centric . . . you can come out different people at the end. And that happened to a very definite extent.'

It cannot have been easy for her. He worked long hours, had odd sleeping patterns, didn't much like company or restaurants, and when he was not working he spent his time studying ancient languages.

'Was it hard hiding the affair?' I ask.

'I never hid it. I told her straightaway,' he says. 'I was never keen on subterfuge.'

For 10 years, he lived with his wife and saw Susie, when he could – not with his wife's blessing, but with her knowledge. Susie tells me she would drive with him from the hospital in the city, all the way up to Pittwater where he lived to spend time with him. She would then catch a bus back.

'I knew that we would be together eventually and I suppose all women in my situation think that,' she says. 'But he told me it would happen, and I knew he didn't lie. I just knew it would take time.'

And so, when he retired, he and Susie moved to Tasmania and his wife stayed in the house in Sydney, on the water at Pittwater.

And now he says of Susie: 'There is no person I would want to live with more. I could not find a person who would be more suitable. She's just a great person and I think she would say the same in reverse. We are just very, very at one really. Still.'

She is like a schoolgirl when she talks about him. They tease each other like a pair of teenagers.

The next time we meet, Ian tells me he found Lisa's story about the Tasmanian Devils very interesting.

'So you finally watched the news?'

'Oh no. I turned the volume down until Lisa's story came on and then when it was over, I switched the television off.'

He may not follow the news, but he is devoted to sport, particularly American football. I learn this after spotting some sports magazines on his table, next to a pile of books written in Chinese. He religiously follows the Green Bay Packers and belongs to a club that mails out a copy of every game for him to watch.

'It's very stop–start but in a way that's the beauty of it because every play is so structured and everybody's got a job to do,' he explains. 'You look at a play and then it stops and then you think about it and what's going to happen.

'Have you ever heard of Thomas Merton?' he asks, reaching into his wallet for a clipping that he carries with him. 'Merton was a Catholic priest who was very interested in Chinese literature. I've had this for years.'

And then he reads it:

ADVENTURES IN CARAVANASTAN

In 1968 the French-born writer and Catholic monk, Thomas Merton, found himself among friends sipping bourbon and watching TV coverage of the Dallas Cowboys going down 31–27 to the Green Bay Packers. Merton afterwards reflected in his journal that the game had a religious seriousness which American religion could never achieve. Professional football, Merton said, had a comic, contemplative dynamism, a gratuity, a movement from play to play, a definitiveness that responds to some deep need, a religious need, a sense of meaning that is at once final and provisional, a substratum of dependable regularity, continuity and an ever renewed variety, openness to new possibilities, new chances: it happens, it is done, it is possible again.

Ian Johnston is a man whose spiritual needs are sustained by eastern philosophy, ancient poetry and gridiron.

He grew to love American football after a stint working in Canada in the 1970s. His love of Chinese poetry and philosophy began at St Andrews University in Scotland, where he went to escape his father. Because Scotland's system was different from England's, he was initially a year ahead and was exempt from many first year subjects. And so he spent a year reading.

'It was the first time I read Confucius, for example, and I read Chinese poetry and that was the start of being interested in it really.'

Frustrated with some of the translations, he became determined to learn the language himself, both the ancient and modern form, and attended night classes. In 1976, back in Australia, his teacher realised he was much brighter and more advanced than the rest of the class and sent him to meet Wang Yachun or Mrs Wang, a Chinese scholar living in a flat in Sydney's Summer Hill.

'It was one of the most memorable days of my life. I went out and saw this woman and the house was like this,' he says pointing to the shelves, 'very simple and full of books, and this woman talked Chinese to me non-stop for three hours. I knew a bit of Chinese but there was no way I could follow what she was saying. I could pick up odd things. She couldn't speak English. Out of it I managed to work out that we had an arrangement and so I used to go and spend two hours with her every week. We would read classical texts and that continued right up until I left. It was wonderful.' She later sent her son, who had qualified as a doctor, to work as his resident.

Ian taught each of his three children an ancient language for their HSC. One Latin, another Chinese. The third wanted to learn Greek so, even working full time as a brain surgeon, he did a quick PhD in Ancient Greek to have the necessary qualifications.

He has so far published five books: a medical text on tumours; a translation of Chinese philosophy; a translation of a classical Greek medical text; and two books of translated poetry from Ancient China. He is working on three more: translations of two ancient medical texts and a bilingual edition (translated into both modern Chinese and English) of Ancient Chinese philosophy.

He is widely read in philosophy but it is the Confucian teachings which guide him, he says. He has just translated two of the four books that were the basis of Confucianism from 1200 onwards and these are soon to be published.

'I've been interested in the philosophy and I do the translations, but it's not just about doing the translation. I deeply believe in the philosophical aspects of Confucianism.'

For him, this means behaving properly towards family members and immediate associates. He kept in contact with his father up until his death, even though he disliked him.

'Confucianism is about the individual person trying to be the best they can. I don't want to use presumptuous words, but as virtuous a person that they can be in their immediate situation. Don't worry about the big issues. It's about what you do in your own life and your immediate associations.'

He combines this with some aspects of Buddhism. He used to meditate on a set of cushions in his study, but Reg now uses them as a day bed. And while he believes in these philosophies he has never been persuaded of the existence of a superior or supernatural being, a God.

So, after a life of witnessing the fragility of life and of having studied the world's great philosophies, what answers does he have for the rest of us?

'Ha,' he says. 'Not many. Live a simple way of life, don't interfere with other people and try to do good. I feel that I have had a functioning life of helping people, which undoubtedly is the case. I was never motivated by monetary factors or reputation. I was very dedicated to doing the best I could for the patients. I did that for 30-something years. So now, on the last little end bit of the life, I live in a way that makes no imposition on other people and on things. I use next to nothing. I try to restore the land here and live a very simple life. If I have contact with anybody I try to make it as harmonious and kind as I possibly can. That's it.'

For his sixtieth birthday Susie gave him three things that he had never owned. She presented him with his first pair of jeans, his first joint and his first pornographic movie. He quite liked the jeans, for a while, but soon got annoyed that he couldn't fit his hands into the pockets and never wore them again. He refused to smoke the joint.

One night when they were in bed together, she slipped the movie into the video.

'Oh my God,' he said. 'My gosh, look at that. What is happening there?'

After a while, he turned to her and said. 'Do you mind if we put the football back on? That should get me in the mood.'

A few days after our last meeting he sends me this email: 'I have added the last lines of a long poem by Tao Yuanming (written in 405 AD) which is to be included in the forthcoming book. As I was reading them in the final preparation of the manuscript, it occurred to me that they offered an excellent and brief summary of the conclusions I have drawn from the material in the "pointy-headed" bookcase, and elsewhere!'

> *Our form in this world is very brief.*
> *Why not follow the heart and let things be?*
> *Why be troubled about what is unknown?*
> *Riches and honour are not what I want.*
> *The heavenly realm is not what I hope for.*
> *I just cherish a beautiful morning to walk alone,*

sometimes to plant my staff as I weed or hoe,
or climb the eastern hill to give a long sigh,
or write verse beside a clear flowing stream.
I must embrace change as I near my end,
and find joy in Heaven's decree.
What is there to doubt?

9

We are beginning to settle into the rhythm of life in a caravan with a toddler. It is unlike any travelling experience either of us has had before. In the old days before I met Lisa, travel generally involved dodgy bus journeys in third world countries, lazy weeks by the beach and searching for cute Catalonians to engage in late-night tango lessons. Life now revolves around Joe's daytime sleep. We see and do things in the morning, come back to the caravan for lunch, put Joe to bed and then head off again in the afternoon. It is travel within strict parameters – it's road haiku.

We have no oven, only a small bar fridge and limited storage space, but we've resolved to eat well anyway. We are working our way through half a dozen cookbooks. Our greatest fear is Joe being scalded with hot water so one of us has to entertain him while the other is cooking.

We bathe him each afternoon in a big bucket outside the van. He loves it. Grey nomads come to marvel at our happy little boy thrashing about in the water. They are missing their grandkids.

After leaving Bruny Island we set up camp in a pretty little caravan park by the water at Snug, south of Hobart, and erect the annexe to give us a little more space.

One night we are woken by heavy rain and howling winds. At about 1 am, I go outside with a heavy mallet to belt the pegs securing the annexe deeply into the ground. The wind is so strong that the rain stings my face.

By 3 am the winds have increased to a deafening howl, like low-flying aircraft. The noise is frightening and we are both getting nervous, me about damage to the annexe and Lisa about our safety. She gets Joe from his cot and puts him into bed with us, reckoning that if something falls on the caravan we'll take the blow and he'll be saved.

'We'll have to pull the annexe down or it will blow away,' I say. 'We have to go outside.' Both of us get dressed and leave Joe in our bed. The wind hits us in great gusts. We hear it before we feel it. During the lulls I drop the canvas sides while Lisa holds tight to the awning, to stop it blowing away. If the wind gets beneath it we are in trouble.

'I've got to go and check on Joe,' Lisa shouts through the wind and the rain, leaving me to hold the annexe on my own. 'Bugger Joe for a moment . . .' I shout, but she is already gone. A huge gust of wind hits and I hold on tight, cursing Lisa.

She re-emerges and we quickly roll the annexe, secure it and scurry back inside. Joe is unperturbed, maybe the rocking of the van is comforting him.

In the morning all is calm but the caravan park is a mess. Every tent has blown over and several vans and annexes have been badly damaged. The radio informs us that cyclonic-strength winds gusting up to 170 kilometres an hour have lashed the coasts of Tasmania and Victoria and dozens of homes and caravans have been damaged. There are widespread blackouts.

In the communal dining room we meet a couple who fled a caravan park further up the road. They had been camped in a tent beneath a tree. During the night, they packed up their tent and moved into their car. Moments afterwards, a huge branch landed on the ground where they had been sleeping. They then parked their car behind an amenities block. They had only been there a few minutes when the man had an uneasy feeling and moved the vehicle again. A few minutes later the roof blew off the building and collapsed right where their car had been.

This caravanning and camping palaver is not for the faint hearted.

10

On 26 January 1777, Captain Cook's *Resolution* sailed into Adventure Bay. On board was David Nelson, a young gardener who had been assigned the task of collecting botanical samples. As other crew searched for fresh water and feed for the animals, Nelson ventured inland and found a large, sturdy tree with rough, string-like bark and distinctive smelling leaves. He took the samples back to London and deposited them at the British Museum.

They sat there for years until a taxonomist, interested in naming new species, opened a drawer. He had never seen anything like them. He named them *Eucalyptus obliqua*, derived from a mixture of Greek and Latin: *eu* meaning 'well' and *calyptos* meaning 'covered', in reference to a part of the flower bud. *Obliqua* is a derivative of oblique, and describes the leaf base where the two sides of the blade are of unequal length. In this way, David Nelson's stringybark became the first eucalypt known to science and gave a name to a tree that dominates an entire continent.

Before I made this journey with Lisa and Joe, much of what I thought about Tasmania centred on one particular stringybark found here. I am not entirely sure if it is a *Eucalyptus obliqua* but I like to think it is – that it is somehow special. It is a tall, sturdy tree with a slight bend in the trunk and it's a stringybark.

It is a tree that broke my heart.

And now that I am back in Tasmania, the old emotions, unresolved for years, have resurfaced like an outstanding warrant. I hadn't ever really wanted to come back to this state. And then one day after we leave Bruny Island and are back on Tasmania proper, Lisa encourages me to take a drive to that tree – the saddest gum in all of Australia.

On the afternoon of 28 April 1996, John Lyons, the editor of *The Sydney Morning Herald*, shouted across the newsroom. 'Greg, Greg. Quick, come here.' A lone gunman had gone on a rampage in Tasmania. Eight people were dead. The editor wanted me to go home immediately, pack a bag, and meet the photographer, Rick Stevens, at the airport.

By the time we boarded a flight, the death toll had risen to 20. When we touched down in Melbourne the word was that as many as 40 people might be dead. We couldn't get a flight to Hobart. They were full of police commando and negotiating teams, so we had to fly to Launceston instead. By the time we arrived it was 10 pm. We were forced to make a late-night dash across the island to the Tasman Peninsula with Rick, a keen animal photographer, swerving deftly to avoid every quoll, devil and wallaby that came into the headlights.

The Tasman peninsula hangs like an earring on a lobe, an hour's drive from Hobart. It is home to about 1000 people scattered throughout villages and small rural blocks. There is only one road in. The ruins of the convict gaol, Port Arthur, sit on a bay at the bottom of the peninsula.

It was after midnight by the time we crossed Eaglehawk Neck to the peninsula, just 10 kilometres north of Port Arthur. Wherever we saw a light we would stop, knock and ask if anybody knew anything. We were both terrified that someone would emerge with a rifle. Those inside must have been equally scared because few answered the door.

At about 2 am we found the police roadblock. It was a few kilometres from where the gunman was holed up in the Seascape Guesthouse, we were told, possibly with hostages.

The editor was desperate for copy and a photo. He sent us out to knock on more doors. One or two people spoke to us and gave us snippets, which I filed back to Sydney.

Back at the roadblock, we considered walking to the Seascape where Martin Bryant was bailed up, but feared we might get shot. Police had established contact and were negotiating with him for the release of hostages. A special late edition newspaper was being held off until 6 am. We were under intense pressure to file. At about 5 am I walked past one of the police caravans and saw a cop inside dressed in overalls, talking on a phone. Written on his back, in fluoro lettering, was the word NEGOTIATOR. I found Rick. He took a couple of quick photos and was told to piss off. The door closed, but we had what we needed.

I phoned the news desk as Rick started processing his film in a canister. We found a bakery and he ran inside to dry his film in a pie oven. At 5.55 am he transmitted the photo. At 6 am the presses in Sydney were rolling.

Sometime after daybreak, a car drove past. The cameramen instinctively trained their lenses on the person in the back seat. A man jumped out and yelled: 'Turn your cameras away. This man has just lost his wife and two kids.' Walter Mikac was soon to become a household name.

Another man, Glenn Martin, waited quietly in the sun. His parents owned the Seascape Guesthouse. Glenn was hoping for the best, but his mum and dad were already dead.

Just after 7.30 am we saw smoke rising over the hill. Bryant had set the Seascape alight. An hour later an ambulance drove past, in no great hurry. Martin Bryant was inside, burnt but still alive.

The devastation one demented man had just inflicted was incredible. Thirty-five people were dead and 21 were injured.

The morning before, Bryant had left his Hobart home and driven down to the Seascape where David and Sally Martin lived. He had held a grudge against the Martins because they had bought a property his father had wanted. He shot Sally and then stabbed David.

He left the Seascape and drove further down the peninsula to the Port Arthur Historic Site, parked his yellow Volvo and made his way to the Broad Arrow Café carrying a large bag. He ordered a meal, ate it and then pulled a high-powered rifle from his bag and started firing at patrons and staff around him. He moved to the gift shop, along the eastern wall of the building, killing more people. In less than two minutes Martin Bryant had slaughtered 20 people.

Bryant then walked outside and began shooting at people in the carpark. A coach driver called Royce Thompson was shot in the back; he rolled under a bus and died later of his injuries. Winifred Aplin, a 58-year-old woman on holiday from South Australia, was shot in the chest as she cowered beside a bus.

Bryant got back into his Volvo and drove up a hill leading out of the historic site, killing indiscriminately as he went. He made his way back to the Seascape. He took a hostage with him. Bryant spent all night at the guesthouse until police arrested him, burnt and writhing in agony.

At about 10 am, a bus arrived to take the media on a tour of the killing grounds. The forensic police were still at work. An officer asked us not to photograph or film any bodies.

Smoke was still rising from the Seascape and a blood-soaked Ford Frontera sat in the middle of the road. The windscreen had been shot in. The driver had lived, we were told, but the impact of the bullet tore off her arm. Beside the road there were a couple of police cars riddled with bullet holes. The first two police officers on the scene had been fired on and had spent hours in a ditch, waiting for nightfall.

At a service station as well as the entrance to Port Arthur, there were blankets on the road, soaking up blood where bodies had been.

We pulled into the Port Arthur Historical Site. From the top of the valley, we looked down on the ruins of the old gaol and the tourist facilities, including the Broad Arrow Café. We walked to within 100 metres of the café and were asked not to go any further.

A police officer, tired and traumatised, tried to explain the carnage that had taken place inside. The bodies were still on the ground and we could see police going about their grim tasks with measuring tape.

A policeman then led us on a walk up a hill, an asphalt drive with a line of trees dotted along it.

On the road were two blood-stained blankets. Nanette Mikac had been trying to escape the carnage with her daughters, three-year-old Madeline and six-year-old Alannah. The policeman told us that Nanette was probably carrying her youngest and pulling Alannah along by the arm. Bryant killed Nanette with a single shot to the head. He fired twice at Madeline, first in the shoulder and then in the chest. It was the second shot that killed her.

I listened to the policeman. I was writing furiously in my notebook, but I couldn't comprehend any of it.

A few metres up the hill stood a big, sturdy Tasmanian stringybark with a bend in it. It was here that six-year-old Alannah had sought refuge after Bryant had shot her mother and sister.

Throughout the morning the policeman had remained composed but now tears began to well up in his eyes. His voice broke as he explained what happened next, while little Alannah, wearing her favourite dress, cowered behind the tree. 'He, um . . . he walked behind the tree and shot the girl at point-blank range.'

Policemen and journalists stood sobbing and hugging one another. No one said a word. What was there to say? The horror of what had happened suddenly became overwhelming.

Behind the tree, four sticks were laid out on the ground in a rectangle to mark the spot where Bryant gunned down Alannah. The police must have run out of plastic evidence markers. This image is seared into my memory. Who laid out these sticks? Who had the dreadful task of scooping up that little girl in their arms?

And then, we went on with our jobs.

My task that week was to do the death knocks. I talked to dozens of grieving relatives and survivors. I hunted out photographs of victims. The more senior journalists, Paul McGeough and Lindsay

Simpson, stayed in Hobart searching for information about the killer.

They are two good journalists with bulging egos. One night we all had dinner together along with the photographers, Rick Stevens and Palani Mohan. We ate lobster and drank a lot of expensive wine and McGeough and Lindsay argued at length over who would write the long colour story to run on the front page of Saturday's paper. Lindsay, a freelancer, kept threatening to resign. 'I've got better things to do,' she huffed. 'I should be off doing a story about platypus.'

People react differently under extreme stress but, to me, arguing over the prominence of a byline seemed pathetic in a situation like this. Both Lindsay and McGeough left the room to plead their case with editors back in Sydney. McGeough won.

And then, after eight or nine grief-soaked days and alcohol-fuelled nights, I flew back to Sydney. Within 12 hours I was back at work.

Thinking about it now, I'm not sure why I went to work. It's just what you did. But I only lasted a day.

After so much chaos, I needed some sort of order. I wanted to get my hair cut, dryclean my suits, pay my bills and maybe even do my tax. Anything but pick up a phone and talk about Martin Bryant. I found myself wandering around the city, not wanting to go to work, but not wanting to be at home alone.

At the time, I lived in a flat near Kings Cross. At the nearby Darlinghurst Police Station, which was then a community centre, I saw a sign advertising a counselling service. I went in, made a booking, and then sat there, with three or four junkies, waiting my turn. I finally got in to see a counsellor and explained what had happened. Three minutes into the session I thought, 'This woman is madder than I am.' I walked out.

I had often noticed a little hole-in-the-wall hairdresser, not far from my flat, and today, I thought, I would duck in. I asked for a haircut. As soon as I sat down I knew something was strange. The posters on the wall were faded and had been torn from magazines. It wasn't long before I realised the woman was not a very good hairdresser. Usually they run their fingers through your hair and then cut above, don't they? This woman was grabbing clumps of hair and cutting below with her unusually large fingers.

It was then I realised the woman was not actually a woman. I later learned that the transvestite who butchered my hair was not actually a hairdresser but an amphetamines dealer.

I paid, walked out with my bad haircut, and knew I needed to find some peace. I rang the *Herald* to say I wouldn't be in for a week. I was going home to Guyra. I wanted to lie in front of the fire and read books. Mum booked a plane ticket. I told her I didn't want to see anybody.

The next day I flew to Armidale and Dad picked me up from the airport. In Guyra, I went down the street to buy a paper. The first person I saw was an old family friend, Gwenny Nielson, who ran up and gave me a hug. 'Darl,' she said. 'Your mum told me that we're not allowed to talk to you, but I just thought I'd come over to see how you are.'

It is a beautiful sunny day. We drive from Hobart to Port Arthur, past green fields and around and over waterways, with Joe chatting to himself in the back seat. As we make our way down the peninsula I try to remember which houses I visited back in 1996. The old bakery, where Rick dried his film, is boarded up. I remember the frantic efforts we made to get the photo to Sydney. From this point on everything comes into focus. I remember it all vividly, like a movie replaying in my head.

Saplings, planted around the time of the massacre, have grown into large trees up around the Seascape Guesthouse. I can place where the police cars were, and the bloodied Ford. Further along I remember where the blankets had been, on the road and outside the service station.

As we drive into Port Arthur, I am still not sure why I am here. Lisa is quiet and is leaving me to my thoughts. Joe, of course, is oblivious.

A new information centre and café have been built and while Lisa takes care of Joe, I walk up to the reception. The place is packed.

I ask if there are people still working here who were working the day of the massacre. Halfway through the conversation a rush of grief overcomes me and I walk away into a corner.

Lisa talks to the receptionist. The woman says she had dated a guy whose parents were killed in the massacre.

More composed now, I return to the counter. The woman tells me not to worry, it happens all the time. Some of the people working that day are still here, she says, but none are rostered on.

'Would you like to call one of them?'

'No. No,' I say. 'It's okay.' What more can they add, I think, and besides – haven't they been through enough already?

We walk outside to the site of the Broad Arrow Café. It has been stripped back to its stone foundations and sits as a memorial.

Out the back, there is a simple little garden with a cross and the names of those who died. I am surprised by how many of those names I had forgotten. An inscription reads: 'May we who come to this garden cherish life for those who have died.'

Martin Bryant's name is not mentioned.

'Geez,' says a man in a tracksuit and an Akubra. 'Shocking, isn't it? Senseless.'

'Yes,' I say. 'Senseless.'

We then take a walk up the hill, the same walk I took with the policeman back in 1996.

I spot the tree. Lisa hangs back with Joe. On the ground are three little plaques you would never notice if you weren't looking. They say, 'Nanette Mikac, Madeline Mikac three and a half, Alannah Mikac six and a half'.

Around the plaques someone has placed some gerberas that have wilted, and some pipi shells. I wonder if Walter, Nanette's husband and the girls' father, put them there. I hope he has found some peace.

Joe crawls over and picks up one of the pipis off Alannah's plaque. 'She'd have been 18 now,' Lisa says.

I look behind the tree. The sticks, of course, have gone. I tear a strip of bark from the tree and put it in my diary.

I have often wondered why these deaths affected me so deeply. As a reporter, I have covered a lot of death in my time; dozens of murders, mine disasters, road accidents, and later, the earthquake in Pakistan, where 80,000 people died. But nothing affected me like this.

Rick Stevens, the photographer, and I have talked about it. He spent a long career photographing tragedies: from Cyclone Tracey, famines in Africa and the Bali bombings but, like me, he thinks Port Arthur was different.

'It was all so senseless,' he said. 'And every one of those people killed could have been your aunt, your mum, your friend, your kid. It was an ordinary day with ordinary people on holidays or at work. It was just so unexpected and so brutal. It has stayed with me like nothing else I've covered.'

Somehow it was different from a cyclone or the tragedy of war. Murder is more comprehensible when there are motives like greed or jealousy. Martin Bryant had no real motive, no sane motive, he was just unhinged, like a dog that kills sheep for fun. But he wasn't a dog and the people he killed weren't sheep.

At first, I thought he should die too – maybe the death penalty was right in this instance. Now I hope he spends every day of his life thinking about the horror he inflicted.

I still don't know exactly what is achieved by coming back here. At least now I can talk about it occasionally without getting upset. But perhaps tears are the only appropriate response to something so terrible.

I prise the pipi shell from Joe's hand, place it back on the plaque where it had been and we walk off into the sun.

11

'Get Real Forest Information' reads the sign out the front of Pru Barratt's house. Here in Maydena, these are inflammatory words and each month a logging truck will veer to the left and send the sign hurtling down the road. Someone has painted a large yellow penis on her fence and, at the entrance to the national park nearby, there's a message written on a boulder which reads 'Kill a Greenie, Save a Job'. Such is life for the only green in the village.

Perched up in the hills, an hour west of Hobart, Maydena used to be a company town. Every house was once owned by Australian Newsprint Mills, ANM, which processed its logs here before they went by train to the paper mill further down the valley. The plant closed in the early 1990s and 250 people, virtually the entire workforce, lost their jobs.

Pru Barratt's grandfather, John, 81, worked all his life for ANM, first as a bridge builder in the forests and later as a first aid man. He still lives here, on a little farm just out of town. Pru's father, Stephen, worked on the company's maintenance crew but lost his job when the plant closed. He survives now doing odd jobs and prospecting for gold. He's still fighting a back injury claim against the company. He lives in a caravan on a block owned by Pru's brother, Nicky.

Nicky is a timber worker. He's employed by a contractor to spray chemicals, burn off, and plant seedlings. Now in his mid thirties, he's been doing this since he left school and yet is still only paid between $16 and $17 an hour. If it rains and he can't work, he doesn't get paid. If his boss loses a contract, Nicky's hours are cut back and he sometimes struggles paying off his house and the few hectares that surround it.

The Barratts are old Tasmania. For John Barratt these forests provided a job for life, free health care and a company house. For his grandson there's no such certainty.

The fortunes of the forests have also changed radically. Up until the 1980s, in operations right across Tasmania, individual logs were selected and snigged out using small bulldozers. This timber went to local mills and was used for furniture, housing and paper. After 10 or 15 years, the forest would recover and you could hardly see where the loggers had been. It was specialised work and labour intensive. Men were admired for their skills as bushmen and they'd take bets on how accurately they could fell a tree.

Now, giant machines are used to obliterate the forest – not a stick is left standing. When the machines are done it looks like a First World War battlefield. Anything that remains is torched. The timber that is harvested is pulped for paper. The ground is then replanted with a single species, the shining gum, imported from Victoria. It can all be done with a handful of men. The forest has become a factory.

Pru Barratt has dedicated her life to stopping the clear-felling of these old growth forests in the Styx and Florentine valleys above Maydena.

Pru is 36 with long dark hair and a sinewy figure. She could be beautiful but the harshness of her character seems to have bleached the softness from her features. She speaks in short, sharp bursts, like a barking dog, and drives a panel van with an Aboriginal flag painted on the bonnet and 'Save Tassie's Native Forests' and 'Ban 1080' plastered on the side. She wears a vest which has a patch sewn on the back declaring that she is a 'non-breeder – I care about the planet'. Even among radical greenies she is thought to be extreme.

I visit her at her house, which sits behind an old church in Maydena's main street. She has a large, covered patio which serves as her forest information centre. Aerial photographs, showing the destruction caused by logging, decorate the walls along with posters of trees, pamphlets and stickers. She sells organic cornflower, jams and small organic onions, ambitiously priced at 80 cents each.

'As the daughter of a timber worker, how did you arrive at this point?' I ask her.

'I grew up in a beautiful town thinking everything was wonderful,' she says, as we sip herbal tea. 'I spent my youth out in the forest, hunting and fishing and we would collect gum nuts to sell. This was a great little thriving community with a youth club, a tennis club and a cricket club. It had a free company doctor and dentist. It all turned to shit when I was about 13 or 14, which was when my father lost his job, and the town just fell apart.'

As a kid she'd never really thought about the logging trucks that hurtled past her house – that's just what happened.

After school, at the age of 18, she left with her boyfriend and moved to the Pilbara in Western Australia. He worked as a boiler-maker in the mines and she drove trucks and trained as a horticulturalist. They split up after two years and she moved to Perth.

As a child, Pru suffered spinal problems and walked with callipers for a number of years to try to correct the condition. In Perth, after a work accident, the pain in her back became excruciating and she turned to massage, yoga and meditation for relief. It was during this reflective period, she says, that she began to question the way she lived her life and the impact she was having on the planet. She concluded that she couldn't continue living the same way. She became a vegan and quit her job at a plant nursery because it used too many chemicals.

'I became aware of the consequences of my actions,' she says. 'Even people within the movement find me alien because I have really strong understandings which I can't compromise.' She volunteers that she hasn't had sex for 12 years and has learned to control desire and use that energy more wisely.

Pru is also against bringing more children into an already overcrowded world. 'For selfish reasons, people want to bring an 80-year consuming nightmare onto the planet,' she says. 'It can't go on.' She has voiced these views to mothers with young children who've not always welcomed her opinions. 'But I can't help it. I can't help but tell the truth.'

'Maybe we should all be thinking about killing ourselves because of the damage we're doing to the environment,' I joke.

'I have thought about it,' she says, without hesitation or humour, 'but it would go against my principles of non-violence.'

After 12 years away, Pru returned to Maydena with new, uncompromising attitudes. But she found the community wasn't the one she'd left behind. 'The logging industry had changed so much, even from my youth,' she says. 'At least in the old days when they raped the forest there were jobs in it. Now it's all mechanised and the men are getting screwed. There used to be 250 people employed just from Maydena. Now it'd be lucky to be a dozen or so and they're clearing more forests than ever before.'

She used to hang out with her brother, Nicky, and his timber worker mates playing pool, but her views put her at odds with them. It all came to a head one day when some of the local boys got drunk and drove out to where the activists were camped in the forest and 'beat the shit out of them'. Pru had the names of some of those involved and reported them to the police. None were charged.

Her brother found out. 'The next thing Nicky comes screaming down the road and crosses my driveway yelling abuse at me, "I don't want your greenie fucking shit in my life. Don't bring it down to my house. You are not welcome on my property anymore – I don't want anything to do with this greenie fucking shit."' That was two years ago and they haven't spoken since.

That afternoon Pru and I drive out to the Florentine Valley. A group of activists has been living out here for more than a year attempting to stop a logging operation in an old growth forest.

They are mainly young kids from the mainland – university students, drifters, dope fiends, idealists, girls searching for meaning and boys hoping to get lucky – who come for a couple of weeks or a couple of months to help the cause.

Pru supports them but doesn't spend much time out here because she just can't hold back about the cigarettes, the pot and the drinking. She is a pacifist, and wonders how much more violent you could be to yourself than puffing on a roll-your-own Winnie Blue. 'Big tobacco and big alcohol are as bad as Gunns could ever be,' she says as we walk down the dirt track towards the camp. 'But it is acceptable within the forest group and within society. I go further than just the superficial. I mean, you can't be out here shouting "save the forests, we need clean air" if you're sucking on a cigarette killing yourself – you're just a hypocrite.'

In the middle of a track in the forest the activists have set up an enormous wooden structure, like a giant double-storied cubbyhouse. Inside the structure a car has been cemented into the road as well as large steel pipes that they can attach themselves to. It is all designed to slow the loggers until other activists arrive as reinforcements. It usually takes the police a few hours to get them out.

Today we stop and chat with a young couple, Owen 'they call me Sunshine' and Leith 'they just call me Leaf'. Leith says her parents are wheat farmers in WA. She quit her job as a video journalist on a sports channel to come to Tasmania. 'My parents don't like it but they have come to accept it.' Saving old growth forests, she says, is more important than her career.

It is hard to argue with her, standing here among these trees. Looking up at them reminds me of coming from the country to the city as a child and walking among the skyscrapers. These are the giants of the Australian forest, *Eucalyptus regnans*. Known variously as the Australian mountain ash, the Tasmanian oak, the Victorian ash or the swampy gum, this is the world's tallest hardwood tree and the world's tallest flowering plant.

Regnans are like whales, awesome and breathtaking simply because of their sheer size. Some of the trees in this valley are approaching 80 metres in height. They're as tall as the Sydney Harbour Bridge, from the road to the top of the giant steel arch.

They may be awesome, but they're not particularly beautiful. Scrappy bits of bark hang from their trunks and the tops of most trees end in a splintered mess – like a bad haircut. They've simply grown too tall and the wind has blown off their crowns. Maybe this is where Australia's tall poppy syndrome began – *E. regnans*: getting above themselves, too tall for their trunks.

Pru takes me further into the forest. Old, dead trees lie rotting on the forest floor, their trunks many metres across. There's a musky freshness in the air. Where trees have fallen, smaller plants – ferns and shrubs – are soaking up the sunlight before the canopy eventually closes over. The forest is bursting with life, all sorts of life. On trunks I see fungi that look like clams. Others look like the faces of old men. On the ground there are mushrooms, fire-engine red, and mosses, fluoro green.

And then Pru points out a line of white pegs with bits of orange plastic on them. 'That's where the road will go,' she says, angrily. 'They've got fuckin' plantations growing all over this state now, going to waste, and they want to clear this. This state is fucked.'

The next day I go out to meet Pru's father and grandfather, Stephen and John. John owns a 12-hectare farm just outside of town, and he and his wife still grow a hectare or so of vegetables and rows of old-fashioned flowers – carnations, dahlias, daffodils, gladioli and jonquils – that they sell at the markets in Hobart. They barter what they have left.

Stephen is waiting outside when I arrive. He shows me into a shed where he is doing up a 20-year-old four-wheel drive that he bought on the cheap. He wears a thick flannel shirt and a dirty, stained cap with 'Tasmania the lifestyle' written on it. His long reddish hair pokes out the back of the cap like Crusty the Clown. On his belt he wears a large hunting knife. He invites me inside and we sit down with his father, John, at a laminated table.

'Prudence was a wonderful shot as a girl,' says John, as we sip tea and make our selections from a packet of Arnott's assorted biscuits. 'She could take the eye out of a wallaby at 100 yards. She loved shooting and she loved fishing. Now, she wouldn't touch a good chop.'

Even as a girl she was different, adds her father Stephen. 'Radical, she was. The art teacher rang me up a few times wantin' to know what was goin' on in her head. When the kids were making pottery she was makin' skulls and things with snakes crawlin' out the side.'

I am expecting these two old timber workers to rubbish the idealism Pru brought back with her from the mainland, but am surprised at what they say. 'I am proud of what she does,' says her grandfather. 'You know she's had dinner with Bob Brown, and all.'

'They need people like her,' continues Stephen, 'to keep an eye on things. The Forestry here's just out of control. There'll be nothing left soon.'

Both men, who have lived in this valley all their lives, tell me the same story I have been hearing from liberal greens all over the island. The timber giant, Gunns, in collusion with Forestry Tasmania and the state government, is trying to clear as much old growth forest as it possibly can before the practice is outlawed. Once a forest is clear-felled it is forever in the hands of the timber companies as a plantation. It is a grab for land, forever, for the benefit of a few.

'When I first started working out here,' says Stephen, 'they brought in one enormous log and the boss reckoned it paid the wages of everyone working that day – 250 men. And now Forestry is taking out 100 times more than that each day and the people of Tasmania get nothing. There is no discount on our taxes or anything. There are hardly any jobs and the only ones making money are the big bosses at Gunns.'

They are worried about Nicky. He's become withdrawn and Stephen thinks the chemicals that they spray on the plantations are affecting his moods. 'He used to have a lot of friends but now . . .

he's got a beautiful pool table out the back of his house that ain't seen a cue for three years,' Stephen says. 'The chemicals, I reckon, have got him.'

He cops it too, for being Pru's brother. 'The other blokes stir him up. It's the same with those kids out in the forest. The bosses will say "bloody greenies, if this keeps up you won't have a job" and the workers go out into the bush and bash 'em and burn their gear. It all comes from the top.'

Nicky, they say, would have a different opinion from them.

'He gets pretty irate about this conservation,' says Stephen.

'Yes,' replies John. 'He doesn't even go much on his own sister.'

'They don't talk and she's not allowed on his property. It is ridiculous. The shit has been put on him. She's not all that pleased with him either. He's into poisons and killing animals. She is dead against the things he does.'

They believe Nicky has a right to earn a living and they can't abide greens going in and wrecking or damaging equipment, but they keep coming back to the idea of balance.

'I tell you what,' says Stephen, 'if it wasn't for people like Pru keepin' an eye on 'em they'd go bloody haywire, I'm tellin' ya. They are rotten blokes, Forestry.'

Old John says he doesn't much like this clear-felling and the waste of it. 'What they leave would make you weep,' he says. 'Beautiful timber – blackwoods, celery pines and myrtles. It all goes up in smoke. They won't even let people in to take it away as firewood.'

For all the logs that are taken the people of Tasmania receive few benefits. Even with the timber royalties Forestry Tasmania does not turn a profit for the people of the state. On the other hand the timber company, Gunns, is the largest and most profitable company in Tasmania. As few as 1200 people are now directly employed as forestry workers in Tasmania, according to an article on the *Tasmanian Times* website.

In the days that I am in Maydena I make several attempts to contact Nicky. His father tells me that he is passing on the messages but that his son just doesn't want to talk. 'He's scared the contractor might get the shits,' he says. One afternoon I stop at his house and knock on the door. A woman, who I assume is his partner, answers. She retreats into the house and I can hear a conversation. 'Sorry,' she says when she returns. 'Nicky's not talking to anyone today.'

Six months later, I am listening to the radio and hear a report that the blockade in the Florentine Valley has been smashed. There have been arrests. The loggers have now moved in. Where those glorious old giants, the *Eucalyptus regnans*, had reigned, there is now nothing.

12

Lisa has become obsessed with maps. As we are driving along, between feeding Joe sultanas and reading him *Hairy Maclary* and *The Very Hungry Caterpillar*, she stares at our touring maps for hours. She has fallen in love with the *shape* of Australia and looks at it as though it is a painting. 'I think it is the most beautifully shaped country in the world,' she says.

In the caravan we have a large, laminated *Australian Geographic* map of the continent and for the past few days she's had it out on the kitchen table, staring at it and writing notes. Something is brewing.

My best friend is an Irish photographer called Patrick, a lovely bloke, who is often as inept at life as I am. His wife is organised, smart and together, as is Lisa. Each time Pat and I meet up we toast our good fortune, at having 'married up' — and drink to Lisa and Cherie, saviours to two hopeless men. And so Lisa organises where we are going and I drive there.

'Babe,' she says when she's finally emerged from the map of Australia. 'We need to be in Queensland soon if we want to make it across the top before the wet season.'

What else can I say but 'Okay'?

We cross the Tasman and motor through Victoria, in a day. The following night we stay with an old school friend, Jeff Ticehurst, in

Leeton. He has two little girls, aged six and eight, who are smitten with Joe. But I have never seen two kids move more swiftly than when the three of them are in the bath and a pea-sized poo bobs up beside our grinning son.

The Ticehursts have organised a babysitter and we leave the kids at home and go out for dinner. After months in the caravan an Italian meal in Leeton feels as exotic as being on the canals of Venice.

In the morning it is lovely to see my old friend crouch down to each of his little girls, give them a big hug and say, earnestly, 'Darling, just do your best at school today.' It will be a ritual I'm sure he'll perform every day until they leave for university.

We leave Leeton early. I really want to stop in Griffith. I've heard it's an interesting inland town with great little coffee shops and delicatessens because of the large European migrant population. Joe falls asleep about 10 minutes shy of Griffith, so we drive on. Nothing in life is more important than his sleep.

As we head north the land gets drier and flatter. Somewhere in central NSW we hit a sign that says we've entered outback NSW. The outback is an odd term and no one seems to be really sure where it begins or ends. One rule seems to be that it's beyond where wheat is grown, but not always. Maybe it should be marked by the first dead emu beside the road.

The outback has to be flat and generally barren. Once you cross the border from rural Australia to the outback, service stations become roadhouses and the cost of fuel rises by a dollar a litre. Roadhouse is, in fact, an old Aboriginal term that translates as 'Charge triple, where else are the bastards gonna get it?'

The outback is also home to some of the world's most dubious tourist attractions. It is on a vast, dry plane along the Kidman Way, 100 kilometres or so south of Cobar, that we find one of them. (In the outback, you only have to say that something is a tourist attraction and it becomes one.)

Gilgunnia is marked on our map and we decide to stop here for lunch and to give Joe a break. He keeps teasing us with the I-am-about-to-take-my-first-steps routine. It gets us every time.

This place used to be a mining town of 1000 people that began with a goldrush in 1895, but there is now nothing left from that time — nothing apart from two old pepper trees. A water tank, a picnic table and a toilet have been recently erected by an Apex club.

The rush lasted until 1907 and a single mine staggered on until 1938. When it closed, the town ceased to exist. Despite this, an enthusiastic committee was formed to celebrate Gilgunnia's Centenary. It is bit like celebrating your grandfather's hundredth birthday, even though he died of a heart attack in the garden at the age of 54.

On a large granite rock that was specially selected and trucked in, the committee has erected two plaques.

The first reads, 'Gilgunnia — Centenary 1895–1995. To commemorate the pioneers of Gilgunnia Gold Fields.'

And the second, 'This plaque is dedicated to Leila and Tom Alderidge of "Burthong" in appreciation for all their efforts for placing Gilgunnia back on the map.'

There is also a really bad sculpture of a miner, made from old bits of steel.

Leila and Tom deserve their plaque because they did a splendid job putting Gilgunnia back on the map. And now, there are five other caravans pulled up, basking in the imagined splendour of Gilgunnia's glory days.

As Joe pushes his Playskool pusher around the dust I chat to three elderly people who are sitting in the shade outside one of their vans. They have been camped here for two days, they say, and may stay a bit longer.

'We love it here,' one says to me, 'the solitude.' That'd be solitude in numbers.

We push on to Cobar.

In Gilgunnia the boom is a distant memory. Here it is in full swing. We park our caravan in the yard of another old friend, Roger Jackson, who is in the mining game. Things have never been rosier and the only problem seems to be finding staff and places to accommodate them. One of Roger's former employees was a drill rig manager. He was living in Indonesia and they would fly him in and out, from Cobar to Jakarta. He left to work for another company that was offering him $200,000, tax free, in Sierra Leone.

The economy has hit the skids in the US with the collapse of the housing market, but China is full steam ahead. People in Cobar just can't help but make money. The town is swimming in the stuff. The boom, they say, could last another ten years.

13

Australians have this view of themselves as being a nation of larrikins. We see ourselves as part Ned Kelly and part Crocodile Dundee, proudly anti-authoritarian but with a sense of humour as well. The truth is we are a most law-abiding nation. Almost all of us live in neat little suburbs by the coast, we wear helmets when we ride our bikes and, unlike Paul Hogan, we generally pay our taxes.

Occasionally we break out and there'll be a hint of larrikinism, like a streaker at the cricket. But Channel Nine will refuse to show it and the commentators will prattle on about batting averages and strike rates while a woman runs nude in front of 50,000 appreciative fans. The hapless 'pitch invader' will be head-locked by police and taken to the cells, conveniently located beneath the grandstand, fined $5000 and banned from the MCG for life. Politicians will make their 'no apologies' speech for the crackdown on this heinous crime.

The reality is that we voted for John Howard for eleven years and only booted him out because someone equally as dull, Kevin Rudd, came along.

Such is life.

Lightning Ridge, the NSW outback opal town just south of the Queensland border, is the most un-Australian of towns. Here, disorder reigns. The official sign as you enter the town hints at what lies within: 'Lightning Ridge, population . . . ?'

This entire joint is a town planner's nightmare. In 1987 the council at Walgett did an aerial survey and found there were 800 camps, all of dubious legality, dotted among the vast opal fields surrounding the Ridge. A camp is a dwelling built above a mining lease and can range from a humpy or a caravan to an elaborate, sprawling house. A crackdown was ordered. There were to be no more camps. By the next survey, in the 1990s, the number of camps had more than doubled to 1700.

If you've ever wondered where the old vehicles of Australia – trucks, utes, cement mixers, caravans, double-decker buses and drill rigs – go to die, it's here. They live on a little longer than they should as old miners coax the last chugs of life from them, but from here there is no escape. Their rusting carcasses seem as natural to the landscape as the gidgee and the leopard woods.

And the Ridge has its own code of behaviour. On Bruny Island, ratting is to pull someone's craypot and the punishment is social exclusion. Here, a rat is someone who raids an opal mine in the dead of night to steal opals. The punishment is a little more severe than a cold shoulder. I was told about an incident, just a few years ago, where explosives were placed under the house of a ratter while he was out. The explosion could be heard 20 kilometres away. 'Nothing useful was left of the house,' grinned my informant, 'not unless you were in need of toothpicks.'

This is a place for dreamers. About one per cent of the people who come to Lightning Ridge to mine opal strike it filthy rich and never have to worry about money again, a long-time local informed me. Another five or 10 per cent will make a lot of money 'like winning-the-lottery rich'. Forty per cent will make a modest living and the rest will live in poverty and 'have to send the wife out to work to pay the phone bill'. The 10 per cent who make it sustain the dreams of the 90 per cent who don't.

For many of those who come here – the Germans, the Aborigines, the drifters, the Croats, the crooks, the mad, the retirees and the greedy – hope sustains them long after reality may have slipped away.

I grew up hearing stories about Lightning Ridge, of how someone or other had gotten into trouble and slipped off to the backblocks of the Ridge to mine opal for a year or two until things had blown over. Or of others, who had supposedly made a fortune.

But that's not why we came. We were drawn to Lightning Ridge after reading a little book that charmed us. Flicking through an old copy of *Granta*, Lisa had come across *Pobby and Dingan*, by Ben Rice.

'You've got to read this and we have got to go to Lightning Ridge,' she insisted after wiping the tears from her eyes.

It is a slim book, a children's fable, both beautiful and sad, and as good a book as you'll read about Australia. 'It is an enormously touching, imaginative and unexpected novel,' says *The New York Times*, 'that just glows in your hands.' We had to visit the town that inspired *Pobby and Dingan*.

It tells the story of Ashmol Williamson and his little sister, Kellyanne who live in Lightning Ridge. Much to Ashmol's annoyance, Kellyanne has two imaginary friends called Pobby and Dingan. The children's father, Rex, is an opal miner who comes home from work 'covered in dust, his beard like the back end of a dog that's shat all over its tail'. When Rex cracks too many tinnies of VB, which is often, he gets emotional and 'it is like the beer is going in his mouth and coming out his eyes'.

One day Pobby and Dingan go missing down an opal mine.

Kellyanne crawled into my bedroom through the car door. Her face was puffy and pale and fuzzed-over. She just came in and said: 'Ashmol! Pobby and Dingan are maybe-dead.' That's how she said it.

'Good,' I said. 'Perhaps you'll grow up now and stop being such a fruit-loop.'

Tears started sliding down her face. But I wasn't feeling any sympathy, and neither would you if you'd grown up with Pobby and Dingan.

'Pobby and Dingan aren't dead,' I said, hiding my anger in a swig from my can of Mello Yello. 'They never existed. Things that never existed can't be dead. Right?'

Kellyanne falls ill with worry and, despite his cynicism, Ashmol figures the only way to help his sister get better is to organise the people of Lightning Ridge to help in the search for Pobby and Dingan.

> *Well I think Kellyanne was pretty amazed by all this, because her eyes were wide open. She turned and whispered to me: 'Are all these people looking for Pobby and Dingan?'*
> *'That's right,' I said. 'Even the Abos.'*

And so Lisa and I set up our camp in a town that is 'full of flaming crackpots . . . like the sun had burned out their brains . . . a place full of holes and criminals and freaks'.

Ormond 'Ormie' Molyneaux and his brother, Joe, look as if they've been transported from the 19th century. Ormie is a tall, rangy man with arms that start off big at the shoulder and are just as big at the wrists. No one ever got arms like this at a gym. They're a product of a lifetime of manual labour. Joe is even bigger.

The brothers, both in their late 40s, wear stubbies and t-shirts and big, heavy boots. Joe, who lets Ormie do all the talking, has a little towelling hat pulled down low over his ears like Wal Footrot, while Ormie favours a wide-brimmed Gray Nicolls cricket hat. Both men have great bushy beards, like the founding fathers.

I was told that Ormie was a man who had 'held a million dollars in the palm of his hand more than once in his life'.

'Molyneaux. That'd be French,' I say to him, not long after we have met.

'Our family got kicked outa France a fuckin' long time ago,' he replies in the broadest of drawls. Ormie is one of Lightning Ridge's leading figures and a big-wig with the Lightning Ridge Miners' Association.

'The old man came out here after the war, shootin' roos and lookin' for opal,' he says when we meet at his place, a comfortable but modest house on a big block in the middle of town. 'His father, my grandfather, was here before the war, scratchin' about as well.'

Ormie, his brother, Lisa and I sit on the verandah in the shade drinking beer, while little Joe crawls around the yard playing with a dog. Ormie's wife also comes outside to chat. She spent some time in Guyra as a kid, and we talk about people that we both know.

The boys are very particular about their beer and an esky full of Tooheys on ice sits at Ormie's side, like a faithful dog. He pats it often. After chatting for a bit they agree to show me down their opal mine. They've assessed that I'm not a rat, or working for one.

The next morning, at 6 am, the brothers drive past the council caravan park where we're staying and I follow them out to the claim.

We turn off the main road and drive out through hard, scrubby country littered with old machinery and mullock heaps. An abused British Leyland truck, with a drill rig on the back, sits above the mineshaft at the Molyneaux claim. Parked next to it is an old pink Ford tip truck.

Ormie starts the generator to run the lights and the hydraulics underground and explains the system he and his brother have created to ward off ratters. It's pretty simple. The ladder into the mine stops halfway down the shaft.

'Hopefully the cunts'll scurry down the ladder, run out of ladder and break their fuckin' necks,' he says.

Joe climbs down and puts the other ladders in place and then when he gives the signal I climb 30 metres into the earth on bits of wobbly steel with my notebook tucked into my pants and my camera over my shoulder.

At the bottom, tunnels spear off in several directions from a large cave they call the ballroom, which is propped with cypress pine logs. The clay here has remained undisturbed since the time of the dinosaurs and as Ormie cracks off a piece of the ceiling with a hammer, to show me something, it releases a musky scent that has remained trapped in the clay for some 65 million years.

He leads me down a shaft where a couple of bright lights

illuminate the textured clay roof. They are looking for a black substance called potch, which is basically silica. Over millions of years, liquid silica has leached down through the earth and become trapped in the clay and solidified. While most of it is worthless, some has formed into opal. When polished it sparkles and shines a rainbow of colours so beautiful that drunk men will weep telling you about it. No two stones are ever the same.

As *Pobby and Dingan*'s Rex Williamson says:

Ashmol, I sensed it today! Tomorrow we'll be on the opal, son, and we'll be bloody millionaires! I can feel those bewdies in the drive just sitting there staring at me.

Ormie points out minute strands of tree roots that look like fine spiders' webs. These roots have made their way down through faults in the earth which is sometimes an indicator of where opals may be found.

'We just have to find the cunts,' says Ormie, explaining the intricacies of his trade.

Most opal miners now have little hydraulic diggers, like a small backhoe, that they operate with a joystick to gouge out the opal dirt. Ormie and Joe prefer to use the old-fashioned method of jackhammering the clay. 'When you drink as much piss as we do you need to keep in shape,' says Joe, in a rare statement.

The two men then lift their jackhammers. For an hour or so they spear the clay, gouging out clods of opal dirt from the walls and the ceiling. It is cool down here but within minutes they have their shirts off and are sweating out last night's Tooheys, the enormous muscles in their backs and arms working in tune with the thud of the hammers.

When they are done, a great pile of earth sits on the floor of the mine. Joe disappears up the ladder and a few minutes later a huge steel bucket is lowered into the shaft. Ormie steers the bogger, a tiny little hydraulic front end loader, with a joystick, scooping up the opal dirt and driving it back to dump in the bucket. When the bucket is full, they hoist it up and it lands in the truck.

They repeat this until the truck is full. They say I can come over to the puddling dam later in the week, to watch the process of washing the opal dirt to reveal the stones.

'You might work months or years before you come across a patch of opal,' says Ormie. 'And then all those opals might be in the one load of the bogger.'

It is why ratting is such a terrible crime. Men could work for years to find the stuff and then have it all stolen in a night. The ratters, they explain, are cunning. They sit and wait. They camp out in the scrub and see who is putting in extra hours. They note who is buying new vehicles and equipment. They watch for the mood of men, pissed at the pub. They reckon there's a certain look that comes over a man who's 'on opal' and it's harder to conceal when drunk. Then they strike, in the middle of the night.

A miner will arrive in the morning to see something amiss. A section of his ceiling or wall that was there yesterday is gone today.

'It fucks with your mind as much as anything,' says Ormie. 'You don't know what you've lost.'

Each morning we are in Lightning Ridge we put Joe in his pram and walk out to the hot spring baths on the outskirts of town. The ground out here is littered with thong-piercing thorns – cats eyes and devils heads – and almost every day we get a puncture in the pram and one of us has to carry Joe.

It's worth the walk though. The baths are a delight. There's no entrance fee or fences and the two cemented pools, one hot and one not quite so hot, sit out in the middle of a paddock. Old Romanians, Greeks, Italians, Russians and Bulgarians bask in the hot waters that bubble up from the earth. They talk to each other in their own tongues or in broken English. If you ask where they are from they'll tell you the old country but almost all of them add, 'but Aussie now'.

We also spend a lot of time wandering around the streets – Opal St, Agate Rd, Silica St and Gem St – popping into shops and talking to locals.

A woman who runs a motel tells us that she and her husband moved to Lightning Ridge to mine opal 10 years ago. After a lifetime of being responsible, having an office job and raising kids, she said it made her feel like a delinquent. 'I felt free digging around there in the dirt all day and then going into the supermarket with clay all over me,' she says.

One day we come across a strange European woman who buys opals for a living. She clams up when we start asking questions. 'That bitch,' we are told later, 'she buys from the ratters.'

'Who are these ratters?' I ask Maxine O'Brien, the hard-bitten secretary/manager of the Lightning Ridge Miners' Association.

Maxine is a woman who doesn't pull her punches. 'They are generally of a certain ethnic persuasion . . . well, let's be honest, they are basically all Yugoslavs.'

There was a big influx from the Balkans following the wars during the 1990s and they formed ratting gangs, she says. 'Some of them are hard men who'd stick a knife in you as quick as look at you.'

One day we meet up with a young miner called Aaron Bruce, a nice bloke. He's 27 and a multi-millionaire. He owns a new Hilux as well as a new souped-up Commodore. He has a spa on his front verandah. It is a winner, he reckons, with the backpacking chicks who arrive each week on the bus. 'Women are rarer than opals in Lightning Ridge,' he tells me.

On the wall in his study, Aaron has a picture of two trays of opals — it's his favourite photo. In one tray there are a dozen large opals and in the other several dozen smaller opals. He and his partner collected them in just one load and it took them less than an hour. They netted almost half a million dollars.

His dad was an opal miner too, but died young and broke after striking it rich as an 18-year-old. Aaron reckons he has learned from his old man's mistakes and is investing his money in units down the coast as well as shares.

'Come back in five or 10 years' time,' says another old-timer. 'I bet you he'll have the arse out of his strides. It's just the way it works.'

And then we meet Bob Hewlett, the unluckiest miner in all of Lightning Ridge, a man as unlucky with opals as Rex Williamson from *Pobby and Dingan*. Rex had 'strange eyes – blue and green with a flicker of gold in them. "Eyes like opals," my mum once said with a sigh, "only a little easier to find."'

Bob Hewlett also has eyes that sparkle, but that's because he laughs a lot. He's just about the happiest man you'll ever meet, despite never striking much colour.

'Bob Hewlett,' people say when we mention his name. 'You wouldn't meet a nicer bloke, but you wouldn't want his luck.'

After our first meeting, Bob invites us for dinner with him and his wife, Donna – she works at the school to pay the bills. They live about 10 kilometres out of town in a place that's been a work in progress for decades. They started with a tent before upgrading to a caravan. And then, as the Hewlett family expanded so did the camp. A room was added to the van, not long after their first son was born. Another room came later, along with a tropical roof to keep the place cool. Thirty years on, the caravan is buried deep within the house – it's now a walk-in-wardrobe. Somehow, it all works beautifully.

Out the back of the kitchen, Bob leads us up some stairs, made of old tyres, to the top of a mullock heap. From here we peer out over a dam that used to be an open cut opal mine. The Hewletts have planted dozens of trees – willows and gums. It is almost pretty.

While Donna and Lisa wander off with Joe to feed the chickens, Bob tells me a bit about his past.

He came to Australia from Wales as a 10 pound Pom in 1962. He was 23. He got a job stacking books at the National Library in Canberra and then decided to go bush. His two options were cherry picking or wheat testing. He chose wheat and was sent to the north-west of NSW. When the wheat season was done he thought he'd check out this place called Lightning Ridge.

Bob ended up dividing his life between wheat and opals. Over the summer, he'd work on the wheat harvest managing the giant grain silos near Walgett and during the cooler months he'd head back to Lightning Ridge.

He met Donna in 1974 on a trip to Brisbane. She was a young bank teller, 17 years his junior, who was charmed by this charming man. They got married, travelled back to England and were going to do the hippie trail across Afghanistan, but then the Russians invaded and Donna became pregnant.

They came back to Australia and Bob did another wheat harvest. When it was over, Bob introduced Donna to Lightning Ridge. 'We found a few thousand dollars worth of opal. It was enough to make us want more.'

But as Bob readily admits, he's never made much more than that. 'My bad luck is legendary.'

He explains that after miners have washed their opal dirt and been through it to check for opals, the remaining rocks are dumped near the puddling dams. A group of Aborigines waits for the trucks and will sift through the rocks for any opal the miners may have missed. It is an accepted practice called noodling. There is fierce competition to be the first when the rocks are dumped. Fights can sometimes break out at the back of the tip trucks.

'They don't even bother standing up when they see me driving in,' Bob says with a great laugh.

An hour later, when Joe has finished cleaning out the Hewletts' kitchen cupboards, had a bath and been put to bed in his portable cot, the four of us sit down for dinner in a cosy room full of well-thumbed books.

Bob, who's the Lightning Ridge councillor on the Walgett Shire Council, explains that he's been fighting for years to preserve camp life for the small-time miners. The authorities just can't abide the disorder created by people building their own dwellings on their own little mining leases.

'They keep thinking that we will be inundated by dole bludgers,' he says. 'But a summer or two in Lightning Ridge will sort them out. This place is unique. We should try to preserve this.'

We ask the Hewletts if they've read *Pobby and Dingan*. Donna has but Bob hasn't. We give him a rundown of the story.

'That little girl wouldn't be the only one in Lightning Ridge with imaginary friends,' he says with a great cackle. 'I've been imagining opal ever since I first came here.

'It's a bastard of a thing, opal. It just gets you in. Each time you go to leave you suddenly find a bit. Most opal exists in your own head. There's always been more opal in people's heads than in their mines.'

Young Ashmol Williamson summed it up the same way:

And the rest of the world thinks we are all total nutters, but they can go and talk to their backsides for all I care. Because they are all just fruit-loops who don't know what it is to believe in something which is hard to see, or to keep looking for something which is totally hard to find.

On another evening, I say goodnight to Lisa and Joe and drive out to one of the remote opal fields, about 60 kilometres out of Lightning Ridge. There are several illegal hotels out here to which police turn a blind eye. I visit the Glengarry Hilton – a pub in a shed in the middle of nowhere.

The night is wonderful. There are drunks and spivs trying to buy opals and farmers getting away from their wives. I meet them all and we drink into the wee hours. I stay in a demountable building out the back for $15.

In the morning, while I am eating breakfast, three old men are having a conversation out the front of the Glengarry Hilton. Two of them are Aborigines.

'Wasn't that great,' one of the Aboriginal men says, about the Prime Minister's apology to Aboriginal people. 'That Kevin sayin' sorry to us fellas.'

'It was good,' the other two reply.

'Me and my cousins were talkin' about it and reckon it'll be good for land rights. My cousin Johnny, he reckons he's gunna claim Arnhem Land. He likes the look of them gins up there and reckons the fishin' is unbelievable. My other cousin, Lionel, he reckons he's takin' Queensland, all them sandy white beaches with them good lookin' backpacker sheilas. Queensland is for him. Me?

I been thinking about this a long, long time,' he says, with a long pause. 'I'm takin' Liquor Land.'

The three men fall about laughing.

On Saturday morning, as arranged, we drive out to the puddling dams, where Ormie and Joe Molyneaux are tailing out.

It's like a scene from *Mad Max*. On a massive mound of dirt surrounding a muddy pond are about 20 old cement trucks. It looks like the past set in the future. As we drive in, a caretaker pokes his head from a shed and must make a judgement call that a man, a woman and a baby in a Volvo are unlikely to be ratters.

High up on the mound, Ormie and Joe are hard at work separating opal from dirt. The dirt is basically clay and so when it is rotated with water in a cement truck, the clay washes away and the rocks are left. These rocks are then tipped out onto a long steel table. Ormie and Joe sift carefully through the rocks with their hands. They go about their task methodically, stopping just occasionally to open another Tooheys. Our little Joe sits on the back of their ute, watching the process intently.

The opal is sorted into two containers. One lot goes into a bucket that they sell by the kilo. The more valuable opal is put into a plastic Napisan container. It is sold by the carat.

I peer into the container and say jokingly, 'I suppose there's 10,000 bucks in there?'

They both look at each other. And then, with a wry smile, Ormie says, 'No, there's a lot more than that'.

Ormie's on opal.

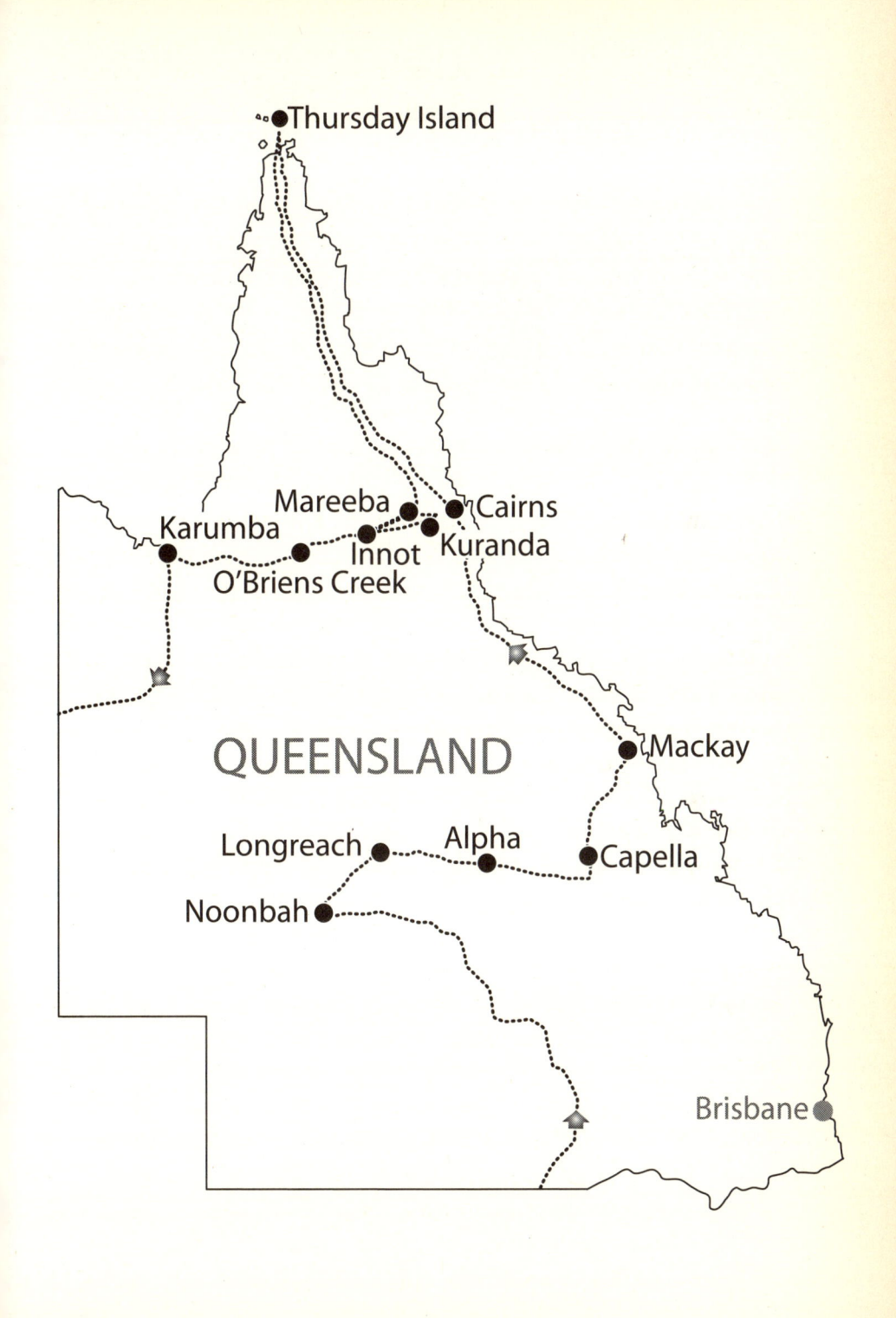

14

As we head north from Lightning Ridge the names of the towns and villages to our east and west sing to us from road signs, rhythmically. It's like a poem recited by an old blackfella – each new line is revealed 50 kilometres or so from the last – Mungindi, Goodooga, Dirranbandi, Nindigully.

We cross the border without much fanfare, just a parochial sign pointing out the many treasures on offer in the grand state of Queensland. I am half expecting the former premier, Peter Beattie, to be at the border with a toothy grin, a bad Akubra and a firm but friendly handshake. Instead, there are just a few droopy-eared Brahman cows munching on sun-bleached autumn feed.

The confidence displayed by the state's welcome sign is on show in each little town north of the border. They all possess one or two grand hotels large enough to stand 500 drinkers or more at any one session. 'XXXX,' they curse in giant lettering from the rooftops. Their main streets are a couple of hundred metres wide and planted with enormous trees. There are ambitious and beautiful town halls, of stone or elaborate timber, and schools of art and buildings to house haberdasheries. They just lack people. Surat and Augathella never quite became the inland metropolises they were meant to be.

We have an enormous two-day drive to make it to the middle of Queensland, to a farm west of Longreach, and the further north we go the drier and harder the country becomes. We entertain Joe by singing endless rounds of 'Old MacDonald Had A Farm' and try to introduce him to native species, but who knows what noise Old Macca's wombat makes, let alone his platypus or his hairy-footed dunnart.

There's a report on the radio about a breakdown on the Parramatta line in Sydney causing commuter delays. Out here, the news seems to be arriving from another planet.

It's not until we stop for supplies that we realise how feral we've become. Back in Lightning Ridge, I stepped on my glasses and they are now held together by a ball of sticky tape. Our clothes are filthy, stained with red dust, and Joe has bits of food all down his front. He has a bump on his forehead from yet another attempt at walking. Lisa has not dyed her hair for a couple of months and the grey roots are inching upwards from her scalp. The demented punk-mother look may be great in Newtown, Sydney – it's not so great in Roma, central Queensland. 'People are staring at us,' she says as we make our way into Woolworths. Joe is intently piloting his pusher in a quest for discarded Coke bottles and old cigarette butts to put in his gob.

At some point we cross from the Murray–Darling catchment into the Lake Eyre Basin. The basin covers more than one-sixth of Australia and yet all the water that falls across this vast catchment never reaches the sea and hasn't for the past 150 million years. It is, apart from the poles, the least densely populated place on earth with just 60,000 people – 30,000 of those in Alice Springs.

We pass through paddocks that extend to the horizon and you can see the curvature of the earth as the sky bends and the clouds drop out of view. The land is harsh and unrelenting.

On the ABC we listen to Tim Winton talking about his new book, *Breath*. Winton tells us about a couple of his characters, British migrants, who are 'kind of emblematic of generations of Australians who have lived in Australia and not really felt that they belonged or who have not even been able to see where they live ... You've got to be mindful of the fact that it takes a while to see and feel where you are and it's pretty common for people to come out to Australia, drive out and just think, "Well, there was nothing out there, there was nothing to see." It's just that they didn't know what to look for.'

It sums up how we both feel out here. The land around is mesmerising but we don't understand it. There are times when it seems there is nothing here.

We pass over a bridge which indicates the gully beneath us is the Thomson River. 'The old Thomson has seen better days,' says Lisa as we look out to see a few putrid water holes on a largely sandy riverbed. Like Winton's characters, we don't really know what we're looking at.

We press on through more and more seemingly empty country, hoping that the man we are about to meet will open our eyes.

Angus Emmott is seated at his kitchen table drinking coffee from a cup his kids bought him in Brisbane at an Andy Warhol exhibition. 'I like boring things', it declares. The kids have nicknamed their dad Nature Boy. As he takes a sip from the mug his wife, Karen, walks in the door and plonks something on the table wrapped in tissue paper.

'Present for you, darling,' she says.

The cattle farmer carefully peels back the tissue. Inside is the body of a small bird with splashes of blue on its wings. Its eyes are closed and it has, understandably, a melancholic look about it.

Karen had been into the nearest village, 50 kilometres away, to attend a course in mosaics. As she was driving home through a patch of mulga scrub, a little blue bird had darted in front of her vehicle and she heard the soft thud as it hit the top of the bull bar. It hurtled over the roof to its death.

Now her husband is examining it at the kitchen table. 'Well, what do you know,' he says, turning it over in his fingers. 'It's a female *Malurus splendens emmottorum*.' He puts the dead bird in his pocket and continues to sip from his cup. He allows himself a smug little smile.

Angus is wearing a grubby old work shirt and is a tad soft in the tummy – the result of Karen's amazing cakes and slices. When he is not wearing his stained cap, his thinning hair is revealed. His top lip supports a 1970s-style moustache, like Rod Marsh's, and he wears those all-purpose spectacles that become sunnies, sort of, when you go outside. If you saw him in the street you'd think this 46-year-old man was a truck driver.

The dead bird in his top pocket, the *Malurus splendens emmottorum*, is a subspecies of splendid wren named by a taxonomist at the Queensland Museum in honour of the man sitting at the table, Angus Emmott, because he discovered it.

The little wren will go into a freezer in Angus's study and from there it may end up on display in a glass case at the University of St Petersburg or at the Academy of Natural Sciences in Philadelphia. It is one of dozens of species that had been unknown to science until it ended up in the hands of this curious cocky.

The world of natural history is very happy that Angus Emmott likes boring things.

Angus's grandfather first settled on this property, *Noonbah*, in 1917. The holding, 140 kilometres south-west of Longreach, now comprises a relatively modest 60,000 hectares of Queensland channel country.

The homestead is a jumble of architectural styles and each new generation has added a piece, but not subtracted from the past. A 1950s double-storied Queenslander sits next door to the original cottage. Just off the house there are stockmen's quarters, built at some other time and in another style. They are now empty. Angus's contribution, a large covered patio with a bubbling water feature, sits out the back of the cottage overlooking a paddock and the water storage dams. Forty people could sleep here, comfortably, and a serious game of hide and seek would take several days.

Angus and Karen's two kids are at boarding school, so the couple now lives alone in this warren of timber. But they have the company of their many pets as well as the frogs in the toilets.

Karen, a nurse who grew up on the coast at Mackay, is warm and engaging and the sort of mum who sends off food parcels and long letters to her kids every other day when the mailman comes.

Angus is the eldest of three children and has spent his entire life here at *Noonbah*. He did his schooling by two-way radio at the School of the Air until he finished his formal education in Year 10, at the age of 15.

We sit around his kitchen table drinking good brewed coffee, while he tells us he's always had an interest in nature and in collecting things. 'My mother wasn't very impressed but as a little kid I would collect snakes and keep them in boxes,' he says. 'At first it was pythons. I graduated later on to the more bitey ones; mulga snakes, brown snakes and death adders.' He also collected birds' eggs, camel skeletons, insects, Aboriginal grinding stones and feathers.

When he was about 10 years old, a man from the Queensland Plague Locust Commission came out to *Noonbah* looking for different species of grasshopper and Angus was shown how to properly pin insects and how to identify minute differences. 'I knew what I collected was only touching the surface,' he says. 'When you walk out in the grasslands in summer there are all these amazingly different species of grasshoppers and they change when you move into a slightly different habitat. I was fascinated by those changes and why one would thrive in one area and not another.'

During these Darwinian awakenings, Nature Boy was born.

A few years ago he was awarded an Honorary Masters degree from the University of Central Queensland for his contribution to desert science. And now a friend who is a professor from Harvard University and a regular visitor to *Noonbah* is encouraging him to go to Harvard to do his doctorate. I wonder how often someone has turned up at the esteemed university to do a PhD having never set foot inside a school classroom, let alone a university.

After coffee and slices of Karen's cakes, Angus takes us on a tour. On one of the verandahs he opens a freezer to reveal an aviary of dead birds of prey: whole eagles, kites, hawks, falcons and bits of an owl that came to grief on someone's Landcruiser. These will go to university and academic institutions around the world. He has collected many of the species, mainly killed by cars or cats and has a network of friends and neighbours who save him their roadkill.

'We had a koala in the freezer once,' he says. 'We'd pull it out for international visitors to have a bit of a cuddle and to take a few photos. It was a hit.'

Inside Angus's enormous study there are dozens of jars with snakes, lizards, goannas, turtles, geckos and fish. Another freezer is stacked to the brim with Glad Snaplock bags containing birds, marsupials, lizards, frogs and large insects. There are a couple of large black drums filled with pure alcohol and one has dead goannas floating about in it; the other, lizards and snakes. Each reptile is tagged with a number and a GPS record of where and when it was found.

In cabinets on the walls are the skulls of dozens of animals, from small marsupials to a giant camel. There are more on the floor.

Angus opens the wide, flat drawers of one to reveal displays of great beauty: hundreds of pinned beetles in one, colourful butterflies in the next, cicadas, giant mantis, cockroaches, flies, wasps, ants ... there are dozens of drawers.

His study is an Aladdin's Cave of natural history.

It is also full of surprises. On a bench in blue plastic tubs is a collection that looks like some sort of animal dung. It is actually owl vomit or, more specifically, regurgitations, known as owl pellets.

Owls, he explains, swallow their prey whole and then regurgitate the fur and the bones. 'I am halfway through a survey for the Queensland Museum which is looking at the distribution of native rats,' Angus explains. 'If there are any out here their skulls will turn up in the owl pellets.'

There are specialists in arid reptiles, birds, trees, marsupials and even cockroaches but few people in Australia have as broad a knowledge of desert ecology as Angus.

From *Noonbah* he has identified more than 500 plant species, 185 birds, 62 reptiles, 30 mammals, 14 fish, 28 butterflies, 25 cicadas

— many of which were previously unknown to science, as were many of the cockroaches, flies and ants. A whole host of animals has been named in his honour including an almost legless skink, *Lerista emmotti*, that he found in the garden, a long-necked turtle, *Emydura macquarii emmotti*, the wren and myriad invertebrates.

And to think you could drive past and think there's nothing out here.

One night recently Angus was in bed reading an article from a science journal about the evolution of mammals when he came across something he thought interesting. He nudged Karen, who was asleep. 'What is it darling?' she asked, used to these nocturnal interruptions.

He explained there is a theory that Australia once went 17,000 years without a monsoon – in these parts that equates to a 17,000-year drought.

'Please don't tell the neighbours,' Karen begged.

A farmer was recently complaining to Angus that he had been 'in drought' for the past 10 years. Angus replied that maybe it wasn't a drought. Maybe it was just normal.

He views the dry times as part of the natural cycle.

'It doesn't help me financially, but it does mentally,' he says. 'Dry is the natural state out here. How we manage that is going to be the big challenge as things get drier and hotter.'

Lisa mentions the Thomson River that we passed on our way to the property and the fact that we thought it appeared to be in bad shape. The Thomson, Angus says, is in fact in great shape. It is certainly in a lot better condition than the dying Murray-Darling.

'A healthy river in this country might be completely dry and empty and barren,' he says. 'That is the nature of desert rivers. But when you do get these big monsoons, the water goes down the stream and covers the flood plain and you get this huge burst of life with insects and fish. It not only supports the aquatic system but is also a very important breeding ground for birds like pelicans and ducks and whatever, especially as so many wetlands around Australia have been drained or cut down.'

Out here, he says, the boom sustains the long bust. In dry times nature retreats to small areas and few survive. When rain does come again the survivors repopulate, quickly. 'If we get rain out here we will have zebra finches building nests within 24 hours.'

During floods, clams and shrimp that had remained dormant in the dusty riverbeds burst into life in the billions. It is one of the most incredible flourishings of life on earth.

'The explosion of insect life after a wet season is equal to any biodiversity you will get anywhere in the world.'

Understanding the nature of this cycle has caused Angus to drastically change his grazing practices. He has fenced off sections of his property to leave as nature reserves.

When his father managed *Noonbah* it ran 10,000 sheep and 1000 head of cattle. 'The old man didn't know it but it was unsustainable,' he says. Angus has vastly reduced the stocking rate and now runs just over 1000 cattle and no sheep.

He says that many farmers simply do not have a great understanding of the land they inhabit.

'They might say they are at one with the land, but they probably can't name 20 or 30 species of plants, let alone anything else,' he says. 'They are just very focused on their stock and the palatable grasses. But you just can't keep pushing and pushing the land because you can tip over the entire ecosystem and you can see that happening now with the collapse of the Murray–Darling system.'

Angus is the chair of the Lake Eyre Basin Committee and a prominent member of other bodies that lobby and advise government. His strong views have sometimes put him at odds with other farmers. Whenever there is a call to turn coastal rivers inland Angus will be on the ABC, patiently explaining that this is not a good idea and would do great harm both to the coastal system and inland systems.

'Some people have told me that I don't represent the majority view of farmers because I am too green. That's okay, people are entitled to that view. I mean, being too green just may mean that we (humans) are here for another 500 years rather than just another 100.'

Climate change will make large tracts of Australia unviable for grazing, he says, and the effect on nature will be devastating.

'The temperature spikes at the top end are pretty scary,' he explains. 'It is almost unbearable out here at 45 degrees and when it hits 50 the birds start to die. If we get a rise of several degrees in temperature then the high-end spikes could go up quite a bit. If it spikes at 55 then the bird population will be severely reduced and cattle won't go out to feed. Everything changes.'

While he is critical of some farmers, he is also angry about policies that allow productive land to be used for housing. 'The east coast is the most productive land we have and yet every year more and more of it is concreted over to make more housing and nothing destroys an ecosystem quite like a slab of concrete. This places pressure on the system elsewhere.'

'Massive changes need to take place everywhere if we are going to save things. And I don't know if it can be done.'

As we are talking there is a great barking of dogs and a squawking of chooks outside.

'Hello, he's back,' says Angus.

We follow him out to the chook pen. The Emmott's two Jack Russells have an enormous goanna, a yellow-spotted monitor, bailed up. The reptile, a metre and half long, is a regular visitor that comes looking for eggs and especially loves freshly hatched little fluffy chicken nuggets. Angus moves behind it while the dogs keep it occupied and then he pounces. With one hand behind the neck and another on its body he brings it close for us to look at.

'Beautiful, isn't he?' he says. We admire the goanna for a while before he puts it gently over the fence to see it scurry off into the paddock.

Angus has a way with animals like Steve Irwin did. The two were friends who bonded over snakes. Where Irwin sought celebrity, Angus courts science.

★

On our second day at *Noonbah*, Angus and I go for a drive across his property in his old semitrailer. He has three rogue cows to take back to a paddock and out here it is easier to truck them than to drove them, the distances are so vast.

As we drive along, he points out various trees, shrubs and birds and how they all interact. I imagine that he views the land in a similar way to Aborigines, before the arrival of whites. He sees it in a different way from you or me, the way that autistic savants see patterns in numbers, perhaps. He is looking for small changes that indicate big things.

He points out the gidgee, leopard wood and beefwood. Birds fly out and, for my benefit, he rattles off their common names: crimson chats, diamond doves, brown falcons and crested bellbirds.

If a plant is in flower he knows what birds and insects it will attract and the marsupials and snakes that in turn feed on them.

It is all interconnected and if the land is overgrazed, he says, this whole system falls down. If the cattle are allowed to eat everything then nature has no chance.

We pass trees that are so beautiful they look out of place in this landscape of desert shrubs and rugged acacia. *Eucalyptus papuana*, the ghost gum, is surely the most beautiful of all gums. It is like a beautiful young Danish backpacker that got off the bus in the outback and decided to stay. The trunk is smooth, like the skin of a child, and glows a brilliant white as though it has lived a life out of the sun. The branches lean out delicately and form little ripples, like folds of skin. Its leaves are vibrant and green and plump as if they were watered daily.

'I think it's important to do this sort of work,' Angus says as we trundle through the paddocks of *Noonbah*, chatting about his documentation of the species. 'The universities don't have the money or the time to be out here. And so if we are going to sustainably manage ecosystems we at least need to know what is out here.'

'Do you become despondent with the drought and with the state of the environment?' I ask him.

'Yes, often,' he says. 'When things get too bad I go out and chase snakes. They have always been my favourite. I love the texture of them and the smooth and graceful way they move. I just love to watch them. Snakes cheer me up.'

His eventual aim, he says, is to cut his cattle numbers right back and to work more with scientists and universities on various projects using *Noonbah* and his expertise in natural history. 'I pretty much do it now, I have just got to work out how to get some bugger to pay me for it,' he says.

One afternoon we sit on the back patio, sip cool drinks and try to keep Joe from falling into the water feature. We chat about living out here, this far from town. Both Angus and Karen say that despite the improvements in roads and vehicles and the arrival of the internet their sense of isolation is actually increasing. There are fewer people living out here than ever because corporations have taken over big tracts of land. Family farms are becoming a rarity.

'When I was a kid this property had three families living on it, plus a couple of single stockmen and all the other farms around here were the same,' Angus says. There were lots of parties, tennis days, picnic races and a great sense of community.

Now, six of the eight farms that surround *Noonbah* do not even have a manager on them. They are owned by corporations or wealthy cattlemen from other parts of the state. They come in once a year for the muster. Any fencing work is done by contractors. The cattle remain but the community is gone.

For those who stay it is tough. Karen says that some of the mothers move into Longreach so their children can attend a local school and they can get a casual job, to ease the financial strain. 'It is just terrible for their family life. I have seen several marriages break down as the husband and wife grow apart, with her in town and him out on the farm.'

The isolation doesn't stop the Jehovah Witnesses, however, who still come knocking even all the way out here. Angus invites them in and gets them started on long philosophical and ethical discussions about souls saved versus their carbon footprint. 'I've had them running out the door,' he says with a cheeky grin.

In other ways, the Emmotts are not isolated. They receive a constant stream of visitors with links to the world of natural history.

The week before our arrival, a scientist interested in the genetics of dingos was out here. The famous bird artist, William Cooper, is a regular visitor. The World Bank has been working at *Noonbah* for a number of years looking at arid trees and shrubs and how they may be grown in parts of Africa for fuel or essential oils.

'Angus's interests certainly make it a very rich life,' says Karen. 'And it's been wonderful for the kids growing up. They've met a huge diversity of people from all around the world. I think they take it as a matter of course that everybody gets possums out of trees and measures them and keeps things in their freezers and collects plants.'

Romance has also blossomed out at *Noonbah*. A woman from New Zealand and a man from the US both came to study cicadas and fell in love. They are now married.

'You wouldn't think two people could base a love and a life on cicadas, but it seems you can,' Angus says.

Karen says the big moments in her life with Angus always involve nature. On the first morning of their honeymoon, on Dunk Island, he woke her up at 6 am to go bird watching.

'Not exactly what I had in mind,' she says.

When she was due to have her first child, her waters broke at 3 am and they rang Angus's parents, who lived next door at the time, to let them know they were heading to town. 'Angus's dad was on the local council and there was a council meeting on that day. He was never one to pass up a lift and so he jumped in the car with his council papers.

'So I am in the front, in full labour, trying to maintain my dignity with my father-in-law in the back with his little pork-pie hat and council papers, chatting about other things as if nothing was happening. I felt every bloody cattle grid on the way into town.'

Finally, she saw the lights of Longreach and felt a great sense of relief that the baby would not be born in the car. 'And then we both saw it, on the side of road – this dead bird came into view. Angus looked at me with these big eyes and I said, crankily, "Oh, you may as well stop. Pick it up." And so we turned around and picked up a bloody dead bird on the way to the birth of our first child.'

It was an Australian Pratincole, a long-legged and graceful running bird that favours the Australian outback in summer and Java and Borneo in the winter, Angus informs me.

We say goodbye to the Emmotts after a few days, and on our way to Longreach come once again to the Thomson River. We look at it with different eyes. It is no longer a fetid ditch. As we pass over the bridge I keep a keen eye out hoping to see an *Emydura macquarii emmotti* poking a head out from its shell.

15

My big sister, Megan, is a milliner who works for the London Opera. She is a committed non-breeder, but not for environmental reasons. She's just not much into kids and I can understand that – neither was I until Joe somehow snuck through. Meg reckons she is going to invent a marker pen for people just like her.

It will work like this: when one of your friends, let's call her Claire, has her first baby you take the pen and run it over Claire's name in your address book so that you can't see it. Her name is effectively erased. After about two years the pen will fade and Claire's name will pop back up in your book and you will think, 'Oh, I must give Claire a call. We'll be able to have a chat now.' That way, Meg reckons, she can avoid the hours of mindless baby talk and her friends won't have to be offended when she is unable to conceal her complete lack of interest. It's best for all concerned.

Alternatively, you could send the doting couple with their baby on a trip around Australia in a caravan for a year. That way the parents can look on in wonder at the development of their child, in isolation, and no friendships need be harmed in the process.

We wake most mornings to the sound of Joe cooing in his cot. It's as beautiful a sound as the morning warble of the magpie. We let him out and all of us snuggle up together for the next hour in our double bed, which folds out at the end of the caravan.

For me, the biggest joy of this trip is being able to witness my little boy's progress each day instead of being in an office.

Today we are in a caravan park in Longreach, sitting outside beneath our awning. Joe is over near the barbecue area, a couple of metres away, playing in the dirt. Suddenly, he stands up and stumbles forward like a drunk. One step. Two steps. Three steps. He is not even aware of what he has done.

To us it is the most amazing feat of human achievement ever witnessed. It's as if he is Moses and has just parted the sea. We smile and hug him and later crack a bottle of wine to celebrate.

Our friends, work colleagues and even Abdul, our local shopkeeper, should be thankful that we are alone in central Queensland and that they are spared the minute details of our little boy's astonishing daily achievements.

He's very advanced for his age, you know.

16

When I was a kid growing up in the bush there was no bigger event than the Guyra Show. We would save our pocket money for months and then climb through the hole in the showground fence behind the cricket nets to avoid the entrance fee. Money was for the octopus, the dodgems and Dagwood Dogs.

One year, when I was about 10, a local greengrocer called Henry Riley organised a junior boxing event and I secretly entered it. I could fight as a kid and was certain I could beat my opponent. It turned out to be one of the most traumatic days of my life. In front of everyone in the district, my mother dragged me from the ring before a punch had been thrown. I have never forgotten the humiliation.

Another year I secretly entered the junior calf ride and came fourth. I was grounded for a week.

And each year, a week or two before the show, a strange kid would turn up in our class at Guyra Central. There would be one or two in each of the other classes.

'Children, this is Leroy,' Mr Skinner would announce. 'His family is with the show. Now I want you to be good to Leroy while he is here and you might even get a free ride.'

They all seemed to have old-fashioned names like Leroy or Mervin. None of them wore school uniforms and they would sit at the back of the class not saying much. You just knew never to get into a dust-up with a Showie like Leroy because they could all fight. And if they lost they'd stab ya, so we reckoned.

The show was such a large part of country life and yet we knew nothing of the people who manned the ticket box at the ferris wheel or made the fairy floss. They were a mystery race.

All these memories are now flooding back because we are in Longreach and the show is in town.

Longreach sells itself as the Aussiest of Aussie towns. There was probably a question on John Howard's Citizenship Test which read: 'Which Australian town most embodies the country's spirit of mateship, ingenuity and undeniable greatness?' You'd have been sent to Nauru if you didn't answer Longreach. The Stockman's Hall of Fame is here as a 'tribute to Australia's outback heroes' along with the Qantas Museum that commemorates the enterprise of the 'founders of this Great Australian Company'. Then there's that iconic outback institution, the School of the Air, which for years has secretly been producing greenie, pinko pastoralists who know Latin names for cockroaches and read Noam Chomsky.

If anywhere in Australia is going to have a great show it surely must be Longreach, we figure, so we head off to check it out.

I can't find a hole in the fence large enough for the stroller so we pay our money at the gate. We are surprised at how few people are here. The agricultural display halls are almost empty and the displays themselves are pretty slim. Outside, there don't appear to be many people competing in the horse events. There is a BBC documentary crew filming a show called *Outback 8*, about kids experiencing the authentic outback lifestyle. The crew looks as bored as the kids.

We take a wander down through sideshow alley.

'Where's the cha-cha?' asks Lisa.

It's nowhere to be seen and neither is the octopus or the hurricane. There's only one decent ride, the zipper, but it stands silent because of a lack of patrons. There's a small merry-go-round staffed by a guy in a grimy shirt and a Captain Morgan rum cap and we entrust our son to him. Joe sits on a little zebra, not really sure if he should laugh or cry.

Yesterday I rang the Showman's Guild and was given the name of Nita Bell, who I was told came from an old show family. We almost leave without seeing her but decide we may as well drop in now that we are here. We track Nita down at her Dagwood Dog stand. She is a short woman in her mid sixties with blonde-grey hair that's pulled back in a pony tail. We talk to her while she serves chips, dogs and waffles.

It is the last afternoon of the show and Nita is packing up in a couple of hours, she tells us, and moving on to a little place called Alpha, two and half hours' drive away.

'Why don't you come and camp with us at Alpha? I'll organise a camp spot for ya, love.'

And so we run away with the show.

Alpha is an old railway town of 390 people, 450 kilometres from the coast at Rockhampton and 250 kilometres from Longreach. The railway yards closed in the early 1990s and since then the town has battled to survive. Its streets are named after the great British writers: Shakespeare, Milton, Byron, Tennyson and Burns. However, the early flourish of poetry in Alpha seems to have faded and the newer roads are named Shortcut Ave, Dip Yards Rd and Northside Truck Detour.

We arrive at the showground, located in a paddock over the railway line, late in the afternoon. The Showies are camped on one side of the ground and the horse people are on the other. They don't mix.

Some of the Showies are living in caravans that look as if they've escaped from the backblocks of Lightning Ridge, as do some of the inhabitants.

Nita, however, is fastidiously tidy and she and her husband, Gary Miller, have saved us a spot next to their neat little caravan. We are tucked up behind the dodgems and the Dagwood Dog stand. On the ground around us electrical leads criss-cross like spaghetti. Nearby, someone has plonked an old washing machine on the ground and it is whirring away.

Workers in stained and tattered caps with teeth to match wander about with sledgehammers, preparing the rides and the stalls for tomorrow's show.

Nita takes Joe while we set up. She feeds him biscuits and he plays with her little dog. Because we are late there are no spare taps or power points so Nita organises adaptors and directs us to the best showers in the showground. She helps out as we bath Joe in a bucket outside. He and Nita take an instant shine to each other.

After a big barbecue dinner, courtesy of Gary and Nita, we tuck Joe into bed and listen to him talk himself to sleep as we settle in around the campfire.

The Showies know how to do a good campfire. Someone stopped off along the way from Longreach and collected a load of gidgee wood. Gidgee is a slow-growing acacia and its wood is dense and dry. On a campfire it burns slow and hot, without any smoke.

We can hear the snorting of horses, the stars are out and there's a grand cast of characters around the fire: misfits, old boxers, a woman who was the World's Smallest Musician, the granddaughter of a lion tamer and a softly spoken young bloke with a guitar who we learn has been recently released from jail for sexual assault.

Gary, Nita's husband, opens up to Lisa about his dreadful childhood. His father was white and his mother was part Aborigine. He was given up for adoption as a baby because of the black 'stain'. He lived in boys' homes until he was 12 and then ran away to the show and got a job with a boxing tent. The show became his family. He started fighting at 14 and turned professional at 16. He was a demon on the grog but one day just gave it up. He now survives on cigarettes and Coke.

The show, he says, doesn't care about your past. 'It's very tolerant. It doesn't matter who you are or what you are. I had every show lady in the country lookin' after me when I was a kid.'

He may have had a limited education but Gary is no dill. He reads newspapers and is a great fan of SBS. 'How's that Hamid Karzai going over in Afghanistan?' he asks at one point when we tell him we lived in South Asia. 'Do you reckon the Yanks can stabilise the joint?'

There's a young guy called Patrick, a big fat kid of about 20, who is an apprentice butcher from NSW, helping out one of the other show families. He's been coming on the circuit for the past few years, to get away for a few months and to party. They say he's a good worker. Patrick has a terrible hacking cough. We offer to lend him Joe's humidifier but later realise it won't do him much good in a swag.

Real estate on the showground is handed down from generation to generation, we learn. Each show person knows, to within a metre or so, every patch they 'own' on every showground around Australia. They'll fight to defend their ground. At any time there are two or three different show circuits worming their way around Queensland, which is why Longreach missed out on the big rides – they were on the Emerald circuit, heading to Mt Isa. Many of the big rides are owned by Nita's twin brother Elwyn Bell. Elwyn is a multi-millionaire, they say, one of the richest showmen in Australia.

I chat to a woman called Terry Foster, who is in her sixties. She grew up in a circus and traces her ancestors back to the gypsies of Europe. In the 1960s and 1970s her family had variety shows and Slim Dusty and Johnny O'Keefe were feature artists.

She's spent her life in the game but doesn't know how long shows like this one at Alpha will survive.

'The world is too fast now. In the 1970s and 1980s we were the number one entertainment out here. You would come out to these little towns that didn't get no entertainment and it was a big thing. The women used to come out all dressed up to the hilt, bring the family. Now we are competing against the computer world.'

'That's right,' Gary chips in. 'There's nothing sensational anymore. We used to have people lining up to see the fat tattooed lady. Now, you get that walkin' down the main street.'

The conversation moves on to having kids on the road. Education is a struggle, but there's general agreement that it's a great life for children. Someone is always looking out for them. And with the babies, the women say, breast is definitely best.

'The true test of a show woman is to be able to feed a baby while driving a truck, and not to miss a gear going up or down a hill,' claims Nita's daughter, Leanne. 'If you had to stop all the time you'd never get there.'

Leanne is a vivacious woman with grown-up kids. She is a 40-something divorcee who has been managing pubs. Nita encouraged her to come back onto the road to cheer her up and Leanne has a little stall, selling snow cones.

'There are three things that show people care about most,' she tells me. 'Dogs, children and tap fittings. Don't ever fuck with a Showie about dogs, children or tap fittings.'

Someone produces a guitar and Leanne, who is polishing off her second bottle of wine, starts to sing. She has a great voice and does a good job of Robbie Williams's 'Angels'. On her next song she forgets the words.

People have drifted off to bed, Lisa among them. I follow soon afterwards. Leanne is looking at me cross-eyed. I can't tell if she is trying to give me the eye or if she is just trying to focus.

Joe wakes early the next morning and we stroll around the showground. We pass the people who have come for the dog show. Everyone on the ground hates the dog people.

'They're all fuckin' queer,' Gary reckons. The dog people exist in another world and have no contact with anyone else at the show. They come with their dogs, parade at the dog show and then leave. They bring their own sandwiches and flasks of tea.

This morning, near the dog arena, there is a woman who has two whippets on leads. It is a cool morning and the dogs are dressed in coats of pink fleecy flannel. The woman is dressed in a tracksuit made of the same material.

'Do what ya gotta do, Laddie,' she commands one of her dogs, 'and it's not a fart.'

We come across a bloke they call Jam Jar. He is an ex-Queensland copper who now travels the circuit selling confectionery from a van. He wanders around the showground sipping rum from a jar.

I'd love to know why he left the force. Jam Jar never looks great and this morning is no exception.

'How's things?' I ask.

'Not good. Got pissed as a fart and put 200 on a nag and blew the fuckin' lot. That's a lot of fuckin' lollies.'

We walk around the pavilions where young station hands are mucking out the cattle stalls and grooming red and grey cattle with great Quasimodo humps at the tops of their spines. The boys put Joe on the back of a placid beast and he squeals with delight, and then fear.

Horsey women in tight jodhpurs and pursed lips gallop their charges in circles. The horses snort steam from their nostrils like fire from a dragon.

As the sun rises higher, town people and farmers gather to do their bit. Men stack bars with beer and ice and women with clipboards earnestly judge the texture of cakes, the quality of paintings and girth of pumpkins.

In a shed of squawking birds, I see two men standing side by side, each holding a live rooster with wings spread. One is a small bird and the other a large white one. The bantam is judged Best All-Breed.

Joe is in heaven – he loves the animals and better still, because we are with Nita, everyone gives him free rides. One of his new words is 'more' and at the Alpha Show it's getting a work out.

He's particularly interested in the Gilmore All Star Circus – a family act that includes mum, dad and their three boys who perform impressive acts juggling, balancing and clowning around.

Thirteen-year-old Lewis Gilmore is one of those kids who looks like he's been wired together with spare parts. He's all odd angles and infectious enthusiasm. Lewis has a whip-cracking act, 15-year-old Zac is a clown, and big brother Zeb, at 17, is the master juggler and balancer.

'My brother Zeb,' brags Lewis, 'is one of two people in the world today who can balance a lawnmower on his chin. My uncle invented the act but he died. There's some bloke in America, they reckon, and Zeb. There's only two.' Zeb, he says, has a 'grouse act'.

The word grouse, long dead in the mainstream, is in common use among the Showies.

Travelling with the Gilmores are seven miniature ponies, two alpacas, a miniature long-haired steer, two geese, five chooks and a host of doves, dogs and goats.

And a brand new Victa lawnmower.

The Gilmores spent many years working on sideshow alley, before putting together the family circus.

'It's great to see them doing this new show,' says Nita. 'We need to come up with new ideas to keep the shows alive.'

She hopes the country shows will continue but admits it will be hard and that some might have to amalgamate, just like the councils.

It doesn't take long for us to realise that our host is the matriarch of the showground. All disputes and grievances come to Nita. She struts around like a bold little terrier, daring anyone to take her on.

She is the head of the Showman's Guild on this run and has to ensure the rents are paid and people have their dogs tied up. She's fighting a losing battle to get all the sideshow people dressed neatly and in clean clothes on show day.

'Honestly, some of them are that bloody dirty they frighten the customers away.' She and her staff are dressed neatly in uniforms that say 'Nita's Snacks – Mobile Catering'.

During the days we spend with Nita, her life story is revealed in snippets.

Her father was a famous showman called Roy Bell who started Roy Bell's Touring Stadium in 1924. She grew up living in a tent and toured all over Australia with her family and a team of boxers and wrestlers. As a little girl, she worked in the tent as a contortionist, entertaining the crowd before the bouts began.

Unlike many show people, Nita got an education. She was sent to a convent boarding school in Sydney at the age of seven. After school she considered nursing, but the lure of life on the road was too strong. She tells us what a wonderful life it has been and how show people are a very accepting lot. She despairs at

Gary's experience as a child and claims he would have had a totally different experience had he been born into the show world.

'His mother was part Aboriginal, his father wasn't and because of that he was given up for adoption,' she says. 'His family never sent him a birthday card or a Christmas card or went to visit him. Had it been a show person we would have opened our arms up to him.'

Despite Nita's rosy view of how accepting the show people are her own experience tells a different story. Show people, at least in the past, weren't entirely colour blind.

Nita was her father's favourite, his 'little princess', but she secretly fell for his champion boxer, a Maori fighter called Lester Karaitiana and, at the age of 19, she became pregnant.

'My father asked me if I was pregnant. He thought I looked a bit fat, and I said "no". I felt guilty 'cause I told him a lie so I went back the next day and said, "Dad, I told you a lie. I am pregnant." And he said, "Well you've got one hour to get out of the place." That's how much I broke his heart.'

Lester may have been his champion in the ring but old Roy didn't want him marrying his favourite daughter. 'Things were different in them days,' Nita says. 'There were no interracial relationships like there are now.' She and Lester were banished from the showgrounds. She ran a Chinese restaurant and Lester drove trucks and while they were away they had four children together, including Leanne.

Nita kept in contact with her mother and would secretly visit. One year at the Bega Show, a gorgeous little girl with soft brown skin came bounding into Roy's caravan. 'Who's this lovely little girl?' the old showman asked. 'It's your granddaughter,' replied his wife. 'This is Nita's daughter, Leanne.'

It was after this that Roy relented and invited them back onto the show circuit. He provided them with a caravan and the relationship with both Nita and Lester was apparently mended.

'Were you ever bitter?' I ask Nita.

'No. It was just the way in them days. That was just the attitude back then.'

Her marriage to Lester ended, but they remained friends. She was single for 10 years until she and Gary got together. That was 20 years ago.

She and Gary have built themselves a nice little house on a block outside Canberra and they've saved for their retirement. They've worked hard and done well.

'It'll be hard for me to retire because I get home and I dunno what to do with myself. I've been on the road most of my life.'

We travel with Nita, Gary and Leanne to the next show, at Capella, where we meet up with other members of the family, who are heading north to Mt Isa. Nita's other brother, Arnold, has made a good living out of shows but hasn't bothered to buy a house – he and his wife live permanently on the road in their caravan and travel overseas each year at the end of the show season.

They will all make their way across into the Northern Territory for shows at Tennant Creek, Katherine and Darwin. We plan to be in the Territory in a month or two and promise to meet again.

But before we say goodbye, Nita insists that Joe try his first Dagwood Dog. He licks off all the sauce but is not quite sure how to attack the battered frankfurt. 'Never mind,' says Nita, who hands him a bucket of chips as a consolation. He has no trouble with them.

Will his generation, I wonder after we leave, be the first to reject the lure of a Dagwood Dog?

17

After weeks of dry heat we leave the Queensland cattle country for the coast. One minute we are in dust with mining trucks clogging the roads and the next we are crossing the divide and seeing cane fields, dairy farms and cockies in gumboots. The air is humid and the country is lush, but this beauty fades as we hit the coast. A lot of Australian coastal towns are exceedingly ugly, particularly in Queensland, where the grand messiah of crooks and spivs, Sir Johannes Bjelke-Petersen, nurtured his flock with love and understanding for two decades until 1987. His followers worshipped at his altar and left their offerings in brown paper bags.

Mackay may have been a beautiful town once, but not anymore. Its outskirts are ringed by kilometre after kilometre of ghastly industrial developments. Signs, as big as cars, scream at you from enormous prefabricated sheds. Bunnings! Bed Shed! McDonald's! Wow Sight and Sound! Thrifty! Harvey Norman! . . . It reminds me of some of the uglier parts of Bali and it's like this from Coffs Harbour to Cairns – 2500 kilometres of strip mall with some token rainforest and cane fields in between.

Soon, our land will be girt by superstores.

We drive through the centre of Mackay to a little place called Bucasia, in the northern suburbs, and find an old-fashioned caravan park right on the beach. The Bucasia Beachfront offers 'camp sites, caravan sites, bbq's, pool, ice, bait, gas, phone – sorry no pets'. Paradise for $28 a night.

But not for much longer.

A flash new sign alerts all who pass that Tempo Lifestyles™ plans to turn it into the 'Bucasia Beach Resort and Spa * Absolute luxury beach houses in a boutique resort * Restaurant * Alfresco lounge and wine bar * luxury day spa * lap pool * resort pool'.

'Bastards,' I say to Lisa. 'Haven't they taken enough already?'

Secretly I'm picturing myself slipping into that luxury day spa with an icy glass of chardonnay. I can see Lisa too has a faraway stare – she's imagining the massage menu.

We check in and are assigned a spot. It is drizzling with rain. I set up the van in the wet and we try to entertain a hyperactive toddler in a confined space. Joe tests out his new walking skills: on the table, on the bed and on my head while I am trying to read the paper. Then he totters into the tiny toilet while Lisa is trying to do a pee.

That afternoon, I meet a guy who is travelling with his young family and picking up short-term contracts in the mines along the way. He's an electrician and he shows me how to use the hot water system.

It's simple really. You turn it on. And so now, four months into the trip, we can have showers in the van rather than going to the amenities block. And we no longer have to boil water for Joe's little plastic bath or to wash up.

That night we sit outside and share a drink with the electrician and his wife. Lisa and I forget to put on mosquito repellent and are attacked by squadrons of sandflies. They leave an itch that could send a man over the edge into insanity.

Before we left we had envisaged wonderful, relaxing evenings when Joe had gone to bed. We would eat a nice meal, recline in comfortable chairs and drink good wine. Then we would read or talk or watch the stars. The reality isn't quite so romantic. Most nights we are so exhausted after getting from one place to the next, buying food, looking for a campground, chasing after Joe, setting up our camp, finding people to interview, transcribing those interviews and then cooking dinner that we're generally in bed by 8.30.

Things run reasonably smoothly if Joe sleeps but tonight he is up from 3 am until 5 am. Our tempers are brittle and if I had an angle grinder handy, I'd take it to my skin to relieve the itch of these bloody sandflies.

Thank God Joan is arriving.

Lisa's mum is our guardian angel. She flies in every two months for a week to see us and to bond with her grandson. She likes a glass of red and is a good cook. She takes Joe for walks in the mornings and lets us sleep in. She minds him at night and insists we go off and have a night out. In a year away we get to five restaurants, each time because of Joan.

Joan travels with us up the coast, staying in cabins next to our van. Her arrival is like the sunshine after rain. I am the only person I know who is happy to see more of his mother-in-law. She and I got drunk once and she said to me, 'I never thought someone like you would come along for my Lisa,' and I have never let her forget it.

On our way north, we stop at Airlie Beach where a colleague and friend of mine, Frank Robson, and his partner, Leisa Scott, have their boat moored. They have spent the past year sailing around the Great Barrier Reef.

Joan minds Joe and we go off sailing with Frank and Leisa in their big old catamaran for a night. The boat is like its owner – old and a bit crusty. Year in, year out it is subjected to severe and prolonged bodily punishments yet somehow it just keeps sailing.

We leave early and cruise out to Hook Island where we anchor in a blue bay with white beaches and high rainforests on either side. We dive off the boat, washing the outback from our system, and indulge in the luxury of reading the weekend papers and having an afternoon snooze. On dusk we drink wine on the deck and watch the sunset.

Over dinner we talk about politics, how to cook fish without drying it out, life on the boat, writing, our time in the caravan and the pain of watching the slow, agonising death of newspapers.

Frank is very opinionated and very funny. There is a particular right-wing, moralising columnist whom he loathes. The woman has many children and Frank has nicknamed her 'the womb with a view'.

Frank and Leisa have a dog called Lucky, a delightful little fluffy terrier. Lucky is paying for the sailing trip. *Lucky for Me*, Frank's book about his friendship with the abandoned Lucky, has been a publishing hit and he is now working on a second.

I leave a card for Lucky with the name of a good agent – I reckon he can do better for himself.

After the sun rises Lisa and I dive again into the clear tropical water. We consume an enormous breakfast of eggs and sausages and beans.

It is the perfect antidote to caravan fever.

We sail back across a choppy channel and I spend an hour leaning over the rail. My breakfast becomes fish burly.

The following day we meander up the coast to Cairns with Joan in the back seat playing peek-a-boo with Joe. We find a caravan park in the hills behind the city. Crystal Cascades Holiday Park – 'Your Place in Paradise' – is surrounded by steep rainforested hills but it is not really our scene. It is just too neat, like the new subdivisions that fan out from Cairns. We prefer the daggy old council parks shaded by mango trees, but Cairns has gone corporate. We hadn't imagined staying in places where the palms are all of equal height and equally spaced, the lawn is clipped like an army haircut and the vans are all spotless. 'Our big Australian adventure is feeling more like a package deal to the suburbs,' quips Lisa.

And then one afternoon she wanders over to the laundry and comes back screeching, 'Greg, we have to leave! There is a woman in there ironing her sheets.'

It is a turning point. We vow that from here on in we'll do a lot more bush camping and spend a lot less time in corporate caravan parks. That evening, after dropping Joan at the airport, we sit outside the van planning our escape to Cape York. While we're examining our map, a man pulls up in a white four-wheel drive and introduces himself. It is Tim Smead travelling around Australia with his wife Kate and their *four* children. Their youngest, Georgia, is the same age as Joe. Their caravan, just a few metres down the road, is a 16-foot Expanda just like ours. The Smeads left their home in Port Macquarie six weeks ago and appear to have been through some of the same teething dramas that we endured.

We have a look at their caravan to see how they manage with so many people in such a small space. Six people in a 16-foot van: it's a logistical miracle. They have opted for bunks rather than a bathroom. They only packed one grown-up chair because they know there will never be a time when they will be relaxing together.

It is a brief encounter. We share a meal and a bottle of wine with Tim and Kate on our final night in Cairns and assume it's the last time we'll see them. We certainly don't imagine running into them again . . . and again. Right now, we're heading to Cape York and they're bound for Alice Springs.

18

Cairns may seem to be somewhere near the top of Australia but there's a lot of north left in Far North Queensland after here. The distance from Cairns to The Tip is much further than the drive from Melbourne to Sydney or even Sydney to Brisbane. It is like driving from London to Berlin, on a goat track. That little pointy bit at the top of the state is almost the same size as Victoria, or England.

And again, all roads lead from Guyra, even the one to Bamaga, Cape York. A few months ago my father had been at the funeral of an old family friend, a gentle and humorous farmer called Tom Davidson, one of the Davidson clan of master storytellers. Tom's granddaughter and her husband, Beck and Damien Hepburn, are school teachers on Thursday Island and, through Dad, they invited us to stay.

In the past few days we've talked to lots of people about the condition of the road and decide to leave the caravan where the bitumen ends, near Cooktown. Last night I called the roadhouse at Bamaga, the town at the top of Cape York, for one final check on the condition of the road.

'Love,' the woman said, 'some people made it through today in a Kombi van if that's any indication for ya.'

It's all the confirmation we need and this morning we rise

before the sun and set off for The Tip, bound for Thursday Island, Torres Strait.

Like the people of Australia, the rainforest clings to a narrow strip along the coast. Just 30 or 40 kilometres in from the Coral Sea the lushness ends and the savannah begins. As we head north, the country constantly changes. We pass through long-grassed open cattle country with termite mounds like Gaudi's spires and stringybark forest with palms and black boys. The creek beds are lined with plump eucalypts. It's pretty, in a scraggy Australian way.

The wildlife seems to be in a tropical torpor. Giant eagles, feasting on roadkill, wait until the last moment before hopping to the side of the road and flap no further than the nearest shrub. A big old goanna waddles across the road and waits for me to get out of the car to take a photo, casually flicking his tongue. At one point we come over a rise and see what appears to be a kangaroo on the road but realise it is actually a bird. I slow down and the brolga lumbers into flight, its wings waving like an airborne manta ray.

The one constant is the colour of the road – it is forever a deep, rusty red and paprika-fine. Whenever a truck approaches we pull over and stop. It roars towards us, a storm of dust billowing out in all directions and we wait until the fury has subsided. The dust stains the trees either side of the road.

At Coen, a little Aboriginal settlement with a post office, school and cultural centre that's closed, we stop at the pub for an icy squash and to stretch our legs. It's called the Exchange Hotel and on the roof some wag has inserted an 'S' before exchange. Lisa says to the barman the road is not as bad as she thought it would be.

'They've taken all the challenge out of it,' he drawls.

After Coen the challenge returns. The corrugations are numbing and go on kilometre after kilometre. When the bumps cease the road is like fine quicksand. The vehicle sinks to the sump but handles beautifully. We joke that we may be the first Volvo drivers ever to attempt a summit of Cape York.

By early afternoon we've made it halfway, to Archer River, and stay the night in a clean room that's like a jail cell. The campground by the river is full of serious four-wheel drives and mates on fishing holidays — an activity that I am more than a little suspicious of following that fishing documentary, *Brokeback Mountain*.

The further north we go the more it feels like we are leaving Australia. At one point we try to tune the radio in for some news. We can't get the ABC but the rugby league results from the highland's competition in Papua New Guinea are coming in loud and clear. The lads from Goroka were just far too good for Mt Hagen.

The road forks — the mining town of Weipa is off to the left and the Aboriginal settlements at Cape York are straight ahead. The better road goes to Weipa.

'Seems bauxite trumps blackfellas,' I remark to Lisa.

She forgets all her ABC/BBC training and reverts to Cowra to describe the road ahead.

'Gee, it's not a piece of piss.'

There's a turnoff to Fruit Bat Falls and we stop for a swim. White-limbed spindly gums line the banks of the wide, shallow and fast-flowing Elliot River. At the falls, the river drops over a 30 metre-wide ironstone cliff and down 2 metres into an enormous swimming hole. It is one of nature's loveliest swimming spots. They say there are no crocodiles here, and if there are they are just the freshwater variety, which are virtually harmless 'unless you tread on them or frighten them'. We wait for others to go in first just to be sure. Swimming is never really relaxing, this far north.

A little further on we come to the Jardine River. It is a big river, 70 metres wide and very deep. This one is definitely full of crocodiles. There's no bridge and so, like everyone, we pay the $88 toll for a two-minute ferry ride. What else could we do? Turn back? Swim the river?

A man so black he shines purple, like a plum, drives the ferry. I try to chat to him but his English is limited.

Half an hour later we've made it to the top of Australia. We are 4500 kilometres north of Ian Johnston's windswept retreat on Bruny Island.

19

Charles Passi is a big, gentle man with flecks of grey in his beard and a deep, authoritative voice. He looks like a leader of men. A few years ago, television producers came to Torres Strait looking for people to cast in a drama centred on a medical clinic on one of the remote islands. They initially wanted Pedro Stephen, the mayor of Thursday Island (locally referred to as TI), to play the island chief opposite the island nurse, sexy Susie Porter. Pedro was too busy being the real chief, so he suggested Charles.

'They asked me to come along for a screen test and talk into the camera about things that I am passionate about,' Charles tells us on a drive around Thursday Island. 'I am passionate about many things. They put the camera on and I just got fired up about children's issues and the health of our people and how important it is to retain our languages. I think I really must have hit a nerve because the woman interviewing me actually stopped the tape 'cause she was in tears.'

Charles got the job and went on to become the star of the SBS drama, *Remote Area Nurse*. And, he got to flirt with Susie Porter.

Today, though, he is taking us on a tour of Thursday Island in his sister's four-wheel drive.

'Just to be a part of that, you know, it was wonderful,' he says of his acting experience. 'We were treated like kings, like royalty. They actually set up a tent city for the crew and they rented houses so us actors stayed in houses and the crew stayed in tents.'

The idea of white people sleeping in tents while the mainly black actors lived in houses appealed to him. And the tucker was great.

'They had a big truck with a kitchen in it and chefs. Every meal was like eating at a restaurant. We all put on so much weight.'

Thursday Island, 40 kilometres north of Cape York, is the administrative hub for the islands of the Torres Strait. The islands are actually the peaks of hills which once formed part of the Great Dividing Range. They were cut adrift along with New Guinea and Tasmania when the last ice age ended. There are more than 100 islands strung out between Cape York and the coast of Papua New Guinea. Seventeen are inhabited.

Around 2500 people live on the tiny island of TI. About 1500 are Islanders, while most of the others are government workers from the mainland. Another 5000 people live on the more remote islands. A further 50,000 people who identify as Islander live on the mainland.

In the middle of TI is a hill and Charles takes us there first, to get a view and to see the old cannons installed to repel the Russians in the 1890s. The Russians never came but the airstrip on nearby Horn Island was heavily bombed by the Japanese during the Second World War.

From the top of the old fort, we can see the much larger islands, Horn, Prince of Wales and Hammond, which encircle TI. This island was chosen as the colonial outpost because it offered the only safe anchorage from the treacherous currents and fierce winds.

Today we all have to hang on to our hats as that strong and constant wind, the south-east trade wind, is blowing. It blows like this for six months of the year from April until October.

We drive down the main street with its rows of wide-verandahed shops on either side. It is like a Queensland country town from the 1950s except most of the people are black and wearing floral shirts. Along the water's edge there are some grand old civic buildings including a customs house. The island supports four pubs – Thirsty Island, they call it.

But the churches far outnumber the pubs. The Anglicans were here first and once ruled supreme, but the market has since been deregulated.

They've been joined by the Catholics, the Uniting Church, the Church of Torres Strait, the Baha'i, the Assemblies of God, the Mormons, the Gospel Church, the Seventh Day Adventists, the Horn Island Pentecostal Church and a breakaway from the Church of Torres Strait, which itself is a breakaway from the Anglicans, but nobody seems to know its name. There are apparently some more, but I am unable to identify them.

We drive around neat little suburbs showcasing houses on steel stilts, 1970s Queenslanders, all with well-kept gardens. Most of these houses belong to the state government and this must surely rate among the world's most pleasant public housing estates. The place beams with civic pride. Almost every house has a water view and a big motorboat parked in the yard.

The thing that strikes me immediately about TI is how different it is from any large Aboriginal settlement on the mainland of Australia. The Islanders, who are predominantly Melanesian, seem to have somehow weathered the onslaught of European colonisation better than Australia's other Indigenous peoples.

There's no public drunkenness, no fights in the streets and no houses burned to the ground. The unrest that flares every few years on Palm Island, Wadeye, Redfern or Wilcannia is unheard of here.

'That doesn't mean we don't have our own problems,' Charles says, when I mention this. 'They just happen to be a different set of problems.'

His father was a mate of Eddie Mabo and one of the claimants from Murray Island in the landmark case that overturned the fiction of *terra nullius* – the legal notion that Australia belonged to nobody until the arrival of the Brits.

Fifteen years later and, according to Charles, 'people have become really big headed. On Murray Island we have family against family now. People are taking people to court over land now that everyone thinks "I am a landowner".'

The problem is universal – too many people and not enough land.

Charles's father may have fought one of the seminal land rights issues of the last century but his real hero is his mother. She set up a refuge for women fleeing domestic violence which is named in her honour. Domestic violence remains a problem, Charles says, and it's exacerbated by a severe housing shortage which sees extended families crammed into one house.

On all the islands, he explains, there are few real jobs and people feel disconnected from their old culture but not part of the new one. This is especially true for educated people like him. Charles's father was an Anglican minister and sent him to boarding school in Brisbane to get a white education. He worked for a number of years on the mainland and now that he's returned he doesn't feel like he fits, especially not on his home island of Murray.

'When I go home to Murray Island I can't even speak my own language and for that I feel deeply ashamed.'

We stop at the cemetery. It is like an old family photo album where the pages of the past illustrate what made the people of today. There are elaborate Japanese tombs for the hundreds of divers who died in the waters of Torres Strait, working to supply pearl shell that made buttons for the wealthy of Europe. Malays, Indonesians, Filipinos, Fijians and Samoans were victims for fashion here too.

The headstones of the well-to-do Torres Strait Islander men tell of their bravery and their seafaring skills, while those of the women extol their virtues as faithful wives, mothers and servants of God.

The grave that catches our eye, however, is a fresh one and its headstone is yet to be erected. The man was buried only a few weeks ago and it is piled high with brightly coloured plastic flowers. Flapping in the breeze next to the temporary wooden crucifix is a very large light blue flag. 'Loud and Proud', it proclaims, 'NSW Blues'.

Nothing inflames the passion of TI residents more than the annual Rugby League clash between Queensland and NSW. This man is cheering them on, from the afterlife.

'Bloody traitor,' Charles complains. 'We may be fighting for our independence and our rights but when it comes to footy, we should all be true Queenslanders.'

'Even dead people?' I ask.

'Yes,' he replies, only half joking.

Each year on the eve of the final game of the three-match series, the Queensland supporters – the great majority on the island – march from Anzac Park to the bowling club to watch the game. A small but vocal band of NSW supporters jeers at them from the side of the road, like Orange men and Catholics in Belfast, but without the rocks. The march will be held in a fortnight.

Tonight the second game is being played. All around the island houses and cars are plastered mostly with maroon flags although there's the odd defiant splash of NSW blue.

Later, I wander down to the bowling club where a giant screen has been set up. The place is packed with a couple of hundred people, mainly Islanders, but also a few white mainlanders – nurses and customs officers and other government employees. An Islander next to me is wearing one blue sock and one maroon sock.

'I got a foot in either camp and whoever is winning I pull that sock up,' he explains.

It is one of the most enjoyable sporting events I have ever witnessed. People are laughing and shouting at the television while children are running around between the tables, playing tipped-you-last. Old women, silent in beanies, watch every move, ignoring the bedlam around them.

There's a local hero, too. Sam Thaiday is an Islander and one of the enforcers in the Queensland forward pack. A great cheer erupts whenever he is on screen. Many people tell me they are related to him or that they know him well, even though he was born in Sydney and lives in Brisbane, 2700 kilometres away.

The man with odd socks has an easy night. His blue sock remains limp at his ankle while Queensland thrash NSW 30 to nil to equal the series.

★

Everyone on TI, it seems, is obsessed with State of Origin football. Everyone that is, except Cate Titasey.

After just a few days on the island we hear about this interesting white woman: lawyer, artist, writer and mother of four who came to TI, fell in love with a black fisherman and stayed. We go for a walk one afternoon and manage to find the Titasey house. It is a big double-storied wood and fibro place where you can glimpse the water from the balcony.

The Titaseys are among the few people on TI who own their home. Cate and Tony live upstairs with their kids while Tony's mother and other relatives live downstairs.

Cate is 39 and 10 years younger than her husband. She is tall and slim with piercing blue eyes and a practical, tomboyish hairdo. I imagine she has looked exactly the same since she was 17. She is welcoming, articulate and warm and just a little bit mad, in the nicest of ways.

Tony is typical of the TI mix. His mum is half Islander and half Samoan. His father was a merchant seaman from East Timor who captained a pearl lugger. He runs a fishing charter and a lawn-mowing business while Cate does the books and organises her husband. She also paints and writes and does free legal work.

Every other house we visit on TI is scrupulously neat and has pictures of Jesus or Mary on the walls. Not this one. There appears to be no need for cupboards in the Titasey house because most things are on the floor. There are lots of books, and a big, succulent vegetable patch out the back.

In the kitchen, within scribbling distance of the phone, Cate has written in Texta all over the wall. There are phone numbers, ideas, the names of books she's been recommended and reminders. The interior reflects her personality: slightly manic, a bit scatty, but artistic, interesting and full of ideas. On a few of the walls hang Cate's stunning pictures of Islander faces.

While Joe plays with the kids inside, we sit on the balcony and chat to Cate about life on TI and how she ended up here. After graduating from university she worked for a couple of years for a law firm in Cairns but became worn down by the 'environment of endemic negativity'.

One day out of the blue, she answered an advertisement in *The Cairns Post*, 'Bar attendant wanted for Far North Queensland island hotel.' She had been planning to travel to Egypt but thought she'd check out this exotic island hotel first. She quit her job as a lawyer to become a barmaid. She landed in the Federal Hotel and hated almost every moment of her seven weeks pulling beers.

A few days before she was due to leave, Tony walked in and ordered a lemonade – an unusual order on Thirsty Island. She liked what she saw in the softly spoken Islander with his long, black spiral hairdo and moustache – picture early Lionel Ritchie.

They chatted and he invited her to go for a ride in his dinghy, to fish and possibly deer hunt on Horn Island.

The only stag she'd get, said the publican when she told him later of the offer, was Tony himself. That was fine by Cate. She didn't fancy venison.

Things went to plan and they spent a passionate few days together before she flew off to Cairo. He thought he'd never see her again.

'A few months later I was walking down on the esplanade and I saw this good-looking woman and I was checking her out and realised it was Cate,' Tony tells me later.

She had returned to TI to take up a job working in domestic violence at the women's centre and was looking for accommodation. 'I said that she could come and stay with me. She said, "Tony, I insist on paying rent" and I said, "We'll work something out".'

Seven weeks later, Cate quit her job and went fishing with Tony as his deckhand. She learned how to gut and fillet fish, how to read the currents and tides and how to siphon fuel without getting a mouthful of petrol.

Tony insisted that he never wanted any more children. He already had two.

He now has six and one of them, a little boy of almost three, has just crawled up onto Cate's lap, lifted her top and is suckling on her breast. 'What can I say?' she grins. 'I got my handsome black prince and my little brown babies as well.'

But like the man with odd socks, she has a foot in either camp – she'll never really be an Islander, but through her marriage and her children she is forever tethered to the Torres Strait. 'I feel like I'm on this razor's edge between the two cultures sometimes,' she says. 'I'm not part of the white community and I'm not part of the black community; I'm just between the two. But that's okay.'

One of Cate's main frustrations is that she can't get an exhibition at the local art gallery because she's white. Her work has been allowed to hang in the gift shop attached to the gallery and the local government even presented one of her paintings to former Premier, Peter Beattie. Despite that, she's been told repeatedly by white workers at the gallery that only Indigenous artists are allowed to exhibit.

'It all gets a bit ridiculous at times,' Tony tells us. 'They allowed another artist, who was Maori, to hang his work, but not Cate who lives here.'

In recent years Cate has turned to writing and now produces a regular column for *The Cairns Post* about life on TI. She has also just finished a novel, a crime thriller set on Thursday Island, called *718 Sections*. A few weeks after we leave it is shortlisted for the Penguin Crime Writing Competition.

One day Tony takes us on a tour in his dinghy, the 6-metre fibreglass *Madam Dugong*, across to Goods Island. Our little Aryan prince could have done with a dash of TI pigmentation. He is wearing a broad-brimmed hat, full-body sunsuit and sunscreen. His head is poking out through the top of a bright orange life jacket. It is a calm day without much chop but Joe is a little unsure as the big, powerful motor bounces us across the water.

Tony is out here almost every day and never gets sick of it. He feels an affinity with the sea and calmness descends whenever he's on the water. 'It might just be getting away from the kids,' I suggest. He smiles.

As a child, he was always on the water and after school he joined the merchant navy and later worked on the tugs at Weipa. He came back to TI in 1991 to fish for crays.

We slice through the water for half an hour until we reach a deserted beach on Goods Island. The rusted ribcage of an old cargo ship that came to grief here pokes from the water. Tony eases the boat up onto the beach and we put Joe in a backpack and walk.

The island is uninhabited but there is an old Second World War fort high up on the hill. It is a 30-minute hike through scrub that is part tropical and part Australian bush. Below we can see the reef through clear waters.

We reach the top of the hill where there is a cement bunker that looks north towards PNG. I imagine the soldiers stationed here during the war, looking out over these waters, day after day, waiting for the Japanese to arrive. Some days I bet they wished for an attack, just to break the boredom.

On the way back to the boat, Tony tells us that it has been hard at times for Cate, not knowing if she was fully accepted.

'I tell her not to worry about it, that it doesn't matter, but I know it worries her sometimes.'

He says that his mother was a bit wary of Cate at first but that she has come to accept her.

'I think this whole notion of being accepted into an Indigenous community is really a European concept,' Cate says, next time I meet her.

In a way, straddling two cultures allows her to be a fly on the wall observer of both. She can have coffee with the white women and listen to them complaining about the colour of their kitchens or the tenants in their investment properties back in Townsville, or their frustration with the lazy locals. They can live here for years, she says, and have no appreciation of the Islanders.

'I turned my back on what probably would have been an affluent suburban existence for an adventure. We are struggling financially and things can be really hard at times, but my life is so much richer than what it would have been if I had chosen that other life.'

But she has also seen some of the brutality of island life and indifference, sometimes, to domestic violence. She has seen the ridiculous rigidity of positive discrimination. There are laws prohibiting fishing by whites to protect traditional fishing rights. Once Cate represented Tony's brother in court after he was prosecuted for employing a white deckhand because he was unable to get any Islanders to work for him.

Tony is quite critical of his fellow Islanders and says that many of them are lazy, unwilling to work and addicted to welfare. He used to employ a couple of locals in his lawnmowing business but now works alone because he says he cannot get reliable staff.

For Islanders, houses are free and if people need extra cash to buy a boat or a four-wheel drive, they go out fishing for crays to top up their work-for-the-dole payments. There's no incentive to work, he explains.

'If you try to get them to work for you eight hours a day for five days they can't handle it. They stress out because they have never worked so hard in their lives.'

Cate looks at all this differently.

'They're not the ones stressing out over a $400,000 mortgage,' she tells me. 'Who's the fool?'

I ask Cate why Torres Strait Islanders seem to have coped better than Aborigines with the arrival of Europeans. She thinks it's because they were never really dispossessed of their land and, apart from TI, there are very few Europeans living on other islands. Their culture and way of life was never completely crushed.

'People have been coming here for 170 years to make their fortune but it was the resources of the sea they were after – the pearls, the bêche-de-mer, the turtle shells and the fish. They plundered the sea but they left the islands and the Islanders pretty much alone.'

Each Friday, the local primary school holds Floral Friday and children and teachers wear loud floral clothes. Our generous hosts, Beck and Damien Hepburn, have invited us to talk to their classes. They are both committed teachers and Damien, in particular, has achieved phenomenal attendance results in his class. Every time a child misses a day, he phones the parents. If a child is away for two days he visits the house. He then sacrifices his lunch hour to make up for lost time when the pupil returns. At 97.5 per cent his attendance rates are unmatched.

Before we go to the school, we head downtown to buy Joe a blue floral number from Mona's Bazaar. Outside the shop is an Islander kid surrounded by some smaller kids. He is about 16 and, with clipboard in hand, is doing some market research for the local chicken shop, Island Rooster.

'So what do you prefer?' he asks the kids gathered around him. 'Dugong or Island Rooster?'

'Dugong,' they shout. 'Dugong.'

'What about Island Rooster and turtle?'

'Maybe Island Rooster,' says one.

'Depends,' says another. 'Is it with chips?'

At the school, Joe is a hit and every kid in the class wants to cuddle him — a little white boy in a sea of black, grinning faces.

For most of these kids, English is their second language after Torres Strait Creole, or one of two distinct Islander languages. They want to know if we speak other languages and are fascinated when Lisa starts talking to them in Urdu. We show them pictures from our trip around Australia — the furthest most have been is Cairns and there are some in the class who have never been to the mainland, just 30 minutes away by ferry.

They tell us they like to go hunting for dugong and turtle with their fathers, or to shoot deer on Prince of Wales Island.

One little boy, Philip Pensio, boasts that he's the best hunter of sugu — octopus — and promises to take us with him when the tide is right.

A few days later, we walk the reef on the back side of the island while Philip pokes down every hole, feeling for the soft flesh of octopus. He carries his spear in his other hand and fires it off at shadowy shapes that dart in the shallows.

There is a naïve view that native people kill only what they can eat, but Philip and his mate Wimple are like boys everywhere. They kill, or attempt to kill, everything they see: crabs, fish and a small shovel nosed shark that Philip spears on the run. We find no octopus.

'What do you want to do when you leave school?' I ask them.

'Work for customs,' they both say. 'They got the best boats.'

On the beach, near where we're hunting, three large turtles have ropes tied around one of their front flippers and then to a tree on the shore. It is hot and they are exposed to the sun without relief. Kids are sitting on their backs and poking them.

'They'll be killed for the sad news,' says Philip, going on to explain that somebody has died and the funeral guests will eat the turtles.

'When is the sad news?' I ask.

'Couple of days,' he says.

'So they will stay out in the hot sun tied up like this until then?'

'Yeah,' says Wimple, as if it were obvious, 'until they kill them for sad news.'

It is too much for Lisa, who once worked on a sea turtle conservation project in South America. She and Joe go off to explore some gentler aspects of island life.

We walk past the beach again two days later and the turtles are still baking in the sun, waiting for sad news.

20

It is a sunny afternoon on Thursday Island and I am sitting in the garden of the Torres Strait cultural centre, Gab Titui, sipping coffee with Cate and Tony Titasey. This is the place that has refused to exhibit Cate's art because she is white but she can't boycott it because it is also the only joint on the island that serves a decent cup of coffee.

A couple with a baby in a pram joins us. I am introduced to Jeff, known as JT, and Jane Tanswell and their baby daughter, Taslyn. They joke about a documentary called *After the Attack*, which has just screened on pay television.

'Oh – my – God,' says Jane, 'it was so embarrassing.'

The program was filmed on TI. Tony had taken the crew out on his boat to do the shoot. They didn't bring real actors and instead used the first two white people they could get: a clerk from the courthouse and a paediatric nurse. It was a hammed-up re-enactment of a crocodile attack and the acting was apparently very bad.

'Who got attacked by the crocodile?' I ask.

They all look at JT and laugh.

'That would be me,' he says.

'Really?'

He shows me the scars on either side of his skull to prove it. There are four neat pincer marks where his head was clamped between the jaws of a three and half metre crocodile.

Coconut Head, the locals call him now – with a nut so tough that not even a croc could crack it.

JT and Jane are both police officers. They live in a spacious government flat on the harbour side of the island and, the day I visit, JT's boat is parked out the front.

He is in his mid thirties, fit and freckled suggesting a life spent in the sun. Jane is a few years younger, with a rounded, pretty face and curly hair. Six-month-old Taslyn lolls about on the floor as we talk.

We settle down on the couch with a coffee and JT tells me his incredible story.

'It happened on 8 January 2007. That time of year, it's the doldrums. The south-east trade winds have left and the northerlies for the monsoon still haven't arrived. Everything is flat calm and every man and his dog jumps in his boat and goes out to explore, fish and dive.

'We decided to head out with some friends. Alpha rock it's called, which is a small rock off the tip of the Cape. We thought we'd go there to do a bit of fishing and try our luck with some mackerel.

'We set off early that morning. Our friends were in a smaller boat and tagged along behind. We spent a couple of hours patrolling around, dragging lures and not really catching much. It was just a magic day. The water was that flat and calm that the horizon just blended in with the sky.

'By lunchtime we were looking for a place to pull up and have a bit of a feed. You can see the Adolphus Islands from this outer rock, and it was the girls who suggested we go across there to have some lunch. So we shot across to Little Adolphus which is the first and the smallest island to the north. We did a slow, slow lap around, just looking in the water for any danger. Sharks were the primary concern because January is smack bang in the middle of the turtle breeding season and tiger sharks love turtles.

'The plan was to dive down and spear a cray and cook it up on the beach for lunch and wonder what the poor people were doing.

'The water was like an aquarium, we could see everything on the bottom of the ocean – the coral, the fish, everything. We all got into my boat and three of us suited up with our cray guns. Jane stayed on the boat as the lookout and we slid off into the water.

'I started diving in water which was probably about 3 metres deep but started to get a bit nervous because I thought it may be where the sharks swim, off the reef, so I went into shallower water.

'I was very close to the shore, 7 or 8 metres away, and in water which only just covered my head. I felt a lot more comfortable in there. I wasn't in the water long – four or five minutes, tops, looking for little hidey holes where the crays would be. I stumbled across this big, wide open patch with coral ledges in a big circle and I remember thinking "This is just about perfect."

'I dived down and stuck my head under all those little ledges, the whole time turning and checking to make sure I was safe.

'After one of these dives I came to the surface, exhaled and was sucking in a fresh lungful of air. Then I just got fucking smashed. The initial impact absolutely stunned me. The only thing I could relate it to, in my line of work, is when you get unexpectedly king hit from behind and you have no idea what's happening.

'I got smacked that hard that everything just shut down. I lost vision, blacked out, lost all feedback from my arms and legs, no feeling . . . but I remember my brain still ticking over, going "what the hell?" I initially thought I was hit by a boat, it felt so hard and inanimate. It felt like it couldn't be an animal. It felt like a hammer or a sledgehammer had hit me.

'That was the first half second, and then for the next two seconds I became aware of the crushing pressure on my skull and I could feel that I was being pulled down to the sea floor by my head. My body was just following.

'I was trying to process this and that's when I started pushing and shoving with my hands and spear gun, still thinking, possibly, "shark". I'm starting to think, "Okay, it's an animal, an animal's got me," and I'm still thinking, "Maybe this is a shark." I had no idea that it could have been a crocodile, so I'm pushing and shoving half to fight it off and half to get some feedback.

'While I'm pushing and shoving and fighting and we're going down to the bottom, all of a sudden it let go and it was like a light in the room was switched on. Suddenly it was day and I've got sunlight, the pressure is off my head and I just shot to the surface and took a deep breath of air.

'For whatever reason I instinctively looked over my left shoulder, and the croc just popped up right behind me. My heart stopped. I thought, "This is a croc attack, I've been hit, this is a croc attack." With my little gun I've aimed to shoot, not that it would have made any difference.

'He has taken off across the surface and sort of half rolled. I remember seeing the side of his flanks, he was really light brown on the top but had bright yellow stripes down his flanks and was really white underneath. He's sort of rolled on his side and took off sideways.

'He then went in a slow arc in front of me and back underwater and I lost him in the coral beside me. That's when the panic started. I thought, "I've read about this; they come back to finish you off." With my free hand, I remember waving and looking at Jane in the boat, it seemed like it was hundreds of metres away at the time. "Jane, get here now, get here now." I was waving my gun back and forth, the mask had been knocked off and I could feel the blood running down the side of my face.

'I was kicking madly, trying to get some leverage to look up above the water to see where he'd gone, and doing circles to see if he was coming in behind me, and sticking my head under, to see if he was coming up at me. The waves of panic were coming from my guts up into my throat, and I'm swallowing hard, pushing it back down saying to myself: "Keep it together. Keep it together. Keep your shit together."

'Within a minute Jane had driven the boat up beside me. For whatever reason, I just didn't think to get in. I just threw my arm up over the gunwale of the boat and pointed the spear gun and shouted: "Just don't let him eat me, just don't let him eat me."

'Jane grabbed me by the back of the wetsuit and flung me into the boat and the next thing I'm aware of I'm skidding across the back of the boat. I thought, "Shit, I've survived."

'Jane swung the boat out to pick up the other two and then we just screamed offshore, about 300 metres, pulled up and all of us just looked at each other and tried to take in what had just happened. I was sitting on the back seat of the boat while Jane wrapped a bandage around me and her legs were shaking that much she could hardly stand.'

Jane speaks for the first time, to give her version. From the boat she saw it all happen. The crocodile approached not horizontally, but swam in vertically.

'I thought, "Gee, that looks like a crocodile, moving towards the back of his head," and then it must have somehow turned, grabbed the back of his head and just disappeared under the water. There was no splash, no screaming, no kicking.'

Then she saw her husband bob up and the crocodile bob up beside him and she aimed the boat for the gap. She can't remember dragging him in.

On the way back to Thursday Island she pulled so hard on the throttle cable that it broke and they had to wait for another boat to take them to shore.

JT was taken to hospital and stitched up. The teeth punctured his cheek and into his skull but there was remarkably little damage. Crocodile experts aren't sure why it let him go, perhaps it was just playing with him, or warning him to keep out of its territory. It could easily have crushed his skull or rolled and broken his neck. They say he's the luckiest man alive.

The doctor who stitched him up gave him a medical certificate to take one day off work. *One day!*

★

Jeff grew up in Cairns and has spent much of his life on the water. Now he'll only dive on remote reefs where there is no chance of crocodiles. And he and Jane fight every time he wants to go back into the water.

'I don't want to cottonwool myself and become a basket case and so I go in every now and again just to test myself,' he says. 'But I can also see Jane's point of view. She says: "You never saw it coming, it just hit you out of the blue, but I saw it come up and grab you and take you under, and every time you go out that's what I see again."'

It's an issue that remains unresolved but in many other ways, they say, the attack has brought them closer together.

'It has changed him,' Jane says. 'He appreciates life more now and cherishes me more and is very good with Taslyn. He used to work lots of overtime but now he comes home early and he is happy just to hang out.'

'It's a cliché,' he says. 'But when something like that happens, you appreciate life more.'

After the attack there was a media frenzy. JT sold his story to the tabloids.

He bought a new motor for his boat with the proceeds.

21

The Savannah Way is the necklace of Queensland, hanging from one shoulder at Cairns and sweeping across to the Gulf of Carpentaria. After descending from The Tip, we set off at a leisurely pace westwards, towards the Territory, in search of any jewels that may hang from the chain.

A few hours inland, just west of Ravenshoe, Lisa directs me into a free camping ground called the Archer Creek Rest Area – a pretty little spot near the road with a fast-flowing creek.

The caravan world is divided into two tribes – the park dwellers, who stick to town caravan parks, and the bush campers, who ferret out free spots in the scrub and in national parks. The latter are like backpackers who used to do Europe on $5 a day – a cult that has somehow come to believe powdered milk is just as good as the real stuff.

Up until this point we have pretty much been park dwellers. In Tasmania it was too cold for Joe, we insisted to each other, and we needed a powered site to run our little electric heater. It then seems we became addicted to mains power not only for heat but to recharge our laptops, phones and cameras.

In our minds, though, we see ourselves as the more adventurous bush campers. You know – as travellers rather than tourists. We decide to stop at Archer Creek to affirm our fantasy.

Besides, we are haemorrhaging cash. We have chosen to drive around one of the largest countries on earth just as the world decides to run out of oil. When we set off we were paying $1.47 a litre for diesel. Up here we are regularly paying $2.20 and in the Territory we will pay a staggering $2.80. Some weeks we burn through $500 on fuel alone. So now we are on the hunt for anything cheap and figure, with a little bit of planning, we can bush camp for two or three days at a time and then come back to 'park world' for a day or two to recharge our batteries and wash our clothes. Archer Creek is the start of the new resolve.

We start to unpack when Lisa points out a problem. 'Greg,' she says in that tone my mother uses when she calls me Gregory. 'Did you fill the water tanks?' I scramble about under the van and discover the two tanks are indeed bone dry. It is not a great problem, I argue in my defence, because I can bucket water from the nearby stream. I spend the next half hour running back and forth to the creek. Unfortunately our bucket has no handle and I am forced to repeatedly walk past all the other serious campers, looking like an African village woman. I can't tell if Joe is laughing with me or at me.

Before setting off this morning we picked up our new Volvo from the dealer in Cairns – the company insists on exchanging vehicles at 20,000 kilometres, apparently for resale value. The new vehicle is even flasher than the last and has a sunroof, cream leather seats and just 35 kilometres on the clock. For some reason Lisa and I are dressed in our only decent clothes and Joe has on a designer t-shirt that someone bought him for Christmas – usually he's top-to-toe Target.

And so, looking like we are off to a Liberal Party fundraiser in Toorak or the rugby at Bowral, we leave the van at Archer Creek and set off to check out some hot springs at nearby Innot.

And there, on the outskirts of the outback, we drive our new Volvo over a rise and into a festival of ferals.

Parked on either side of the creek are dozens of bongo vans and panel vans painted with flowers, Aboriginal flags and rainbows. I manoeuvre our gleaming silver Volvo into a spot between two battered vans.

Down in the creek, there are about 60 semi-naked young people lolling about in the warm waters that bubble up from the earth. Here we are in our smart casuals surrounded by body piercings, tattoos and dreadlocks – it's like a knotted hair convention.

'I told you Queensland was mad,' I say to Lisa.

'Can someone please light me a joint,' begs a guy sitting outside the van next to our shiny Volvo.

I unhook Joe from his sparkling, white-leathery kingdom and we wander down to the sandy creek bed to check things out. We know there has got to be a good yarn here, somewhere. Besides, I reckon any time spent with near-naked 20-year-olds is time well spent, even ones with plaited armpits.

And then we realise how conservative we look. Joe even has his hair combed. People are looking at us as though we are Pauline Hanson and David Oldfield at the Aboriginal tent embassy.

'There's no way I can break through,' I confess to Lisa. 'You haven't shaved your underarms or legs for weeks, you go down.'

When she doesn't budge, I remind her that she was a vegetarian for 15 years and once wore a navel ring. She even dragged me to hypno-birthing classes before Joe's birth.

'Yes,' she says. 'But that was all in the past and the hypno-birthing was a definite mistake.'

The horrible reality is unavoidable. To these young anarchists we are middle class and middle aged. We *are* the enemy! We walk tentatively about the fringes of the group until finally Lisa has an epiphany. 'What are we worried about? There are a lot of middle class people here. In ten years' time half of them will be in business suits climbing corporate ladders.' And so we plunge in.

What we have stumbled into is the fag end of a trance music festival, The Winter Solstice and Lifestyle Gathering, a four-day binge in the scrub where hippies take drugs and wear really bad clothes and don't have to worry about getting bashed up. It had finished yesterday, at a venue about 20 kilometres away, and the stragglers have gathered to recover in Innot's hot springs.

The first person we meet is a guy called Alistair who appears to be pleasantly stoned. I am a little unsure just what a 'trance music festival' is and ask him to tell me.

'Trance music,' he explains, while rocking back and forth, 'is kinda getting back to an earthy tribal-type beat. People, you know, can go into a trance and some can dance for 24 hours in a blissful state. I danced for about eight hours at one time.'

'Were the drugs that good?' I ask.

'Man, I did it all on chai and chocolate.'

Alistair tells us that the police pulled him and his mates up on the way to the festival. The cops defected the vehicle because it had no back seat and there were passengers sitting on the floor. He is complaining that this was very unfair.

'Lucky it wasn't 25 years ago in Sir Joh's day,' I say. 'Back then the Queensland cops would have beaten the shit out of you and run you out of the state, seats or no seats.'

'Nooo,' he says.

'Yesss,' I respond.

The next person we meet is Ben Speirs. Ben looks out of place, mainly because he's recently cut his hair short. He's not wearing a shirt and is both broad shouldered and incredibly lean. He looks like a private school rowing boy in need of a feed. An English girl called Emma, who is dressed in a bikini and has a stud through her bottom lip, is hanging by his side.

Ben has a van with two large plastic drums strapped to the back and a sign which declares 'Powered by Vegetable Oil'. He has driven almost 50,000 kilometres on fish and chip fat that he's collected from cafés for free. I am impressed and wonder if we could pump some through the Volvo. He goes into great detail about why this would be a very bad idea.

I am keen to talk to him some more, but Ben and Emma only met this morning and it seems that Ben is keen to get to know Emma a little better.

We have missed the trance music festival but we are told the Kuranda Roots Festival is being held just outside Cairns in four days' time. Many of the people we see wallowing in the creek will be there, including Ben. We arrange to meet him. The Territory can wait a week or two, we decide. We are off to dwell in a land of *no woman, no cry*.

22

We pack up and retrace our steps across the Savannah Way. We have days to spare before the reggae festival and are mulling over how we might spend them when we drive into a little village called Tolga, just out of Atherton on the tablelands behind Cairns.

There, shimmering on the side of the road opposite Tolga Pump and Irrigation, is a motor home emblazoned with a big sign: 'Jade Hurley Rockin' In The Jayco Motorhome Tour'.

'Did you just see that?' I exclaim to Lisa. 'It's Jade Hurley, in a Jayco. Jade Hurley is on the same gravy train as us. I've gotta talk to him.'

'Who's Jade Hurley?' she asks.

'Jade Hurley! Jade Hurley! Surely you must have heard of Jade Hurley?'

I pull around to swing our Jayco in behind his Jayco.

Anyone who was forced to wear a clip-on red bowtie and spent a slice of their youth working beneath the neon glow of any workers/bowling/Returned Serviceman's club in Australia would know Jade Hurley. He is the Elvis of the RSL, the King of Middle-of-the-Road.

And here he is on the road at Tolga, trying to get mobile coverage to call his daughter back on the Gold Coast, when I poke my head through the window of his motorhome.

'Hello,' he says in a deep and reassuring radio man's voice. 'I am Jade Hurley and this is my lovely wife Barbara.' We chat for a few minutes and he invites us to his concert that night at the Mareeba RSL Club.

Back in the car, I give Lisa the rundown on Jade Hurley. He played at the Inverell RSM Club when I worked there in the late 1980s and he seemed old then. I am amazed that he is still alive, let alone still performing. He was among the first wave of Australian rockers who came after Johnny O'Keefe. O'Keefe discovered him as a 14-year-old in a Sydney pub singing Jerry Lee Lewis's 'A Whole Lot of Shakin' Goin' On' and put him on *Six O'Clock Rock*. But his career was washed up before the 1960s were over, before I was born, and he went off to work at a service station in Deniliquin.

His career was first rekindled by a rock'n'roll revival tour, *The Good Old Days of Rock and Roll*, which hit the road in 1974. This guy has had more comebacks than John Howard, who I am sure would be a fan. When it looked as if it was over again he struck showman's gold – a fortnightly segment, *Jade Hurley's Golden Oldies*, on the popular daytime program, the *Mike Walsh Show*. His slot ran for almost 15 years and on the back of that, every record he released went straight to gold, some even to the dizzy heights of double platinum, both here *and* in New Zealand.

And, now, all these years later, our Jayco is following his Jayco into Mareeba.

We had already checked out Mareeba, on our way back from The Tip. It is an old-fashioned rural town of 7000 people, a little too far out of Cairns to get many tourists. Thousands of US troops were camped here during the Second World War and it was the main staging post for operations in New Guinea and the Pacific. The fertile volcanic soils surrounding the town grow plump tropical fruits – bananas, avocados, mangoes and paw paws. And while good coffee is grown in the area we couldn't find a place that served it in a cup. It had been Lisa's birthday the following day and all she wanted was to sit alone in a café and read for the day – Mareeba didn't possess such a joint, so we had pressed on to Kuranda in the rainforest above Cairns.

Now we are back for a concert at the RSL. Jade has smoothed things over with security. It's fine for us to camp out the back, on the street behind the club. 'You're a lucky man, Greg,' Lisa says to me, as we're setting up. 'I don't think you'd find many women who would be prepared to camp with you out the back of an RSL club.' I know she's right.

While we get organised, Jade works his way through his sound check and Joe dances around in front. From the poetry of Les Murray to the glitz of Jade Hurley – the little bugger better appreciate this.

It is nearing show time. The crowd is trickling into the auditorium with most having dined at the buffet – 10 bucks for genuine *cordon bleu*. The tickets to the show are $17 and $14.50 for members. 'How many tickets have you sold?' I ask the lady at the door.

'Two hundred or so, love,' she says. 'Double the Elvis impersonator we had in a few weeks ago.'

In the motorhome, parked just outside the stage door, Jade is preparing for the show. He is 65, with a paunch and thinning hair that he keeps long, swept back and bleached blond. He looks like John Farnham, ten years on. Barbara tells me that she makes him bleach his hair because he can't go out on stage looking like a grey old man. They look as if they share the same hairdresser.

He is billed as a cross between Little Richard, Jerry Lee Lewis and Liberace – Liberace won out when it came to costuming. Jade is wearing a black satin shirt sewn with hundreds of diamantes. Over that he wears a white leather jacket with tassels. Around each wrist hang large chain bracelets – one which reads 'Jade' in sparkling stones. Around his neck a pendant hangs from a chain with the letter 'J' in diamonds. On each of his fingers he wears enormous, garish rings.

He points out a ring on his pinkie and tells me it was given to him by 'a certain well-known Sydney socialite, who shall remain nameless.' Years ago he was doing a show in Sydney and the woman had requested that he sing 'Great Balls of Fire'.

After the show she came into the dressing room and locked the door behind her. She had another request. He tells me it was one he could not fulfil.

'She respected and admired me for knocking her back,' he says as he fastens his diamond cuff links, ready to take the stage. 'We got talking and I said I loved her ring. She said you can have it if it fits and it fitted my little finger.'

He stands for a moment, admiring the glistening ring and remembering his act of gallantry. 'Does it still happen?' I ask. 'Do women still throw themselves at you?'

'Course they do. Every night. Occasionally, so do men.'

Adam, his roadie/soundie/only crewman, sticks his head in the door and hands him a glass of liquor. Jade looks at it and sends it back.

'The deal was half a glass, not half a nip,' he grunts.

He takes to the stage with a concoction called Jade's elixir, which is half Green Ginger wine and half brandy – it's in the booking deal, along with a bottle of wine for Barbara. Nearing show time I leave the caravan, to allow Jade to get into the zone, and go to sit with Barbara at the rear of the hall beside a table stacked with CDs. The audience is old, very old. Some are in wheelchairs, although I am surprised to see a smattering of people in their thirties and forties.

'Ladies and gentlemen, put your hands together for Mr Jade Hurley,' booms the pre-recorded voice as Jade bounds onto the stage. There is no band, just Jade's keyboard and Adam on the side controlling the backing music and the lights. Jade greets the crowd with a toothy smile and then attacks his keyboard with a raucous rendition of Status Quo's 'Rockin' All Over the World'.

The audience forgets they are old. There is whistling and clapping and people join in for the chorus. Jade promises them a night of fun, a night where they will know all the words of every song, and he delivers. He reels off Buddy Holly's 'Oh Boy', Marty Robbins's 'The Story of My Life' and Del Shannon's 'Runaway'.

'He shot himself,' says Barbara to me when I ask who sang 'Runaway'. 'Suicide.'

Jade works the crowd with some gay jokes, which go down well here. He claims that everyone on the *Mike Walsh Show* was a 'horse's hoof' and if you dropped $50 you'd have to kick it out to the safety of your dressing room before bending over to pick it up. The audience seems to overlook the fact that the man delivering these lines would not look out of place in the Sydney Mardi Gras parade.

'Ah, the Mike Walsh days . . . television was television in those days. Now, ya just got Jamie Durie diggin' holes.'

Jade has a sore throat, but the crowd doesn't seem to notice, or care. Barbara sits, impassively, with a glass of wine in her hand. She doesn't clap and winces when he misses a note.

'We've got a drunk here,' she says, pointing out a man in a flannel shirt, dancing with his partner, a fat girl in vinyl pants. 'I hope he's not going to be a bloody idiot.'

'Do you enjoy the shows?'

'Oh yeah,' she says. 'I also like to people watch.'

At half time Jade retires to the motorhome while Barbara stays at the table, flogging their self-recorded CDs – $30 for an album, $35 for a double. On each seat they have left a photocopied list of the songs on every album. The oldies just tick off which albums they want and hand it to Barbara – saves time with people saying, 'I want the one about the starlight, the moon and the river. What's-it-called?' This is where they make their money and there's no middle man.

In the van Jade tells me he loves the thrill of performing and being on the road. He gives the impression there is nothing he'd rather be doing.

'I am doing what I love. This is my passion.'

But earlier, Barbara had told me there's another reason. There have been money problems. She and Jade are on the road because they have to be.

Jade was the President of the Tweed Valley Chamber of Commerce and owned eight investment units from Sydney to the Gold Coast, as well as a big house on 11 hectares above Tweed Heads with 'JH' written in tiles at the bottom of the huge swimming pool. He ran as an independent for state parliament and narrowly missed becoming the Member for Tweed.

Jade Hurley was on top of the world. And then he went into business with a sharp-talking salesman, in a venture that sold personal alarm systems for elderly people who might slip in the shower or have a heart attack. The combination of Jade's good name and his partner's business nous was supposed to be a winner. The partner turned out to be a conman who ripped off not only Jade, but dozens of elderly people around the Gold Coast. He went to Grafton Jail and Jade was left to pay off the creditors. He narrowly avoided bankruptcy. He paid back every cent and in the process lost almost everything he owned.

It was 1999, the year he was awarded the Order of Australia Medal for his services to music – it should have been his moment of glory but he couldn't even afford the extra ticket for Barbara to go to Government House in Sydney for the presentation by the Governor-General.

And so, it was back to the road.

'I'd prefer to be home, but this is what we're doing now, that's it. I'm resigned to the fact, that's the way it is,' Barbara told me earlier, with more than a hint of bitterness.

During the second half of the show the audience is swaying in tune, with their arms in the air, to Jade's keyboard solo of 'Chariots of Fire'. They stomp their feet to 'Great Balls of Fire' and sing along to 'Running Bear'.

After the show Jade makes himself available for signings and I sit and watch. Barbara sells the CDs and Jade signs them. When she gets to the front of the cue, a frumpish woman in her fifties suggests that he might like to come home to her place after he's finished.

'There's two of us too,' she grins, motioning to her girlfriend.

Jade laughs it off and says to me, 'Did you hear that? Did you hear what she said?'

Barbara rolls her eyes.

Another woman approaches him with a poster and asks him to sign it 'from Jade with love' to her granddaughter, whose name is Chelbie.

'That's an unusual name,' he comments. 'Where did that come from?'

She explains that when her daughter got pregnant things were rocky between the young woman and the father of the child. The woman was anxious all the way through the pregnancy but her favourite uncle keep reassuring her, saying, 'She'll be right love, she'll be right.'

'So when the baby arrived everything was perfect,' the woman explains to Jade. 'So she named her Chelbie, as in chel-be-right.'

'That's wonderful,' replies Jade, earnestly. 'But why didn't they spell it Sh, rather than Ch?'

'They were going to,' the woman says, 'but then they thought it'd be far too common.'

We retire to the motorhome which is parked next to the stage door. Jade grabs a couple of beers from the fridge while Barbara opens another bottle of wine. They'll sleep here tonight, to save on park fees. Without the sponsorship from Jayco, which includes a fuel card, it is unlikely that the tour would be viable. Their roadie, Adam, has also been supplied with a motorhome. Each night before he goes to bed, Jade does a couple of late-night radio interviews, plugging his show and putting in a word for the sponsor.

Barbara says her big fear is that venues will just stop booking him.

'It'll happen one day.'

But Jade is confident they will be able to keep going, especially because they now have a fantastic booking agent.

'She a real character,' he explains. 'She's hardly got a tooth in her head.'

'The first time I met her she came to the show in Rockhampton and we had a lovely night,' Barbara chips in. 'She describes herself as ugly but beautiful on the phone. She's fabulous and she does have a beautiful voice.'

We talk some more about them almost going under. At one stage things got so bad that Jade snuck off to a pawnbroker to sell all his jewellery – the rings and necklaces he'd been collecting for forty years.

'It broke my heart,' he recalls. 'They were valued at $120,000, for insurance purposes, and the pawnbroker gave me $4500.'

A friend found out what he had done and went to the pawn shop. The pawnbroker called Jade up and said he needed to see him. He arrived and his friend handed over a brown envelope with all his jewellery in it. Jade broke down and wept with gratitude. And shame.

Barbara says their office was in a high-rise unit on the coast and there was a period where she wouldn't allow herself to go out onto the balcony. 'I just couldn't trust myself.'

Jade had to return to what he does best, but it's been a hard slog. He has a genetic heart condition and suffers from chronic chest pains. Once a week the pain will be so severe he has to take a cocktail of Rohypnol and Panadeine Forte just to get some sleep. It wipes him out the following day.

'But the show goes on. If people knock on the door of the Jayco and want a CD or a DVD or a look through the van or want an autograph I put on the smile; the face and the showman come into play. I've got to smile and be happy and give the lady a cuddle and shake the hand of the guy with a smile on his face and I'm feeling absolutely fucking shithouse.'

The next day we follow them down to Cairns for their show at Cazalys, the Cairns Aussie Rules Club. We set up our van next to theirs in the carpark and go off to explore Cairns.

When we return Jade is polishing his motor home – Barbara says he is obsessively neat and tidy and later we find him repainting the big black sign which hangs behind him on stage. Otherwise, she says, he spends his time between shows scouring through op-shops looking for t-shirts and shorts. 'Every year I'll bundle a heap up and take them off to the Sallies,' she says. 'He just can't walk past a second-hand shop or a market.'

After the sound check Jade and I sit in the auditorium and chat. I had heard that he used to visit dying cancer patients in hospital. I ask him why. He tells me he watched his mum die of breast cancer when he was 14. It had affected him ever since. Despite that, he had no real intention of becoming a comforter to dying cancer patients – it just evolved.

One night he was playing at the West Wyalong RSL Club when someone put in a request for him to sing a song for a mate who was dying of cancer. The song was Johnny Mathis' hit 'Twelfth of Never'. The next night he was playing at the Bankstown Sports Club and his manager came in and said 'You are not going to believe this.' A woman had sent him a note saying she was there with her mother who had cancer and only had a few days to live. She also requested 'Twelfth of Never'.

'It freaked me out. From West Wyalong to Bankstown . . . What are the chances?' Word spread among his fans and soon he was getting regular requests to visit dying cancer patients. He did it for years out of a sense of duty, turning up with a smile and a couple of signed albums. He never enjoyed it.

'It got too much for me in the end,' he explains. 'I did this gig down at Panthers in Penrith and when I was doing the sound check this guy was waiting for me. He said he had split with his wife, but they were still close because of the kids. She was dying of cancer. "Jade, it would mean a lot to her if you could visit."

'I walked into Liverpool Hospital and as soon as I walked into the room I knew I didn't want to be there. I could smell death and could see she was about to die. The relatives were all standing around smiling and the lady was so happy to see me and I just couldn't wait to leave. I smiled, gave her a hug and kiss, chatted for a bit and then left. I said to my manager, "I can never do that again," and I haven't.' He makes polite excuses these days.

That night we go back for our second concert. There are about 200 people at the show, including a group of seven or eight university students. It looks like they must have won their tickets in a raffle and are along for the laugh and to ridicule the performance.

Lisa does the first half of the show and comes back into the caravan all fired up. She explains how condescending the students have been and how much attention they've drawn to themselves. 'Little smart arses,' she says. 'One of them called me darling.'

They are still there for the second half – dressed in Vinnie's clothing, jackets and hats, and acting cool and then dancing stupidly up the front. I want to punch them in the chops. After a time a doorman arrives and asks one of them to leave. There is a bit of a kerfuffle but he does eventually walk out and the others follow.

'Good riddance,' I say to Barb.

To be honest, when I first saw Jade on the road my attitude was probably not too different from the students'. I had initially come along for a bit of a laugh. But after a couple of days with Jade and Barbara I've come to like them both. I realise what a good showman he is – he knows how to work a crowd and he gives them exactly what they want. I admire them for clawing their way back.

Towards the end of the show, an old lady with an aluminium walking frame comes up to the counter where Barbara is sitting. She's clutching her photocopied album list with a couple of ticks on it.

'How many songs to go?' she asks Barbara excitedly, like a little girl.

Barbara tells her there are three songs left.

'I'll wait here, then, to be first in line. I don't want to miss him. He's my idol. Him and Elvis.'

23

From Buddy Holly and bain-maries in the bistro to gluten-free lentil pies and 'psychedelic Afro-futuristic-roots' – the difference between the weddings and functions room at Cazalys to the Kuranda Amphitheatre could not be greater.

'Welcome Dreadsters, Funkrats, Soulmamas and Dubheadz,' says the program for the Kuranda Roots Festival. In the amphitheatre the sweet smell of pot hangs in the humid air.

It is probably one of the best outdoor venues in Australia. A series of grassed terraces slope down to a stage at the bottom of the valley. It could easily accommodate 3500 people. It sits right on the edge of the Barron Falls National Park, 20 kilometres west of Cairns in the hinterland, and is surrounded by enormous rainforest trees and palms.

The mood of the crowd, which swells to 1000 or more, is mellow and inviting. There are lots of dreads and purple velvet and breasts being flopped into the mouths of kindergarten-aged children.

It's Joe's first festival and he loves it. We sit up on the slope of the amphitheatre as he dances away on grass in front of the stage. Occasionally he gets a little too excited and we have to stop him crawling up the stairs and onto the stage with Billy Dreads and The Nomads.

At one point, there is a scuffle between two men in the crowd. The band stops playing and the lead singer shouts, 'Hey, take that negative energy outside. This is no place for violence.' The two combatants skulk from the venue followed by security. 'Peace,' says the singer, and then the bongos resume.

We meet up with Ben Spiers, the man who has driven 50,000 kilometres for free on fish and chip oil, and some of his mates. Ben is intelligent and intense. His father is a hippie and his mother is a woman called Susan Davies, a former left-leaning independent who, for a time, held the balance of power when Jeff Kennett was Premier of Victoria. Ben is a mix of politician and hippie.

He explains how he has travelled around Australia, surviving on about $80 a week, camping for free in national parks or on the side of the road and how he gets his fuel for free. We would have trouble feeding Joe for $80 a week. Ben survives through wit, the generosity of others and not paying for much – like the entrance fee to the concert.

'I basically pull into every café that I pass and ask them if they have any waste oil from their fryers stored out the back,' he explains. 'I offer to buy it. Most people, if they have any, will give it to me for free, although I have paid 20 cents a litre for oil.' It is a lot less than the $2.20 we are paying for diesel and is only 4 or 5 per cent less efficient.

There's a merry band of hippies, like Ben, travelling around on chip fat. They compete with a company called The Fat Man which collects the waste oil commercially. Sometimes competition is fierce, but Ben has never failed to get oil.

'It is a bit manic-depressive, the search for oil,' he says. 'Just when I think I will have to pay, I'll stumble across some. I found great oil in Broome. The drums had warmed in the sun and all the dross had settled. It was perfect fuel and I didn't even have to filter it. I pumped it straight out into all my barrels, and that got me from Broome to Esperance with one fill – three and a half thousand kilometres from the top of the continent to the bottom.'

His system is very basic. He pumps the oil into big plastic tanks on the back of his van, a 1980 Nissan Urvan, and leaves them in the sun. All the solids fall to the bottom and can be easily filtered. He starts his engine on diesel and then switches to filtered vegetable oil. He switches back to diesel before turning off the engine so the lines don't clog.

'I am on a mission,' Ben tells us. 'My mission is to educate people about alternative sources of power. I am not actually a biofuels proponent. It is just that this is a waste product that can be used.'

Ben studied mechanical engineering and has invented a low-cost solar thermal collection device that he is attempting to get manufactured. 'It's a bit more like a solar tube heater but it's also a roofing material,' he says. 'The idea is that you'd have 50 square metres — you could make your whole patio out of it, or half the side of your roof. Once you've got that much thermal energy you can do lots of interesting things with it — heating, air conditioning, electricity.'

Ben is a generation younger than me and it is interesting to spend time with him and his mates. They are the carbon generation — acutely aware of the environment and their impact on it.

For a couple of days we hang out in the Kuranda caravan park and explore the local markets and drink good coffee. For a change, there are lots of young couples with kids in the park. We come across several who have given up their jobs, sold up their houses, and are drifting around Australia, looking for a place to drop anchor and start a new life.

One night we meet up with a few of these people. Ben, who has his van parked just outside so he doesn't have to pay, joins us. I make a big fish curry and others bring dhal and salads. Two of Ben's mates, a couple called Clay and Georgie, have ukuleles. They are joined by another guy with a guitar. And then another couple arrives carrying more ukuleles. And so we sit and listen as people sing late into the night, backed by an orchestra.

24

We are camped beside a river, almost halfway between Cairns on the Coral Sea and Karumba on the Gulf of Carpentaria, on a cattle station called Mt Surprise. About a dozen caravans and tents are spaced out along a wide, sandy creek with half a metre of clear, clean water running through it. The surrounding cattle country is dry now but almost every year this river receives a monsoonal drenching and the eucalypts in and beside the river all lean obediently downstream.

There's a different feel to the country this far north. There's something optimistic about it. In the arid centre and the dry lands further south, the country has taken on the lean appearance of a dingo that never knows where its next feed will come from – it's all ribcage and wary glances. Here, it gets dry too and the soils aren't great, but the landscape carries itself as though everything will be okay.

The north offers a softer outback. People come here to Mt Surprise to relax and to fossick in the sandy soils for semi-precious stones like topaz, aquamarine and quartz. Some may stay a month or more. We decide to stay a couple of days, to swim and to write. It is $7 per adult, while Joe stays for free.

We are back on the trail with the grey nomads. It's an accurate term because there are literally tens of thousands of older

Australians on the roads and they are basically nomadic. We've met dozens of them.

Back in Gloucester we became friendly with a woman called Bev Welsh, who was turning 70. She had five children and 12 grandkids and had spent 20 years 'squashed' in an unhappy marriage until she divorced.

In 2005 she set off in a little converted bus and fell in love with the lifestyle. A year later she sold her unit in Geelong and bought a $100,000 motorhome. Bev now lives on the road permanently, and may spend a couple of months in Western Australia for the wildflower season, or three weeks exploring a particularly pretty national park in North Queensland. She manages to do all this on her $12,000 annual pension.

She returns to Geelong for a month or two each year, to see the kids and the grandkids, before heading off again. After a lifetime of caring for others, she's decided that time is now her own.

'If I'd stayed in Geelong I'd have ended up in a nursing home, staring at four walls.'

Bev mainly stays in bush camps for free and if she needs company she chats to one of her fellow campers.

There is an intimacy about these bush camps that you don't get in the caravan parks. People look out for each other. Just up the river from where we're camped is a Welsh couple. They live in Cairns. We chat a few times and then the woman arrives with fresh damper.

'Here love, I thought your little fella might enjoy some of this.'

Joe doesn't get a look in.

Immediately to our right, about 40 metres away, there are two couples travelling together. They are on the booze at midday and play cards all afternoon. They say they are here fossicking, but never seem to make it out to the gemfields.

Off to our left, there's an old-style 1970s caravan and Lisa and I notice that the couple in it seem very odd. She looks like a scared possum and sits timidly in a chair while he potters about inside. Sometimes she just stares into the distance for hours and they seem never to talk. I wonder what sort of marriage they have.

On our second afternoon, Joe and I go off to collect firewood for our campfire. The woman is sitting outside when we return and I ask her if she would like any wood. She just stares at me blankly and a few seconds later her husband comes out of the van, a bit flustered. He says that everything is okay, they don't need wood.

He follows Joe and me back to our van.

'I am sorry,' he says. 'My wife has dementia.'

The man, Barry, is in his early sixties and his wife Maureen is just 59. They own a little dairy farm in Tasmania and this will be their last trip away together. After this Maureen is going into a home.

'This was always her dream, to do this trip and she can't remember anything about it.'

Barry starts to cry as he talks to Lisa and me about his wife's illness. She was diagnosed just three years ago and has regressed to the point where he has to escort her to the camp toilet, just 150 metres away, because she forgets where she is and can't find her way back.

'The terrible thing is that she has moments of clarity where she realises what is happening to her. She gets all weepy knowing what a burden she is and knowing that she is losing her mind.'

I ask Barry if they would like to join us around the campfire, after we put Joe to bed. His face lights up.

'I would like that very much. We don't get out very much.'

He asks us to keep the conversation with Maureen simple. She can remember minute details from her childhood but not where they were yesterday.

After dark I walk over to collect them and give them a hand with their camp chairs. Barry tenderly sits Maureen beside the campfire with a glass of water in the chair's cup holder.

We chat about where they have been and their farm in Tasmania. Maureen chips in occasionally. Most of the time she just stares at the mesmerising dance of the flames.

At one point Lisa asks her how many children she has.

'Oh dear,' she replies, flustered. 'I'd have to count them.'

Later Barry gently points out that she has a glass of water sitting in the arm of her chair. She looks at it, surprised, and then takes a sip.

He tells us that he is not a great cook because Maureen used to do all the cooking while he did the farmwork.

'We eat a lot of baked beans these days.'

'Beans are okay dear,' she says. 'There's nothing wrong with beans.'

In the morning we pack up to leave and Maureen is sitting outside with a cup of tea.

'Hello. How are you this morning?' I ask.

She has no idea who I am.

At a place called Georgetown, we stop for supplies and Lisa asks the woman behind the counter what the next town is like.

'Croydon,' she tells us, 'it's not as big as here.'

'What about Normanton, what's it like?'

'Indigenous,' she says, as if that explains everything, and in a way it does. She means dysfunctional.

We drive through Croydon and Normanton and camp in the famed fishing town of Karumba, at the base of the gulf. Each year thousands of retired Victorians sit out the winter months here, fishing, camping and eating fresh prawns for $10 a kilo. It is also home to a large commercial prawn and fishing fleet.

At night I check out the infamous Animal Bar where the deckhands who've been out at sea for weeks at a time, come to unwind. There are dozens of very big men with mullets and those homemade tattoos that are doodled to pass the time in gaol. You don't often see people without teeth these days and it's probably because they've all moved to Karumba to work on the trawlers. People are walking around smoking joints, but there's none of that hippie, peace vibe from the amphitheatre. A pretty Maori girl, in ugg boots, is prancing about causing trouble.

I get chatting to a young Indonesian guy called Roy who is over here on a work permit and earns around $2000 a month – a fortune in his village in Java. The other crewmen treat him well, he says, and he enjoys his work. What an odd view he must have of Australia, I think. He's never been beyond Karumba.

'Are you Muslim?' I ask.

'Yes,' he laughs, holding up a cigarette and a beer, 'but not a very good one.'

At least he's sipping his beer. Others are guzzling.

Over Roy's shoulder I can see a fight brewing between four enormous men. It starts off with some harmless pushing and ends up with one of the men holding another around the scruff of the neck and deciding if he should let him go or smack him in the head. The two barmaids with tight shirts and enormous breasts, backpackers I guess, stand around not knowing what to do. Suddenly, an older woman emerges from somewhere in the premises and puts herself between the two men.

'You. You. Fuck off.'

She speaks with authority that makes them listen. One of them tries to reason with her.

'We were only fuckin' muckin' around.'

She says she couldn't care less and that they can come back in an hour, after they've been for a walk to cool down. The tension leaves with them.

In the morning, Joe makes a new friend after running into his tent. The guy's name is Rick McLean. Lucky Rick is a bushy from central NSW near Condobolin where he manages a wheat silo. This year, for some reason, the fish just aren't biting for anyone, anyone except Rick. Every day he returns with half a dozen enormous jewel fish or barramundi and luckily for us, he doesn't like the taste of fish. We leave Karumba with a freezer full of fresh fillets.

And then there's two enormous days of driving. Our route could easily be the song list from a Slim Dusty album: Burke and Wills Roadhouse, Cloncurry, Mount Isa, Camooweal and over the border to the Territory. We roll out our swag in Tennant Creek.

We've driven almost 2000 kilometres in less than a week. It feels as if it was a Sunday afternoon spin.

NORTHERN TERRITORY

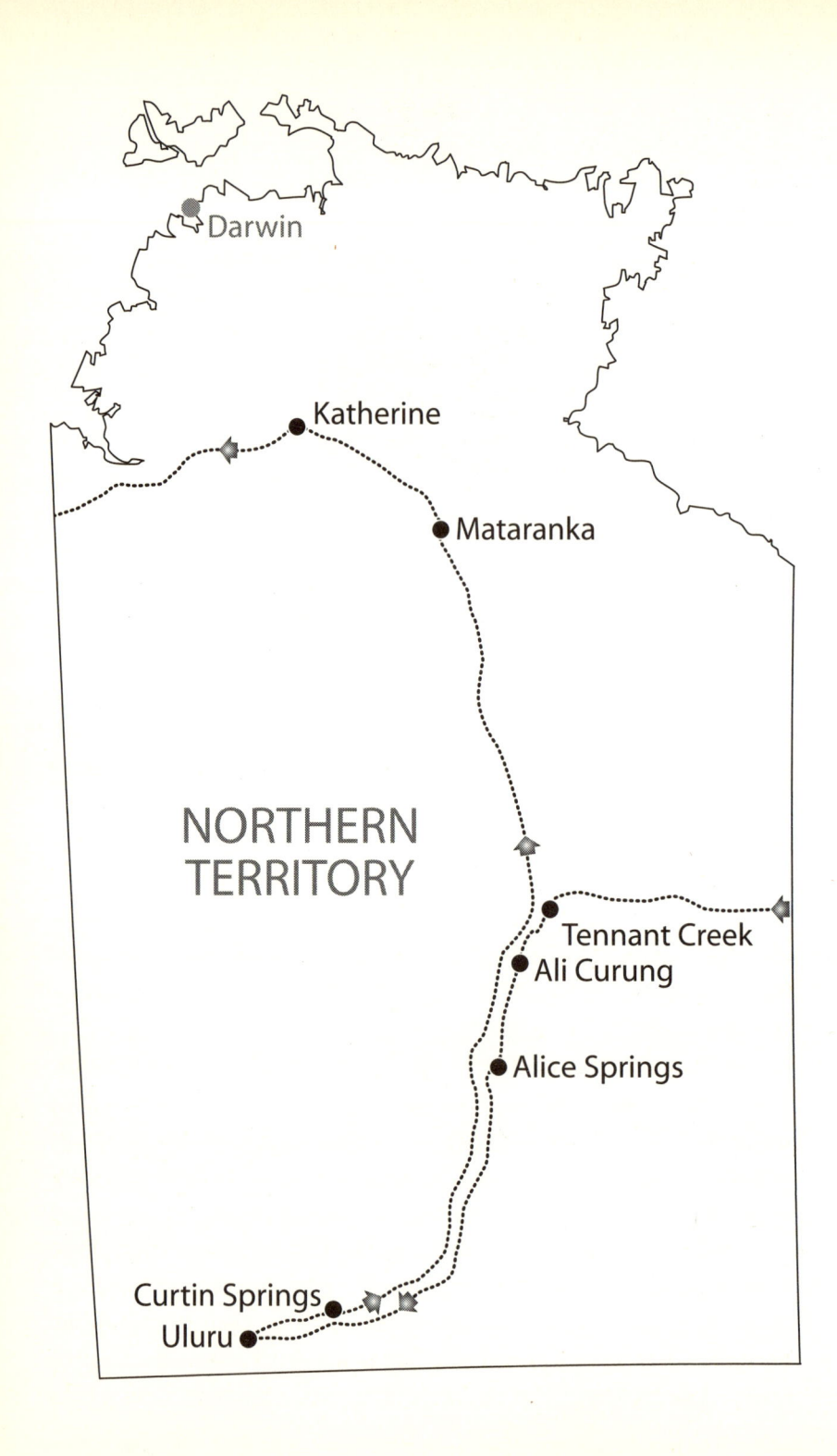

- Darwin
- Katherine
- Mataranka
- Tennant Creek
- Ali Curung
- Alice Springs
- Curtin Springs
- Uluru

25

Tennant Creek is one of those towns that white Australia avoids. Tens of thousands of tourists pass through here each year on their way to Darwin, to central Queensland or to Alice and the Rock. There's some mining history here, from Australia's last great rush in the 1930s. There's a well-funded Aboriginal cultural centre, a few interesting buildings, like the corrugated church, and a craggy, ancient range just out of town. Its location should make it a tourist hub, but the few people who actually stop here do so warily. The wife stays in the car while the husband goes into the supermarket for supplies. They then drive off to the Devil's Marbles and Uluru to experience authentic Aboriginal history and culture, largely without Aborigines.

Tennant Creek is 1000 kilometres south of Darwin and 500 kilometres north of Alice. It has a population of 3300 people of which more than half are Aboriginal. You don't see the whites. They are working in the mines, or at the hospital, on the railway maintenance crews or in the police station.

The main street is filled with Aborigines. Some live here. Others have come in from remote camps to shop, to visit relatives or to get on the grog because many of their own communities have recently been declared dry. The main street is a meeting place and people sit around in circles on the footpath. East coast whites just aren't used to seeing this many black faces and figure it spells trouble. They'd be perfectly safe during the day. The night, however, is another story.

A grog ban is due to be implemented here in a few months' time which will make it illegal to drink in public and police will have the power to seize and dispose of alcohol. The hours that takeaway alcohol can be sold will also be severely restricted. Everyone hopes it will make a difference because now it is a living tragedy.

The rates of violence here among Aborigines are akin to strife-torn nations in the third world. The Night Patrol staffed by Aboriginal men, cruises the street looking for passed-out drunks. It takes them home or to the safety cell at the police station to sleep it off. Between the Night Patrol and the police more than 15,000 pickups are made each year. That's an average of 40 people too plastered to crawl home every single night.

'The nightshift at Tennant Creek Hospital can be a bloodbath,' wrote Dr Dean Robertson in an article published in *The Australian* just before we arrived in town. '"No swearing, fighting, spitting or biting," reads the sign on the front door, but most people are too drunk or wounded to care.'

The first thing we do when we pull into Tennant Creek is stop by the hospital to try to find Dr Robertson. He's already left town. Young doctors and nurses fly in for a few months and then fly out again. It's like a tour of duty.

We drive down the main street to buy groceries. Out the front of the supermarket, amazingly, we spot Nita Bell's daughter, Leanne, who is doing some shopping. The show is in town. We hug like old friends and chat about what we've been doing.

Moments later Nita rings.

'Don't you be booking into the caravan park,' she orders. 'I'll get you a spot in the showground.'

We buy some groceries and drive over. It is a big show with dozens of rides and we set up camp behind the cha-cha and Nita's Snacks and reacquaint ourselves. I volunteer to cook for everyone, a big pot of Stephanie Alexander's chicken noodle soup as it should be.

The Showies have just come from Alice Springs and over soup and wine that evening, tell us that everyone's takings were down 10 to 15 per cent. They expect Tennant Creek will be the same, maybe worse.

The Federal Government's intervention in Northern Territory Aboriginal communities is in full swing. The intervention was begun in the dying days of the Howard Government and has continued under Labor. In an attempt to stem alcoholism and family breakdown in Aboriginal communities, half the welfare payments of some Aborigines have been quarantined and can only be spent in designated shops, on essential items such as food or clothing.

It has slowed take-away grog sales and spending on groceries has increased. It has also had a drastic effect on businesses that have been deemed non-essential, such as fast food outlets.

The Showies are likewise affected but Nita is philosophical. 'If the kids are getting a proper feed, well then it's a good thing.'

We talk about our plans to go out into the Tanami Desert and Nita insists on lending us her satellite phone, just in case.

Throughout the night Gary is unusually quiet and sits off to one side smoking cigarettes and sipping on Coke.

'He's a bit nervous,' Nita explains. 'He's off to meet his daughter for the first time next week.'

Forty years ago Gary had a fling with a young Aboriginal woman who was travelling on the show circuit – they were both aged about 17 at the time. The show moved on and the woman moved back to Western Australia. He says he never knew about his daughter until he got a phone call a few months ago.

The woman's name is Brenda. She grew up in Halls Creek in the Kimberley and now lives in Kununurra. Brenda and her family are driving over to meet Gary in Katherine.

'She's obviously been brought up well and has done well for herself,' Gary explains with pride. They have spoken several times on the phone. 'She's got a Bachelor of Arts from the University of Western Australia. Apparently she manages something for the health department in the Kimberley. 'We'll just see how it all goes.'

In the morning, Nita takes us on a tour of the showground before the crowds arrive. She's like a rooster in a chook pen.

Outside the pavilion, she stops at a stand called Nuts Galore.

'Are you the man who owns this?' she demands, curtly.

'Yes,' he replies, almost choking on a handful of nuts.

'I'm Nita Bell.'

'Yes ... I know who you are.'

'Well you've taken my site and you won't be doing it again!'

'This is my site, I've got photos of myself here,' he protests.

'Listen, this is my site, I've been here for 15 years and I've already made sure you won't be here next year ...'

With that Nita turns on her heel and totters off into the pavilion, leading Joe with her. Half an hour later, our toddler walks out weighed down with free show paraphernalia – pens, stress balls, an orange balloon, a green balloon, Smarties, drink bottles, an Aussie flag, an Aboriginal flag, a Torres Strait Islander flag, a power saving plug, a bag from the Australian Electoral Commission, two videos on making the transition to parenting and a couple of tubes of lip gloss.

Inside, I chat to a woman from the Electoral Commission who is manning a stand with the purpose of getting Aborigines to sign up to vote – she isn't at all hopeful.

'We got none last year and we got none the year before that.'

Late in the day I see her again and ask how many she had signed up.

'Two,' she exclaims. 'Two more than I expected.'

Six years ago Lisa came to Tennant Creek to make a 30-minute TV documentary for the SBS program *Insight*. It was about a group of Aboriginal students who had opted to go to boarding school in Townsville. More than 40 students got on a bus and drove 1500 kilometres to the east coast.

The boarding program was controversial because it highlighted just how bad life in Tennant Creek had become. In previous generations black children were forcibly taken from their parents, and now a group of teenagers was choosing to leave. One 14-year-old boy, when asked if he missed his parents, said: 'No. They are alcoholics. I just want to be on my own.' The mass exodus was also embarrassing for the local high school.

In Townsville one night, Lisa took three of the boys, aged 15, along to Pizza Hut. None of them could read the menu.

One of the main characters in the program was a 16-year-old student called Jana Williams, a tall, athletic and temperamental teenager. Jana was good at basketball, a popular and confident kid who had hopes of going to university or becoming an artist. She was intelligent. Of all the kids who went to Townsville, Jana was the one most likely to succeed.

'Jana was the brightest and everybody could see that she had potential,' Lisa tells me. 'There was a collective desire to see her do well. People bent over backwards for her because they were desperate for someone to succeed.'

Jana would now be 22. The day after the show we decide to try to track her down to see how things have turned out.

We take a few wrong turns before Lisa finally remembers where Jana's family used to live. It is in one of the better parts of Tennant Creek in a reasonably modern subdivision. It is a world away from the squalor of the camps on the edge of town.

We park out the front of the house and can see Jana, her sister and some kids sitting in the shade of the patio. Lisa approaches and at first Jana does not recognise her, but her sister does. 'It's Lisa, from the TV,' she exclaims. Jana smiles and giggles and greets her like an old friend.

'My father, he watched that program over and over,' she beams. 'He showed it to everyone, he even took it to Queensland so our relatives could see it.'

Jana and Lisa chat for a while and we agree to come back tomorrow to talk at length. She has died her hair red and Lisa says she likes the colour and that she needs to dye her hair soon.

'I'll do it for you,' volunteers Jana. And so we promise to return.

★

The next day we come armed with L'Oreal light mahogany. It's hot and we all move into the shade on the patio.

The house is a big, modern design with galvanised tin walls. The large patio out the front is caged in with steel mesh and a steel-grill door that can be bolted and padlocked. It's a common feature in Aboriginal communities, designed to allow people to sit and sleep outside where they can be cool and safe. There is rubbish scattered all over the floor – old Coke bottles, a discarded pack of cards, broken toys, the packaging from a mobile phone.

Jana and I go into the house to fetch something to sit on. I can hear a television in a bedroom down the hall. A couple of family photos hang from the walls, the only decorations. The floors, which are cement, need sweeping and there's grime on the walls. There is virtually no furniture in the big living area of the house, apart from two old wheelchairs, which belonged to Jana's father, Lawrence, before he upgraded to an electric chair. We wheel the old push models onto the patio so that we can sit down.

Jana stands. She is tall and her movements are graceful and feline. She speaks softly. She has smooth, chocolate-coloured skin, a broad nose and long, elegant fingers. She tells us she was once offered work as a model, but was too shy to be photographed in swimmers. She is unusually beautiful in a raw and athletic way. Clinging to her side is a little boy with a cheeky grin. It's her son, Miguel, who is three.

Joe plays with Miguel while we chat about Jana's life since she and Lisa last met. She puts Lisa in a chair and mixes the hair dye as we speak.

Before she went off to boarding school, she regularly wagged school. Her father, Lawrence, sent his daughter away because Tennant Creek was a mess.

'There are a lot of kids in Tennant Creek that don't like going to school,' he had told Lisa, for the program. 'The thing is, they like, you know, hanging around late at night, getting on the booze, like, on the alcohol, smoking, smoking drugs, you know? It's just not a good thing for them.'

And so Jana went off to Townsville halfway through Year 10. She missed her family terribly and didn't think she was going to last. But then she became friends with some girls from the Atherton Tablelands, got involved in sport and started to enjoy all the new experiences.

'It was the first time I seen the ocean,' she explains. 'I was scared to go in the water because of the jellyfish. I found a lot of jellyfish on the sand and I thought, I'm not getting in the water.'

Of the 43 children who left Tennant Creek most dropped out within the first few months. Jana was one of the few who went back after the Christmas break. She was enjoying her studies and doing well at school and thought she would finish Year 12, as her parents wished.

But then, at the end of first term in Year 11, she went off to some celebrations for Naidoc Week (National Aboriginal Islander Day Observance Committee) at Elliott, a tiny Aboriginal settlement, 300 kilometres north of Tennant Creek.

'I fell in love,' she declares. 'It was love at first sight.'

And so, instead of returning to school in Townsville, she stayed with the family of her new boyfriend, Eddie, in Elliott. Her parents were not happy, but they didn't go to Elliott to pick her up, or force her to go back to school.

After she and Eddie had been together a year Jana became pregnant. She was 19 when her son was born. She named him after Miguel Lopez-Fitzgerald, a character in *Passions*, a long-running and bizarre US soap opera which screened on Channel 7.

'My mum and dad were really happy,' she offers. 'Mum said, "At least you didn't have him when you were 15 or 16," like most of my friends did. They were happy.'

She, Eddie and Miguel now live with Jana's parents. They have applied to get their own flat and have been told it may take a year or two, but that they will get one.

Jana has been offered several jobs, but has knocked them back, saying she doesn't want to work until Miguel is at school. One was as an Aboriginal teacher's aide at the high school and the other was at a childcare centre. With the childcare job she was told that Miguel could come to work with her and she'd be with him all the time. She never got back to them.

Jana spends her days watching television and movies and taking her son for walks. She used to have a car but sold it to pay for Miguel's third birthday party. She is an urbanised Aborigine who knows little of the traditional ways and says she is not really interested in them. Eddie works 30 hours a week for the Commonwealth Development Employment Program cleaning up rubbish.

In a town where alcoholism is rampant, Jana drinks only occasionally. Eddie is not a big drinker either.

Jana works the dye through Lisa's hair and when she's finished Lisa goes into the kitchen to wash off the excess dye. The kitchen is mostly empty. There's no fridge.

The following day we meet up with Jana's mum and dad, Lawrence and Rosie, who are minding their niece's flat in the centre of town. She works for the local land council. The flat is clean and well furnished. The niece lets them stay while she's away at conferences. They water the plants.

Lisa is shocked when she sees Lawrence. Six years ago, he was an active, able-bodied man. Now his arthritis is so bad he's confined to a motorised wheelchair. His joints have seized so much that three fingers and a toe have had to be amputated. He looks like an old man. He is 46, crippled by the twin demons of bad diet and 'lifestyle'.

Lawrence and I sit in the lounge room talking while Lisa and Rosie chat outside. The football is on in the background and he glances over every so often because Hawthorn, his favourite team, is playing.

Until a few years ago, when his arthritis got too bad, Lawrence worked for the Night Patrol, picking up the drunks. He saw how bad things could get in Tennant Creek, which is why he sent his daughter to Townsville.

'She came home and then I heard she had a boyfriend,' Lawrence recalls. 'I wasn't very happy 'cause I still wanted her to get more schooling, to learn more education, to get a good job in the future.'

He says that he and Rosie have since offered to look after Miguel so Jana could work at the school, but she didn't want that.

'I'm proud of her but she could work. We could look after Miguel.'

In many ways Jana is a great success. She is raising her little boy in a loving environment with an extended family and she has not succumbed to the temptations that have ruined the lives of many of her friends.

But she's also been cocooned by welfare. She doesn't have to work because everything she ever needs is given to her. In a couple of years she, Miguel and Eddie will move into their own place, provided by the government. If the toilet breaks, someone will eventually turn up to fix it. If the yard needs cleaning, the CDEP truck will arrive every few months to take away the rubbish. All responsibility has been assumed by the state.

The Aboriginal leader, Noel Pearson, argues this is precisely what is killing Aboriginal Australia, 'The irony of our newly won citizenship in 1967 was that after we became citizens with equal rights and the theoretical right to equal pay, we lost the meagre foothold that we had in the real economy and we became almost comprehensively dependent upon passive welfare for our livelihood. So in one sense we gained citizenship and in another sense we lost it at the same time. Thirty years later we find that life in the safety net for three decades and two generations has produced a social disaster.'

One afternoon while we are in Tennant Creek, we drive out to Lake Mary Ann. It's an old mining dam which was turned into a recreation dam in the 1980s.

We let Joe out of the car and he runs straight into the mud.

Down by the water, a black man is fishing with his two kids, helping them cast and threading their hooks with bait. It is a lovely scene and I am intrigued – it is unexpected.

Joe becomes inquisitive and disturbs the fishing while the man and I get chatting. He is not Aboriginal but from a small village in the Solomon Islands. He has come to Australia to work on the railway gang based in Tennant Creek, which carries out maintenance on the Adelaide to Darwin railway. There are 40 men employed on the maintenance crew.

It's hard to believe that in a town with chronic unemployment they've needed to bring in a labourer from the Pacific.

'Are there any Aboriginal workers?' I ask the man.

'There were two, but they didn't last very long. I don't know what happened to them.'

It's time for us to leave Tennant Creek, but before we do Lisa buys a box of chocolates for Jana. We drop around to her house to say goodbye. There's a little bit of small talk about keeping in contact but Jana doesn't have access to a telephone or email. We'll only see her again if we come back to Tennant Creek. Lisa hands over the chocolates and we say goodbye.

26

We make our way slowly down to Alice Springs, camping a night in the splendour of the Devil's Marbles, Karlu Karlu, surrounded by those giant granite mushrooms of the desert.

Karlu Karlu has recently been handed back to the original owners and ordinarily an Aboriginal elder, by the name of Black Hat, gives a talk to the tourists. They gather around a campfire and he tells them about the Aboriginal dreaming stories.

Black Hat is ill tonight and so the talk is delivered by a fat, pinkish park ranger. The ranger, Pink Face, explains to the gathering that the desert Aborigines are not at all like the Aborigines of the east coast who are generally 'half-caste no-good shit stirrers'. Nearly all the ones out here, he assures us, are 'full-bloods and good blokes'.

When it comes to explaining what the Aborigines believe about the formation of Karlu Karlu, Pink Face adopts a broad, blackfella accent, as if channelling Black Hat. 'Way long time go, 'for 'em white fella come . . .'

I can't quite believe what I am hearing. It's the verbal equivalent of smearing his face with boot polish for the performance.

At the end, when he's reverted to an ordinary Australian drawl, someone asks him about Aboriginal art, and if there is somewhere nearby to buy it.

'A new art centre has just opened at Ali Curung,' Pink Face explains. Ali Curung is an Aboriginal settlement just 50 kilometres from here, 20 kilometres off the Stuart Highway. 'You could go to Ali Curung, if you are brave enough. If I go there, I just park outside the police station or the bakery, do what I need to do, and then get out.'

We decide to ignore Pink Face's advice and visit Ali Curung for ourselves – we figure that with endorsements like his the new art centre needs all the support it can get.

Ali Curung is a small desert Aboriginal settlement at the end of a gun-barrel road – a messy mob of two dozen houses surrounding a footy oval and lots of dogs.

We find the arts centre without too much trouble and park the caravan outside. Inside there is a good selection of paintings and as it happens a few of the artists are here. They explain the significance of each piece.

We get caught up in the moment and buy a painting. One of the artists, Maureen, who is dressed in a stylish trenchcoat, a beanie and runners, asks if we would like to see the studio.

We follow her and another woman called Valerie across the settlement. They are fascinated by Joe's white skin and hair. Yet again he has provided an entry card into another world. Valerie and Maureen are old friends and tell me they went for a trip to Sydney once, when they were at school. They are both 40, but look much older.

'I remember dat big bridge,' Maureen says.

'An da ferry,' says Valerie. 'We rode da ferry.'

Outside the studio an old Aboriginal woman has a giant canvas in front of her, which she is meticulously covering with small dots – she doesn't look up when we pass. It is as though she's in a trance.

Maureen and Valerie take us inside to see more paintings. One catches my eye and I ask what it means.

'Dis one here Greg,' says Maureen, pointing to the painting. 'Dis one 'ere mean bilby dream ...'

Valerie cuts in, 'Dat's no fuckin' bilby, Maureen, dat's a wallaby.'

A broad smile breaks out across Maureen's face and she says, without missing a beat: 'Dis painting here Greg, dis be wallaby dreaming.'

The two women erupt in great cackles.

27

Joe has been teething for days. We are in Alice Springs camped in the MacDonnell Ranges Holiday Park, an enormous caravan city on the edge of the actual city. It is high season and the place is packed but after a few days we are an island. There's a ring of empty spaces around us as our fellow campers flee the noise. Thank God Lisa's mum, Joan, is arriving soon, as are my parents.

We endure Joe at night and explore Alice by day, waiting for the reinforcements to arrive.

Alice has a reputation for being an outback frontier town filled with larger-than-life ocker characters. The reality is that ABC Radio National is among its highest rating stations and the town is rumoured to have more doctorates per head than anywhere in Australia. It is the centre for arid zone and desert research and home to a large scientific community. There's a battalion of US spooks, spying on the Russians, the Martians, the AWB and whatever else they do at Pine Gap.

It is the hub for desert art and its main street is packed with galleries displaying the very finest Aboriginal paintings. There are cafés serving fresh food and good coffee, staffed by stern and efficient lesbians. Its Cultural Precinct houses, among other things, the Albert Namatjira Gallery and the Strehlow collection of

Aboriginal artefacts and is surely one of the country's best regional museums.

To top it off, Alice is a starkly beautiful city. The imposing and barren MacDonnell Ranges surround the city while the Todd River, with its imposing red gums, cuts through the town.

We experience all this in sleep-deprived trances, like truckies on amphetamine hangovers.

One night Joe wakes at 4 am and refuses to go back to sleep – he wants to play. I get up and pull the curtains that divide our bed from the rest of the van so that Lisa can rest. I unzip Joe from his cot. Our little electric blow heater wheezes against the cold as I read him *The Very Hungry Caterpillar*. After 10 minutes Joe crawls in behind the curtains and snuggles into bed with Lisa.

I figure he's gone to sleep and I depart to the toilet block with the only newspaper on offer in these parts, *The Australian*.

Ten minutes later, when I return, a distressed elderly woman is knocking on the door of the caravan and I can see Lisa, wide-eyed and frantic.

'Excuse me, but there is a little boy down the road and I think he may be yours,' she says.

We race through the park, our hearts thumping, to find Joe a couple of hundred metres away. He has a mobile phone clamped to his ear and is chatting away contentedly.

We bundle him back to bed but Alice has more drama in store.

The following night Lisa wakes with a start.

'There's someone in the van,' she says. I wake groggily out of a deep sleep. I can hear voices, whispering. I stick my head out to see two or three people, kids, running off through the park. It takes a moment to realise that they had in fact been inside the caravan. Our caravan!

My first panicked thought is of Joe. I race to his cot but he is, for once, fast asleep. My second thought is our computers. Everything from our trip is on them – notes, photos, diary entries. They are gone! Shit! Lisa! Shit! This is a disaster! Call the police!

'They're under the table,' she says, calmly.

Our wallets are gone, but that seems like a bonus.

The next day, as the real drama begins – dealing with the banks to get our cards back – a Landcruiser towing a caravan pulls up in front of our camp. It's the Smeads – Kate and Tim and their four kids – whom we met in Cairns a couple of months ago. They are packed up to leave but stop to chat and tell their own traumatic tale.

Back in Queensland they had just left the remote Lawn Hill National Park near the Northern Territory border when it seems a rock must have bounced up and cut through the brake cable on the caravan as they bumped along a dirt road.

'We were cruising along fairly slowly into a dry creek,' Tim reports. 'As I went to apply the brakes the van just didn't take. I remember looking at the mirror seeing the van swing around to 90 degrees. It was pushing the vehicle into a bank. When I hit the brakes, it just jack-knifed and it spun us around 180 degrees.' Kate and the kids were screaming, their car almost tipped over. But in the end, no one was injured.

'I think I turned to Tim and asked whether we were going to die out here,' Kate says, laughing at her melodramatics.

They managed to limp into Mount Isa, but the van was written off. Kate says she feared they'd have to call it off and go home.

'I didn't want it to be over,' she says. 'It had become like a mission. I was very emotional about it and knew we had to go on.'

They searched the internet and finally found another caravan that could sleep their tribe and had it trucked to them.

Like us, they had come too far to turn back. Circumnavigation had become like summiting a mountain – the view from base camp would never be enough.

28

And then you see it, and you are instantly transfixed. There, in the middle of a memorable and imposing emptiness, stands an eminence of exceptional nobility and grandeur . . . Uluru is, no matter how you approach it, totally arresting. You cannot stop looking at it; you don't want to stop looking at it.
Bill Bryson, Down Under

Writers have compared Uluru to the Mona Lisa, or to the most beautiful sunset they have ever witnessed. It's been looked upon with 'breathless awe'. It is spoken about in religious terms, as if the soul of the continent resides deep within the belly of this giant sandstone beast.

'I was thunderstruck,' enthused Robyn Davidson in *Tracks*, as she came upon it on the back of a camel.

> *I could not believe that blue form was real. It floated and mesmerised and shimmered and looked too big. It was indescribable . . . The power of that rock had my heart racing. I had not expected anything quite so weirdly, primevally beautiful.*

The Rock has assumed a mystical quality. If you look at it long enough something spiritual will be revealed or, as one travel writer said, it is 'the kind of place where magic can happen'.

We've no real affection for any cathedral or mosque in this country. There's no Bodhi tree. Uluru is our holy place.

My parents, Helen and Dave, and Lisa's mum, Joan, flew into Alice Springs a few days ago. We travelled out to the Rock together and are now ready for our Uluru Experience.

'David, can't you get any closer, we're a bloody long way away,' complains Mum.

'No,' he replies. 'There's a sign saying we have to park in the designated carpark.'

'We'll hardly see anything from here. Did you bring the nibblies?'

'Yes.'

'What about the wine? Oh dear, it looks cold outside. Do you think Joe will be warm enough? I don't think he'll be warm enough.'

'Yes, he has a jumper.'

'Is it a warm one?'

My mother believes in freedom of thought — that is, every single thought she ever has must be set free. Bless her.

We drive along and there are dozens of four-wheel drives and hire cars and then finally, almost at the end of the designated parking area, we find a spot and squeeze in.

'David, you forgot the picnic blanket. What are we going to sit on?'

We all assure her that we can perch ourselves on the bonnet, without the blanket.

Dad gets the esky from the boot. He has red wine, white wine, gin and tonic and two types of beer. You just never know how long it will take the sun to set, these days. We all worry that he drinks too much but, after a week with Mum, I fear it may be too little.

He pours us all a drink in plastic cups. There are people, right next to us, who don't have a drink. My father is a generous man and I can see that he is not sure of the protocol — should he offer them a drink, and then, if he starts, where does it finish? The car after that? Does he have to do the whole row? He stands confused for a moment and then takes a large slurp of beer, which seems to calm him.

Joe, meanwhile, has taken off into the scrub at full belt, like a late-afternoon streaker at the Bathurst picnic races. He makes it a good 100 metres into the spinifex before I capture him. As soon as I let him go, he's off again.

Mum has struck up a conversation with some hippies next to us who are sitting on top of an old Range Rover with 'NO COAL' painted on the side. They are smoking joints but I hear them tut-tutting us for drinking alcohol and how 'disrespectful' that is to the traditional owners and the 'spirits of the land'.

On the other side there is a German man and his son. The son is about 13 or 14 and has just been stunned by puberty. His father has obviously started a new relationship with a much younger woman who is extremely attractive. The father and his girlfriend are kissing and canoodling while the pimply son is trying to act cool, although he's obviously embarrassed.

My mother is giving her Guyra spiel to the hippies, telling them what a wonderful place it is and how they should consider a visit.

'It used to be famous for potatoes,' she remarks, 'but now we also have the largest tomato greenhouse in the Southern Hemi —'

She is walking backwards while she speaks, and clips a treated pine car-stop, bolted to the ground. Her legs fly up in air and the red wine she has in her hand is sprayed all over the bonnet of the car, where the rest of us are sitting.

'My hip,' my mother cries. 'My hip.'

We all rush to her aid, except Dad, who gets a towel out to wipe the red wine from the bonnet, before it stains.

Mum is okay, but Joe takes advantage of the confusion and bolts into the scrub. As I take off after him, I look up to catch the last rays of light disappearing down the face of Uluru.

It is beautiful.

29

Ashley Severin is a short, stocky man who feels the need to fudge an inch or so with Cuban heels. The 55-year-old grew up on what was, at the time, about the most remote place on earth — a two-day, 400-kilometre trek down a rutted dirt track south-west of Alice Springs, which was then itself just an isolated outpost. In 1956, when Ashley was a young boy, he and his parents, Dawn and Peter, moved to Curtin Springs to take up a vast cattle lease in the desert. That first year they saw just six other human beings. Two were friends who came to check they were still alive, two were stock agents wondering when they'd be paid for their cattle and two were intrepid tourists who had come to see Ayers Rock.

Last year around 400,000 people visited Uluru and during the peak of the season 30 to 40 buses a day stopped at Curtin Springs. It offers basic accommodation and a roadhouse that serves bad coffee and overpriced beer. Its bowsers pump the dearest diesel we could find in all of Australia at $2.80 a litre — $196 to fill a 70-litre tank.

Curtin Springs is still a working cattle property which runs somewhere between 2000 and 3500 head, but it would have been lucky to survive without the tourists who come to see the Rock, just 85 kilometres away. The tourism side of the business employs 15 people at the peak of the season.

On our way from Uluru back to Alice Springs, the women and Joe go on ahead in one vehicle while Dad and I stop at Curtin Springs to chat to Ashley Severin. I have no idea what to expect. I know only that his family has been out in this country since the 1950s.

We are greeted in the bar by Ashley's partner, Lyndee, a hard-looking woman in her forties with curly hair. Lyndee arrived at Curtin Springs four years ago, as the bookkeeper, and now performs 'other household duties'. She leads us out to the house which looks onto a clipped green lawn with a swimming pool. Ashley is sitting at a cluttered kitchen table with a big buckle and pocket knife on his belt. His collection of beer cans and stubby holders sits on a picture rail which rings the inside of the room.

When Dad and I are seated, I ask if his father saw the tourism potential of Ayers Rock when he took up the lease. No, he says, no one knew anything about Ayers Rock and possibly only 50 people, white people that is, had ever been there before his father.

'No fucking blackfellas lived there either,' he fumes, just moments into our conversation. 'You can forget all the mythological bullshit that goes on now. You need water to survive in this country and there was no water at Ayers Rock. The old blackfellas will tell ya – not these fuckin' cancerous white mongrel do-gooders that are out there now and those useless half-caste yellafellas – the old blackfellas will say they only went there in a good season, which may have been every 10 years or so, in an exceptional season.'

Even if this were the case and they did just visit every few years, that does not mean Uluru and Kata Tjuta, the most arresting landforms for thousands of kilometres, were not culturally significant to the local tribes, I argue. No, I'm wrong, according to Ashley Severin. It has all been made up by 'cancerous white bastards' to keep themselves in a job.

In the 1960s his father was contracted to build the chain fence that now, controversially, takes visitors to the top of the rock. The local Aborigines ask people not to climb it but thousands do. Ashley Severin says they should because the view is spectacular and there were never any objections when his father first belted the steel poles into the sandstone.

'There wasn't a fuckin blackfella out here and when they did go out there they couldn't give a shit,' he claims. 'They used to look at the whitefella climbing and say "he rumma rumma" – mad in the head. Why would you want to climb up there? No kangaroo, no water, no wild tucker. The blackfella didn't climb something for nothing, he was normally chasing food. There were no fuckin' spirits.'

At this point there is a noise outside. Ashley rushes into a room next to where we are sitting and comes out carrying a shotgun. Dad and I become a little nervous but he bolts out into the yard. Boom! Boom!

He walks back into the room. 'Fuckin' hawks. Cunts are in-a-me chickens.'

The source of Ashley's anger appears to be the various run-ins he's had with government authorities and Aboriginal groups over the sale of alcohol.

Up until 1987, he and his father had flatly refused to serve 'grog to the blacks'. They just couldn't handle it, the Severins reckoned.

'They got equal rights in 1967, so we were only 20 years behind the eight ball,' Ashley explains with a laugh. 'No one worried about it and it was a good thing. Then, one day, the old man got a telegram from the Minister for Abo Affairs saying that if he didn't serve alcohol he'd be in court for racial discrimination.'

So they started serving alcohol to Aborigines. Just a few years later they were being accused by the 'cancerous white bastards' of selling too much grog to blacks and 'causing damage to their way of life'. For more than a decade they fought case after case to try to retain their liquor licence.

Finally a settlement was reached. They now have a licence which explicitly states they cannot serve any alcohol to Aborigines. 'Full fuckin' circle – right back to where we started.

'I keep referring to the cancerous white bastards 'cause the cancer lives on the host body until it kills it,' he adds. 'Now the whites who work for the blacks keep them down so they're always assured of a job. They come here, think they have done a good job, then piss off and we are left with the problem.'

Ashley says he was a big fan of Mal Brough, the former Minister for Aboriginal Affairs in the Howard Government, who pushed through the Northern Territory Intervention. He says they corresponded regularly and that Brough had sought his advice.

'He's got balls as big as Ayers Rock.'

But he fears the good work will all be undone by the current Labor government.

According to Ashley Severin, blackfellas should be made to work or left to starve, although he hasn't employed an Aborigine since 1974.

'And I won't be employing another one while my arse still has a hole in it and points to the ground.'

I ask to go to the toilet and am pointed to a room just off the living area. There's no door, just a sheet hanging from two nails. I go about my business quietly and can clearly hear the conversation just on the other side of the sheet.

Lyndee is explaining to Dad that she gives all new staff a little talking to before they start.

'In the induction I say that history has many interpretations, but here you are going to be living with one interpretation,' Lyndee says. 'This is not the most politically correct environment you'll ever work in, but you don't have to be working here long to understand why.'

I flush, wash my hands and soon after we are back on the road to Alice Springs.

30

There are a series of signs leading up to the campground at Banka Banka Station, a vast cattle spread on the Stuart Highway, 100 kilometres north of Tennant Creek. The country here is brown, flat and dry and the signs are placed kilometres apart, allowing time for contemplation. The first reads 'Cool Drinks', the next 'Hot Showers'. It is the third, though, that gets me: 'Green Grass', it promises.

After weeks in a land of a thousand shades of brown, a patch of irrigated lawn is too delicious a temptation to pass up. We stay overnight and Joe frolics in the greenery, without any shoes. Our parents have flown back 'Down South', as the rest of Australia is called in the Territory, and we are on our own on the road. We push north early the next morning and the brown continues.

Somewhere north of Elliott, where Jana found love, we come up behind a little van, chugging along at 80 kilometres an hour and a sign that informs us it's 'Powered by Vegetable Oil'. I can see Ben Spiers inside, with a girl. I honk the horn and wave and initially Ben thinks I am just another impatient motorist, beeping him for driving too slowly. He turns around to deliver the bird, then smiles.

He pulls over to the side of the road and we are introduced to his companion, a young German woman called Kathryn whom

Ben tells us he met in Cairns. He struck oil too, in Mount Isa. The shop owner charged him 25 cents a litre and for $40 he got enough oil to get him to Broome.

We arrange to meet in Mataranka.

Lisa and I have a bet in the car. I am sure he's shagging this girl, Lisa is certain he's not. She wins, we discover later. Ben always likes to travel with companions, to share any costs and to reduce waste. He left a note at a backpacker hostel asking if anyone wanted a lift to Broome. Kathryn answered. It turns out she's a dour German, and not much fun as a travelling companion, but Ben is too nice a guy to turf her out.

Just before Mataranka something amazing happens – the neverending desert finally ends. The grasses become tall, palm trees appear and the air moistens. Suddenly we are in the tropics of northern Australia.

That afternoon we wash the dust from our system in the Mataranka Hot Springs. Joe gurgles happily. The north does swimming holes like nowhere else and Mataranka is up there with the best. From the campground you wander down through a grove of lush palm trees which shades the pool. The water bubbles up from the earth at a constant 31 degrees into a deep, clear swimming hole.

We spend the night at Mataranka and then two more at the magnificent Katherine Gorge, walking and swimming, before setting off for the Kimberley.

WESTERN AUSTRALIA

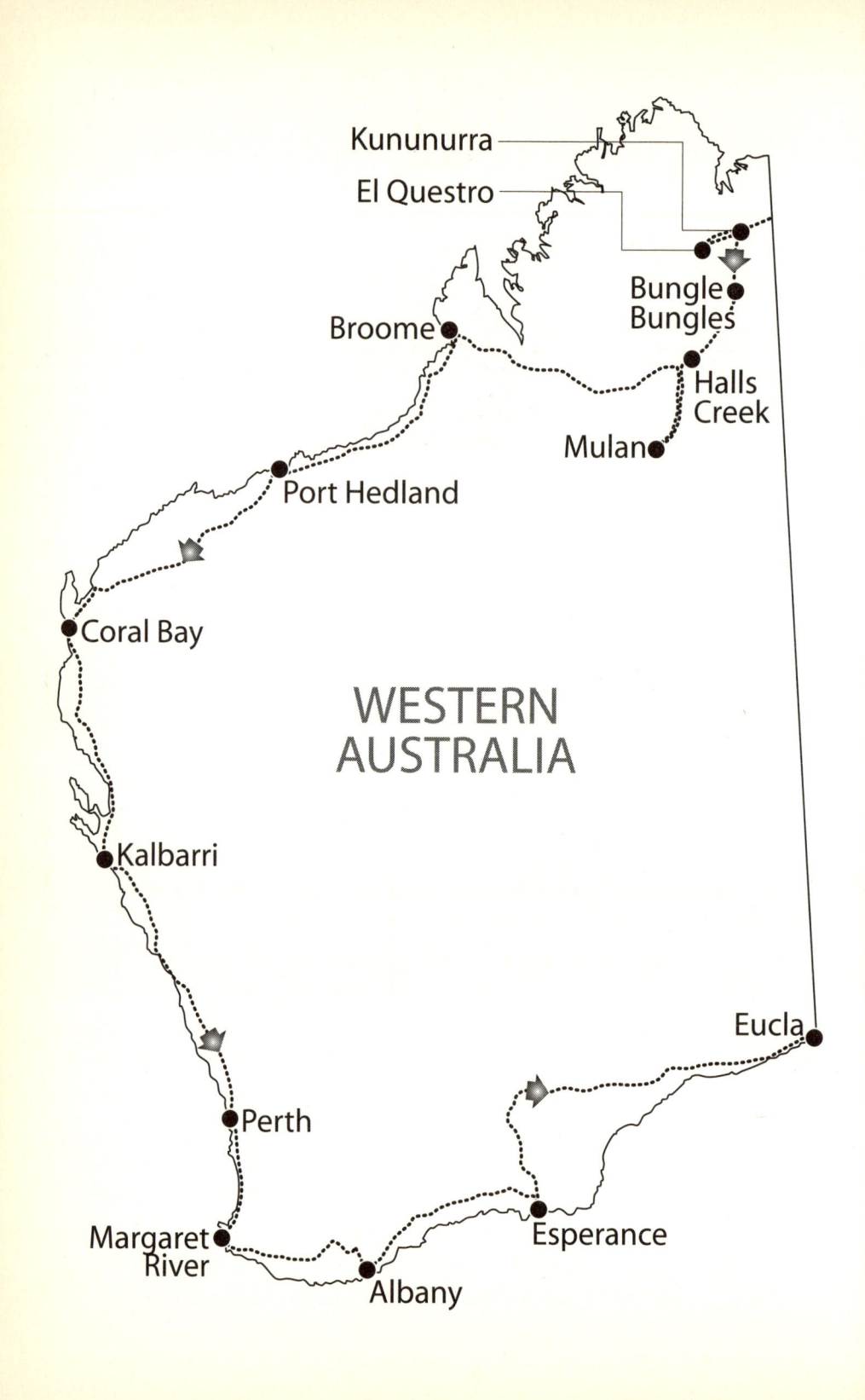

- Kununurra
- El Questro
- Bungle Bungles
- Broome
- Halls Creek
- Mulan
- Port Hedland
- Coral Bay
- Kalbarri
- Eucla
- Perth
- Margaret River
- Albany
- Esperance

31

Woolworths and Coles have buggered hundreds of Australian rural towns. We have driven through town after town in state after state torn asunder by the arrival of the new shopping complex. Like cane toads, they have consumed everything in their path and appear to have no natural predators.

The supermarket shonks have convinced local councillors, somehow, that it is a great idea to build a new shopping mall away from the town centre. It is a 'divide and rule' strategy that has been devastatingly effective. The old main street, with buildings of character and charm, withers and dies along with the town's identity and sense of community.

It has happened in Kununurra. On one side of the CBD there's an expensive Coles supermarket surrounded by a small, sad shopping mall. On the other side there is an independent supermarket called Tuckerbox. A few shops struggle to survive in what was once the old high street but there is no town centre, no focus. The village green is effectively the Coles carpark.

Despite this, Kununurra somehow gets away with it. Like Sydney, it's been badly frocked, but that doesn't hide the pretty girl underneath. Natural beauty compensates for many sins.

The town sits in a valley in the far north of Western Australia, 30 kilometres from the Territory border and 100 kilometres south of Joseph Bonaparte Gulf. The massive dams of the Ord River supply year-round water to irrigated crops of melons and mangoes and even sandalwood trees. The valleys are fertile and lush and the surrounding hills are red and dry. It is a base for tourists to explore the fascinating Bungle Bungles and the gorges off the Gibb River Road.

We are staying in a caravan park shaded by enormous old mango trees that dangle with plump green fruit. A national park begins where the lawns of the caravan park end. The Kimberley is on full display, just down past the amenities block. The soils and the rocks are a deep, rusty red and the hill we can see from the comfort of our camp chairs looks as though it's been formed by man, neatly stacked at some point in the ancient past and then left to slowly decay.

It is the dry season and yet there is lusciousness here — the greens of the trees and the shrubs are as vivid as the reds. Even the spinifex seems to glow. But when you get up close there is not much ground cover and what's there is spindly and unpalatable.

The Kimberley is where the tropics collide with the desert. The country blooms for a few months each year with the arrival of the monsoons and then, for the rest of the year, the desert claws its way back.

We settle in and find the one joint in town that serves decent coffee, the Boab Bookshop Café. The owner is an odd man, creepy in an evangelical kind of way. He looms around the store getting in the way of his waitresses, pretty Danish and German travellers. There are various copies of Christian newspapers strewn about, but not *The Australian* or *The West Australian* or even the local rag.

I ask if he has Paul Toohey's *The Killer Within*, a book about Bradley John Murdoch who murdered British backpacker Peter Falconio and tried to abduct his girlfriend, Joanne Lees. Much of it is set in the Kimberley.

'No, I don't carry anything about crime or murder,' says the bookseller.

'What, no Shakespeare?' I say.

He looks at me blankly.

I wonder too if the Bible would pass this odd censorship clause.

We plan to base ourselves in Kununurra for a few weeks to explore the East Kimberley and to visit El Questro, the giant wilderness park along the Gibb River Road.

But first we want to meet the daughter of showman, Gary Miller, who is here in Kununurra.

Gary's daughter, Brenda Garstone, lives not far from where we are staying in a quiet suburban street in a middle-class part of town. We first contacted her a few days ago and, while nervous, Brenda has agreed to speak to us.

We knock on the door and her husband, Chris, invites us in. He's a solid, handsome man from Broome, a blend of Aborigine, Malay, Filipino, Indonesian, Japanese and British. His accent is broad Aussie with a blackfella drawl. He works for a local Aboriginal organisation coordinating various community projects funded by mining royalties.

Brenda is sitting at the kitchen table, an attractive 40-year-old woman with softened Aboriginal features and a serious frown. Her maternal grandmother was a full-blooded Aborigine, while her grandfather was a white man, a contract fencer. She grew up in Halls Creek, now a dysfunctional town on the edge of the Tanami Desert, halfway between Kununurra and Broome. She holds a senior position with the Department of Child Protection, working with troubled Aboriginal families.

Brenda and Chris's children carry in their DNA a map of human history in the Kimberley. The three kids – Jodene, 11, Tex, 10 and Shakana, six – seem to have plucked the best features on offer from their ancestors and are lithe, brown and beautiful. All three have a future as newsreaders on SBS television. Brenda has another child from a previous relationship, Rhys, who is 15. He is away at school in Perth.

The kids play with Joe and he becomes instantly obsessed with Shakana. For weeks after this first meeting he will lie in his cot softly speaking her name. 'Kana. Kana. Kana.' She is his first true love.

We make small talk while Chris puts on a pot of tea. The nearby Argyle Diamond Mine is at full lick producing its unique pink stones and the town is in the midst of a real estate boom. Prices here are ridiculous they say, on a par with Sydney. They recently bought this house, put in a new kitchen and had it tiled throughout, to make it cooler. It's a big, open-plan place with a swimming pool. Brenda worries about how they will make the repayments. Chris says it'll be right.

When the tea is ready we settle down around the table to listen to Brenda's incredible story. It is like a grand Indian saga set over several generations with a plot straight from a Rohinton Mistry novel.

Baz Luhrmann chose the wrong Kimberley epic.

Brenda's grandmother, Daisy, was an Aboriginal woman born beneath the desert stars and raised in the old ways of the bush. She is said to have been incredibly beautiful. Brenda's grandfather was a digger called Bill Grant who returned from the battlefields of the First World War to set up a fencing business in the Kimberley, which is where he met Daisy.

It was an era when white men had their way with black women and then moved on. But Bill was different and when Daisy became pregnant with his child he did an unusual thing – the right thing – and married her. They went on to have four children together and the family followed Bill around as he worked on remote cattle stations, building fences.

Not long after the birth of their fourth child, Daisy became ill with tuberculosis, Brenda tells us as we sip tea – she's a good storyteller and her husband, Chris, listens intently, chipping in if she misses a vital detail because he knows this story almost as if it were his own.

Daisy, Brenda continues, and her new baby were sent off to the hospital at Wyndham, a port town north of Kununurra. Daisy died not long after being admitted. Her baby was immediately taken by welfare officers and put into a mission for half-castes. Bill, heartbroken by the death of his wife and the removal of his newborn baby, refused to give up his other children, including Brenda's mum, Angelina, who was only two at the time. He was a good and caring man and continued to run his fencing business while raising his young black family.

A few years later tragedy struck again. Bill and his kids were hitching a lift on the back of a truck near the Bungle Bungles. It was Christmas Eve and they were coming into town to go to church. The truck rolled. The kids survived unscathed but the vehicle crushed one of Bill's legs. He was flown to Darwin and after weeks in hospital one of his legs was amputated. The authorities stepped in before he returned and sent his children to the Anglican mission at Forest River, north of Wyndham. There wasn't much the one-legged fencer could do to stop them this time.

Angelina was five and would not see her father again until she was 12, when she came home for Christmas holidays at the end of primary school. She was then sent to another mission school at Derby for three years of high school.

After her schooling she returned to live with her father in Halls Creek. She worked as a shop assistant and in the hospital.

Then, when she was about 17 or 18, the show came to town and she got temporary work with a family which ran merry-go-rounds, laughing clowns and games of chance. Angelina was a good worker with an education and they offered her a full-time job. She discussed it with her father who gave his approval. The show took her all the way to the east coast, which is where she met a kid called Gary Miller who was making a name for himself as a tent fighter and professional boxer.

Gary and Angelina had a fling as the circuit weaved its way up the east coast from northern NSW into Queensland. At Longreach, she got a telegram to say her father was ill with cancer, so she set off for home. In those days it was an epic journey by train and bus, thousands of kilometres across the top of the continent. At some point during that trip home she realised she was pregnant.

Angelina made it back to Halls Creek and decided not to return to Gary. She got on with her life and he got on with his.

It was 1968 when Brenda was born. Not long afterwards Angelina married a local Aboriginal stockman called Stan Bedford. They went on to have six children. They have adopted and raised four other children and fostered seven or eight others. They are close. Brenda says she always considered Stan to be her father, and still does, but she also knew that Gary, her biological father, was out there somewhere.

She had made a few half-hearted attempts to find him over the years and then one day she and Chris were watching a documentary about tent boxing. One of the men interviewed was Allan Moore, a member of the family that Gary used to fight for. Chris contacted him and explained the situation and, after the showman's suspicions were overcome, numbers were exchanged.

Just a few weeks ago Brenda, Chris and the kids drove from Kununurra to Katherine in the Territory to meet him. Brenda is still emotional about the meeting. Not all her questions have yet been answered, but it has flung open doors that had been tiny peepholes all her life.

At the time, Rhys was home from school. He was the only child she had told about Gary. She didn't want to confuse the younger ones if it all went wrong. So Rhys and Brenda met him at a café, as arranged. They hugged and kissed and Brenda looked at Gary and at Rhys and could see the grandfather in the grandson.

The younger kids came in later and Gary hugged and kissed them too.

'That's your grandfather,' Brenda said. She had to explain that beside their Poppa in Halls Creek and another in Broome, they now had a third whose name is Gary who works with the show.

'It was lovely in the end. We bought Tex a skateboard and Gary insisted on paying for it. We drove down to the river and Chris took the kids for a walk. Gary asked what type of childhood I'd had. A good one, I told him, a stable one. 'Mum was never bitter, she never blamed you, there's no bitterness at all.'

Gary asked, nervously: 'You and I, we're okay?'

'Yes,' Brenda replied. 'We're okay.'

The next day they went to the show. Gary and Nita ensured they never paid for a thing and the kids ate Dagwood Dogs and fairy floss and rode the dodgems and the dippers until they were almost sick.

Meeting Gary, Brenda says, has fitted a missing piece. It has opened up other wounds, though, and she is preparing to tell her adoptive father in Halls Creek about the meeting. She hopes he will understand.

Lisa asks what she would like to get out of the relationship with Gary.

'I'd like to get to know him,' she replies. 'But slowly, slowly. I'm not pushing anything.'

The talk moves back to her childhood in Halls Creek. Angelina brought her children up strictly, Brenda says, and the Anglican Church played a big part in their lives.

'The church was the hub of the community in Halls Creek,' Brenda explains. 'You were either in the church or you were on the grog.'

Angelina's husband, Stan, drank, but only a few beers after work and he always had a job, first as a stockman and then checking bores for the local water authority. Things weren't as they are now in Halls Creek – it was then a functioning community. 'The big difference between then and now is that in the old days most people went to church and a few people drank. Now most people drink and only a few go to church.'

Brenda was a good student and spent a few years of her secondary education at school in Perth, but dropped out in Year 11. She trained as a nurse's assistant and worked in various medical jobs around the Kimberley and then she fell in love with a young southerner who had come to Halls Creek to become a mechanic.

They met in 1992, Brenda fell pregnant and they split in 1993 when her son, Rhys, was just three months old.

Brenda was 25, a single mother and stuck in Halls Creek.

'It wasn't the life I wanted,' Brenda recalls. 'I remember thinking, no man is going to treat me like shit again and dictate the course of my life. In a way, him leaving me with Rhys gave me strength.'

And so, with her 10-month-old baby boy on her hip, she moved to Perth and enrolled at the University of Western Australia.

'I set myself a goal of having a degree by the age of 30,' she says. She'd achieved her dream by the age of 28, majoring in anthropology and history. In just three generations her family had gone from hunter gatherers to arts bachelors. She is one of only a few Aboriginal people from Halls Creek to get a university degree.

Brenda met Chris in her last year of university in Perth at a theatre show called Corrugation Road. He worked on a gas rig off Karratha, a fortnight on, a fortnight off, and would fly into Perth for his holidays.

'He was goin' with one of the actresses,' says Brenda. 'I thought, that'll never last.' A few months later she met up with him again and the actress was gone. They went on a few dates. He was keen and wooed her with tickets to Tina Turner. Seems Brenda was better than all the rest.

We chat away for hours, while the kids play and Chris and Brenda invite us to come with them tomorrow for a barbecue on the Ord River.

'That would be great,' says Lisa. 'What do you want us to bring?'

'Have you ever tried kangaroo tail cooked in coals, the blackfella way?' asks Chris.

'No, but we'd love to.'

'That Volvo ever been spotlightin' before?'

'No, but I'm sure it's up to it,' I say.

It's getting onto dusk and Chris hooks a couple of leads to the battery of the car and loads a rifle and a shotgun into the back along with a set of skinning knives, rolled up in oiled cloth. I drop

Lisa and Joe back at the caravan park and then return to pick up Chris. Jodene and Tex climb into the back.

'Don't come home with no wallaby either, like last time,' Brenda insists. 'I want a good kangaroo.'

'Yes dear,' says Chris.

We head off into the wilderness, out of town and down a dirt road which takes us over the border into the Northern Territory. Once we are out of town, Chris gets the guns from the back of the vehicle and leans them next to where he is sitting, pointing into the ground. He pokes the spotlight up through the sunroof of the Volvo.

Chris and I chat about the intervention in the Northern Territory and the problems with grog in communities in Western Australia. He says he took up drinking at 15 and gave it away at 19. He hasn't touched a drop since.

'It makes you cry to see some of these places and what grog has done to them,' he says.

He supports any measures that will reduce the amount of alcohol in Aboriginal communities. He says some families are so broken that children should be taken away for a bit and put into nearby boarding schools, until various problems with their parents are worked through. It is a drastic problem that needs drastic solutions.

'It's reached a crisis point up here, Greg. It really has.'

Chris loves the bush. He and Brenda moved back from Perth so that he could teach the kids how to hunt and take them out bush of a weekend. They want their kids to feel connected to the country, to their Aboriginal heritage and to their relatives in Halls Creek and Kununurra.

But, he says, it is a difficult balance to live in two worlds: a white world that offers a good education and employment opportunities and a black world that offers something equally as rich.

'Do you think it will work? Will the kids feel a connection to the land and will they feel accepted by their cousins?'

'That's a good question. I dunno. Probably not, but we gotta give it a try.'

Just then Tex shouts from the back seat, 'Turkey. Turkey. Turkey'.

Chris spins the spotlight around and we see a huge bustard lumbering out of a gum tree and into flight. He can't get a shot in.

'Bugger. Them bush turkeys are my favourite, them and magpie geese. Beautiful eatin'.'

The kids agree.

We drive for an hour or two without seeing any kangaroos and finally we come across a mob of wallabies.

'Brenda will just have to be satisfied with wallaby,' he says as he reaches for the rifle.

I hold the spotlight and Chris leans out the window. Boom. The wallaby falls to the ground, kicking. Chris fires off another shot at a second wallaby but misses.

The kids then scramble out of the car with a torch. It takes us a while to find the dead wallaby. When we do, Chris sets about removing its tail. I tell him that I will cook the leg. There's a recipe in Stephanie Alexander's *The Cooks Companion* for wallaby and I want to give it a try.

The two kids look on as Chris lops off one of the legs, skins it and then breaks it on the tow bar so it can fit into a plastic bag.

'Cut his balls off, Dad,' says Jodene, an 11-year-old who could be Australia's next supermodel. 'Cut his balls off.'

'Yuck, you are disgusting,' says her little brother, Tex.

'All male mammals have balls,' she replies. 'Even you.'

I rise early in a panic. Stephanie has several recipes for wallaby and kangaroo, but nothing that can really be cooked on a barbecue by a riverbank. I search the internet for wallaby and roo recipes, but come up with nothing satisfactory. Finally I settle on a heavily bastardised version of Stephanie's 'twice cooked wallaby shank with young ginger'. In fact I just use the marinade, or what I can get of the marinade; Tasmanian mountain pepper berries and rice wine are in short supply in Kununurra. I slice the wallaby leg into thin strips and toss it in with the marinade of ginger, pepper, garlic, shallots, soy sauce, Chinese five spice, Hoisin sauce, red wine and lemon – and hope for the best.

After Chris and Brenda and the kids have been to church we head out of town to a beautiful spot on the Ord River called Ivanhoe Crossing where there's a cement road across the river. The river is fast flowing and there are some small rapids above the crossing.

Chris lights a fire and digs a hole next to it to use as a bush oven. He looks like a competent bushman but I can see some grass near the fire which looks a bit dangerous. I don't say anything. I figure he must know what he's doing. A few minutes later we are both desperately trying to stop a grass fire, first by stomping it with our boots, then with the shovel. Finally Chris grabs a blanket from the car and attacks the flames. Lisa and Brenda look on, laughing.

With the fire under control, he singes all the hairs from the wallaby tail and then wraps it in foil. He places the tail in the hole a metre deep, and then packs hot coals around it. Finally, he covers the coals with sand so no smoke escapes.

'There, that should take an hour,' he says.

We look at each other, relieved, knowing how close we have just come to starting a bushfire.

We sit in camp chairs and chat while the kids play by the river.

There is a seriousness about Brenda that I remember seeing in many of my Pakistani friends. Her Aboriginality is something she is very proud of, but it comes with a great and neverending sense of responsibility. She has a good life, but the lives of so many of her people, *her relatives*, are so miserable that she cannot rest. She is serious because the situation is so serious. I tell Brenda that we, as whites, feel sorry when we see homeless or poor white people, but we don't necessarily feel an obligation towards them.

'We do,' she says. 'Or, I do. I think that when you are an educated black person you feel a great sense of duty to do something for Aboriginal people. Sometimes though I would just like to run away from it all with Chris and my family and go and work in a café and have an easy life.'

'That's never going to happen is it?' I say.

'No.'

She and Chris are ambitious, though, to get ahead. They have ordinary, middle-class goals to be financially comfortable and to give their children a good education. When they left Perth they kept their house there, as an investment property, and have since bought their place here in Kununurra.

'The thing is, the more ambitious you are, the further it takes you away from your Aboriginal culture,' Brenda says.

They have relatives come to stay almost every week and there is an expectation that she and Chris will pay for everything. It's hard sometimes to fulfil the obligations to the bank and the obligations to family.

Brenda says it saddens her now to go back to Halls Creek, a predominantly Aboriginal town of about 1200 people with 22 police. The place is drowning in alcohol.

Just recently a local doctor, David Shepherd, went public to say that 80 to 90 per cent of mothers who give birth in Halls Creek got drunk regularly during their pregnancies. 'Therefore 80 to 90 per cent of those kids are going to be affected,' Dr Shepherd told the ABC. 'They are all drinking in an unhealthy manner and how badly those children are affected is just a matter of degrees. There are certainly some that are very, very badly affected, who can't grow, don't speak, are difficult to toilet train and will never learn to read or write. I think those are the ones that we would put into that hard diagnosis of Foetal Alcohol Syndrome disorder.'

'It was different when I was growing up,' Brenda says. 'The mothers didn't drink. The fathers did, but not all the time. They all had jobs. Now, everyone drinks.' And if people want to get off the grog the only real option for them is to seek the support of a church group, she says.

Brenda says she has often pondered why she was able to break out of Halls Creek and not be pulled into the despair that took so many of her friends and relatives. She had some good role models, she says, kids who had left Halls Creek to go to school in Perth.

'They would go on a bit, and reckon they were top dog, but when they'd come back from Perth they'd changed a bit. They had ambitions to go on and do things and I looked up to those kids. I wanted to get out and explore the world.

'But it all goes back to Mum, I suppose,' she says, reclining in her chair by the river. 'She gave our lives structure. We were safe. We were made to go to school. There was no booze in the house and we went to church each week and out bush, camping. Unless Aboriginal families can get that structure back, there's not much hope for the kids.'

Chris says his wallaby tail is almost done, so I put a hotplate over the fire and cook Stephanie's 'bastardised twice cooked wallaby shank with young ginger', cooked only once. It frizzles away on the fire and after five minutes it is done. I hand it around. Everyone is very polite and says it tastes good. I try it. It's okay.

Chris then removes his wallaby tail from the coals and passes it around. It is delicious. The meat is soft and tasty and falls away from the bone.

Joe chews the end of the tail and won't let it go. For the rest of the afternoon he clutches it like a lollypop. He occasionally takes a bite. He will only share it with his true love, Shakana, who spends the afternoon trying to escape our little boy and his piece of slobbered wallaby tail.

After lunch we all go down to the river for a swim.

'Are there crocodiles?' I ask, half joking.

'Yes,' Brenda admits. 'But they don't like the rapids.'

There is a gap of about 20 metres between the fast flowing water and the not so fast flowing water. I like a gap of several hundred kilometres between me and any crocodiles.

'Don't worry,' reassures Brenda. 'People have been swimming here for years and nobody has ever been taken.'

I make sure there are several children in the water before jumping in and then jumping straight out again.

We towel off and drive back into town. It's been a special day.

★

About a week later we are returning from a disastrous trip to El Questro, a vast wilderness park off the Gibb River Road in the East Kimberley.

The Volvo is on the back of a truck and we are sitting in the front seat with Neville, the driver. It has been a traumatic two days since I drove it into a creek and ruined the motor. Joe is asleep, dribbling on Lisa's shoulder.

We had eventually been rescued by a retiree in a Landcruiser who pulled us from the creek and towed us to nearby El Questro station. We had spent last night in a tent. Neville had arrived this morning with his truck and is taking us back to Kununurra.

Neville tells us that he and his wife have been on the road for four years. He moves from fishing spot to fishing spot and picks up odd jobs where he can. The fishing around Kununurra, he says, is about as good as it gets.

As we approach town, we drive past the turnoff to Ivanhoe Crossing, where just last week we were swimming with Brenda and Chris and the kids. Neville points to the river and tells us it's a great spot to fish.

'I had me tinnie in there a couple of weeks ago and saw a bloody enormous crocodile – must have been four metres long,' he explains.

'Where?' I ask.

'Not far from the crossing, half a mile or so.'

'So you wouldn't swim there at the crossing?'

'Wouldn't let me dog swim there.'

We trundle back into Kununurra.

32

The very generous and understanding people at Volvo are sending up a new car *from Adelaide* – I still can't quite believe it. It will take a couple of weeks.

In the meantime we have to get to Mulan, a remote Aboriginal settlement in the Tanami Desert. It is the only part of the trip we planned in advance because we knew we could not turn up without an invitation. A white woman called Kim Mahood is to introduce us to Aboriginal people in this remote community and we need to arrive in Mulan while she is still there. Kim is an artist and writer based in Braidwood near Canberra who spends three months a year up here. She grew up on a remote Northern Territory cattle spread called Mongrel Downs. Some of the men from Mulan used to work for her father as stockmen. She left, after boarding school, to pursue life as an artist, over east. A decade or so ago she was drawn back to the land of her youth. She has written a book about it, *Craft for a Dry Lake*, and also contributes to publications like the *Griffith Review*.

We have been warned the road, the Tanami Track, is extremely rough, so we decide to leave the caravan in Kununurra and hire a four-wheel drive with camping equipment. We get the last one, it seems, in the East Kimberley – a 10-year-old Toyota. For the price, we could have almost hired a helicopter and flown out. But

Mulan is our Mecca — we must make the pilgrimage, no matter what the cost.

We set off early and four hours' drive south of Kununurra stop at Brenda's home town of Halls Creek. The main street is ordinary enough with a butcher, a couple of little supermarkets, a service station, a roadhouse and a hopeful tourist information centre. The town also has a sparkling new hospital.

Around the streets there are a few people, sitting in the shade or walking around. Then we come across a crowd of two dozen or more. They are milling outside the bottle shop, waiting for the doors to open. There are five full-time doctors working in the town and later tonight they'll be flat out patching up this crowd. Like Tennant Creek and Alice Springs, Halls Creek is an exceedingly violent place. If you are black, there's a fair chance you will be stabbed, bashed or raped.

The town also has a brand new swimming pool and I stop, hoping to take Joe for a dip, to break up the day. It is a magnificent pool, the sort of complex you would expect in an inland city of 20,000 or 30,000 people, not in an outpost of 1200. It has manicured lawns, shade sails, diving boards, children's play equipment and an enclosed basketball court.

The Halls Creek Aquatic and Recreation Centre cost almost seven million dollars to build and was opened two years ago by the then Premier of WA, Alan Carpenter, who said it would, 'have a very significant impact on the quality of life for people in the Halls Creek region. Apart from giving kids a lot of physical activity and fun, it is well known that swimming in a well-managed aquatic centre helps to prevent eye, ear and skin disorders. It will also play an important role in the education of young people in the area with the "no school, no pool" policy being adopted.'

But, today — a sunny Saturday — there's no one in the pool. There'll be no impact on anybody's quality of life or health because the centre is closed.

I knock on a thick glass screen in the pool's ticket office to get the attention of a pimply white kid to find out why it is closed. He drags himself away from a computer game.

'Pool's closed,' he says. 'Manager's away.'

The pool is regularly closed, I later learn. The law in WA requires two qualified lifeguards to be on duty and while the manager is qualified he always struggles to get a second trained lifeguard. He has tried to train the partners of police, teachers and other government workers but their turnover is high and many of the public servants are single. He's tried training local Aboriginal people too, but he says they are unreliable.

And so on a lovely sunny day, this seven million dollar pool with its inviting and healing blue waters remains shut – a good intention that doesn't quite work. It seems the only entertainment the snotty-nosed kids of Halls Creek will get today is watching adults get pissed after the bottle shop opens.

After a sandwich we head out of town, turn off the bitumen of the Savannah Way and onto the dirt of the Tanami Track. We leave the red hills of the Kimberley and enter the desert proper. The further south we drive the more desolate it becomes – flat and arid. The monotony is broken by abandoned and burnt out cars left by the side of the road. We pass more dead cars than live ones.

Late in the afternoon we turn off the Tanami Track and find Balgo, a dire Aboriginal settlement of about 500 people. An emaciated camel is walking down the street through rubbish and wrecked cars and dilapidated houses. We could be in Somalia.

The road from Balgo to Mulan runs directly west and I drive the 44 kilometres with my head out the window because the sun is blinding through the windscreen. Joe is getting distressed, having been in the car for far too long, and it makes both of us tense.

Finally, just on dark, we arrive in Mulan. It is bitterly cold and a harsh wind is blowing.

The settlement has a population of about 160 Aborigines and 14 white people. It consists of a high water tank, a school, a store, a dirt Aussie rules pitch and 30 or 40 houses arranged in no particular order. Mangy-looking dogs roam the streets and every house has one or two vehicles parked out the front, up on chocks, with the wheels and various other parts removed. There are few trees and no grass.

We find where Kim is staying, in a compound with a wire fence around it and a few demountable miners' quarters surrounded by barbed wire.

We make our way inside. Within a few minutes Kim Mahood makes it pretty clear she would rather we hadn't come.

33

Kim Mahood is a small, slim woman in her mid fifties with short black hair. She often covers her head with a scarf and wears red lipstick with matching red spectacles. She is intense and self-absorbed. She rolls her own cigarettes, skilfully, with just a few strands of tobacco. She looks a bit like the fashion designer, Jenny Kee, but with European features. Mahood's surname is of Irish origin, not Afghan or Arabic as it may suggest.

Not long after we walk into her quarters she tells us how busy she is, that this is not a good time for her. We are a bit taken aback, after eight hours in the car and months of corresponding. But it's dark and cold and too late to set up our tent at the campground, which is 10 kilometres away. I ask if we can stay in one of two spare rooms overnight and she agrees but wants us out early because a friend is coming to stay the next day. Mulan is a closed community, so we ask about permits. She says she will fix it up tomorrow.

We thank her for the room and I offer to cook dinner, which she accepts. We bought some good steak in Kununurra and fresh salad, knowing how hard it would be to get out here. We hand over bottles of wine, gin, dips and other supplies that she had requested.

We put Joe to bed in his portable cot and over dinner Kim lectures while we listen. She's not the type to ask questions of us and doesn't appear to do two-way conversations. She tells us about some of the work she has been doing which pays for her trips. The Australian Governance Story was designed to explain to Aboriginal communities how government works in Australia. She shows us a big laminated book she has produced using many traditional symbols and motifs. Canberra is represented by lots of dollar signs.

Kim has also worked on cultural mapping projects to record the stories and knowledge people still hold about their country. She's helped map sites that were traditionally important, such as the location of soakwaters, dreaming tracks and campsites as well as the precise areas to which people's ancestors held entitlement. The stories have been recorded on video and the sites painted on a giant canvas so they won't be lost as the people move further away from their old ways.

She has been coming to Mulan regularly since the late 1990s and over the years has built some good, solid friendships. She explains that those friendships are complex and fragile and that in any dispute, even if she were clearly in the right, the people of the community would stick together rather than take her side. 'Gardiya' is the local word for white person and no matter how close she gets to the locals she will always be a gardiya, she says.

We learn that the source of some of Kim's angst tonight is due to the arrival of new community administrators, a husband and wife team. There are 14 gardiya in the community and the new administrators have been putting noses out of joint since they arrived, just six weeks ago. While Kim is not funded by them, she says they can make it hard for people like her to operate out here. She fears that our presence could cause her trouble.

'I have written about this place over the years but I've always been able to fly under the radar,' she tells us.

That night we also meet another gardiya, Wade Freeman, a man with long wavy hair tied in a ponytail and a squeaky voice. He is the Paruku Indigenous Protected Area ranger. A vast area of 430,000 hectares around Mulan has been handed back to the traditional Walmajarri owners and Wade is like a park ranger for those lands.

We come to learn that he also sees himself as the protector of Aboriginal people from evil outside influences, like us.

A big delegation of local Aborigines and various gardiya is about to set off on a trek down the Canning Stock Route to look at its tourist potential and to identify sites that need to be protected. Wade is organising all the food, the camping equipment, the cars, the fuel – everything, basically. These are all gardiya jobs. The locals just have to turn up, maybe.

It's the way things work in Mulan.

In the morning, Lisa and I pack up our things early and load them back into the four-wheel drive. Kim says she will show us over to the camp area later and in the meantime we go for a walk. It is cold and a hard wind is blowing tumbleweeds in from the vast desert plains, adding to the bleakness. We skirt around the settlement, a little unsure of where we can and can't go and what we can and can't do.

The houses are generally in good condition, with galvanised tin walls and roofs, and the newer ones particularly seem to be well designed for the stifling summer heat. The dominant features, however, are the rubbish and the cars. Outside each house there are two or three; some have doors removed, or seats, or whole engines, while almost all have been liberated of their tyres. Mulan will never get a gig as a Tidy Town.

We follow a sign which points out of town to the rubbish dump and decide to follow the road. As we stroll along, with Joe in his beanie pointing out the crows, a ute stops beside us – inside is another gardiya, a man in his late forties with a long goatee. 'Jump in,' he says, 'I'll show you around.'

The guy's name is Peter Lockyer and he's an architect and builder from Victoria who comes to Mulan for three months each year to work on building projects. Everyone calls him Lockie or Lockyer.

Lockie is in a state. The new administrators are making life difficult for him. We hear all about it as he takes us on a tour of

Mulan. He has independent funding to build a childcare centre but the administrators apparently don't like the idea and don't want it built. He is fuming.

We drive past the school which is in good condition. There's a principal and three teachers for 30-odd students. There's a medical clinic with two nurses and one shop. We also pass something that looks like a big shipping container – it contains fuel bowsers. The bowsers gained national media attention in 2004 when the Howard Government agreed to provide them under a program called a Shared Responsibility Agreement. The people of Mulan had to commit to washing their children's faces twice a day and other hygiene measures to combat trachoma and various other health problems. There are still a lot of dirty faces but the bowsers remain.

We stop at the new community centre which Lockie built with some trainee Aboriginal workers. He organised the funding for the project himself – more than $400,000 – through Lottery West, the WA lotteries office, and is proud of what he's achieved.

He shows us through. There's an indoor basketball court, meeting rooms and a space for a games room. It is not being used much yet, he says, and needs someone to run it.

We tell him we're journalists, here to try to learn something about remote Aboriginal Australia. We tell him we're going to set up a tent out at the campground.

'It's too cold,' he says. 'You'll get blown away. I have a spare room at my place. You are welcome to stay.'

It is a generous offer and with the wind howling in from the desert one that we are keen to take up.

We return to Kim's and tell her of Lockie's offer. She seems pleased.

A group of archaeologists is conducting a dig just a few kilometres out of Mulan and she invites us to have a look. Lisa stays with Joe for his morning sleep and I go with Kim.

Along the way we stop to pick up some elderly Aboriginal women dressed in frocks and beanies and with legs so thin I am amazed they don't snap.

Out the front of one of the houses two men are fighting. Both are drunk and the fight is taking place in slow motion. It is almost cartoonish. A dozen or so men watch on, cheering. The three old women get into Kim's vehicle. They say the fighters have just returned from a long drinking session in Halls Creek. The old women are glad to get away for a few hours until things settle down.

We drive out to the dig. I chat briefly with an archaeologist at one of the sites and take a few notes. We then go to a second site where another archaeologist, Dr Mike Smith, is overseeing things. Wade Freeman, from the Indigenous Protected Area, whom we met last night, is also here. Dr Smith has used an excavator to cut a cross-section from a dry creek bed. I jump into the hole with him to have a look. His talk is getting a little technical so I get out my digital recorder, to ensure I don't misunderstand what he is saying.

They haven't found much, he tells me, mainly discarded chips of stone left in the process of fashioning tools such as an axe head – artefacts that came to rest in the soil between 10,000 and 15,000 years ago. 'Basically, what we are looking at are the cigarette butts of history.' It helps with the bigger story but he isn't getting too excited about what he is finding.

However, unbeknown to me, Wade Freeman is getting very excited. He and Kim are waiting for me as soon I climb out of the hole. Wade's already squeaky voice goes up an octave. I feel as if I'm getting a bollocking from the Bee Gees. He says I have no right to record the archaeologist and will need the permission of the tribal elders of Mulan before I can use any of 'their stories'. I say it is Mike Smith's story. No, Wade tells me, it belongs to the people of Mulan and to reprint it without their permission would be akin to 'theft'.

This is so ludicrous I don't know what to say. Surely there's a statute of limitation on stories, possibly a millennium or two, I think. And how do they know that these people are direct descendants of the people who lived here some *500 generations ago*. Maybe that mob moved to greener pastures, to the coast at Broome or Brunswick Heads, and a new mob moved in.

There's no room for joking. Wade is deadly serious. I am a cultural thief and he has caught me red-handed.

Kim says she doesn't want me to use the name Mulan when I am writing about Mulan and that I should identify it only as a desert community in Western Australia. They both say that before I talk to any Aborigines the community council will need to sit and give approval for people to tell their stories.

The three Aboriginal women who have accompanied us to the dig sit on the ground chatting, oblivious to the grave offence I am committing against them, their people and their ancestors.

'I'm not a gatekeeper,' Kim says as we drive back into Mulan. 'But . . .'

I sit beside her, stewing. I know that if I start to talk I will explode.

Back at Lockie's house, Lisa calms me down. 'Great,' I say. 'We've driven thousands of kilometres and spent thousands of dollars to hire the four-wheel drive and I am not allowed to speak to anyone who is actually black.'

That afternoon we follow Kim into the scrub with some old Aboriginal women who are collecting bark which they burn. They mix the ash with tobacco and chew the paste. We drive through a landscape with thousands of anthills a metre or so high. It is like a vast graveyard of red tombstones. I am allowed to photograph the women but apparently can't interview them.

About 10 kilometres from Mulan we drive along the shores of Lake Gregory, known as Paruku. It is enormous and one of the few permanent lakes this far inland. It is also one of the most important arid wetlands in Australia.

Thousands of corellas take to the sky as we pass. We come across a herd of 100 or more wild horses. This used to be a working cattle station and there were hopes that it would continue as one when it was returned to the Walmajarri people of Mulan. But the cattle venture has failed. Wild cattle and horses now roam around the lake – the people shoot cattle for meat, but they don't target the horses. Horses are held in high esteem from the stockmen days – cowboy dreaming, they call it.

The horses are now in plague numbers and are causing terrible problems with erosion and overgrazing, but they are beautiful as they gallop along the shores of the lake in the late afternoon sun.

Tonight there is a get-together in Wade's compound – he's built a pizza oven and we all bring various toppings. Sitting around are the visiting archaeologists and some other gardiya who are going on the trip down the Canning Stock Route. There are a few Aboriginal people as well as Lockie, Kim, Wade and his girlfriend.

None of the schoolteachers are here and I wonder why. I discover later that Wade's girlfriend had been a teacher at the school, which is Catholic. When Wade and the teacher started seeing each other the school took offence at the 'illicit relationship' and made it hard for her and she quit. Wade's girlfriend now has a job with him at the IPA. His group doesn't have contact with the school. It makes it awkward for the other teachers to socialise with them.

The administrator and his wife aren't here either, even though they live next door. The storekeeper and his wife keep pretty much to themselves. Also missing are the nurses from the clinic.

In this community of 160 Aborigines and 14 white people there are several distinct camps among the whites. I wonder how this affects the running of the community.

Recently, I am told, the school got a plumber out to do some work but didn't tell anyone else he was coming even though there is always plumbing work that needs doing in the community. It cost $5000 just to get him to drive out from Halls Creek, with labour costs on top. The plumber did his job at the school and drove back. The next week another group had to pay $5000 to get him out again to fix a couple of broken toilets.

The next morning Kim asks me to write a letter to submit to the council meeting. In 20 years of journalism I have never encountered anything like this, but I type it up anyway. I am unsure exactly how the permit system works and the fact that we don't have them hangs over our heads.

While we cool our heels, I decide to interview Lockie. He's a good man with a good heart and for the past six years he's travelled up to Mulan building outstations and the community centre and doing basic maintenance on people's homes. He fixes locks and re-hangs doors. He is respected for the work he does.

Lockie explains that he is seen in the community as the 'boss of tools'. It is a job that only a white man can hold. If a local was in charge of the tools he couldn't refuse an uncle who wanted to borrow a drill or a hammer and pretty soon everything would be lost. Lockie is able to be selective about who can borrow a tool and demand that it be returned.

His hope is to build up a team of people who are able to do basic house maintenance and assist in the construction of any new homes. New homes are currently built by outsiders who come in every few years and build three or four at one time. Lockie would like to provide continuous employment and build one house each year using local labour. It takes years and years of patience to build up people's skills but because of his run-in with the new administrators it doesn't look like he'll be back next year.

There is always talk about closing down communities such as Mulan, because they are so expensive to run. From the outside it seems sensible. Mulan has little hope of ever being economically viable. There are few real jobs and its extreme isolation means there probably never will be. But, Lockie explains, apart from the fact that this is Walmajarri land and the people have a right to be here, closing the community would create serious problems.

'I think you need to look at the consequences of the alternative to answer the question of whether it is viable,' he says. 'The evidence is that the smaller communities are healthier.' If Mulan were closed the locals would be forced to places like Balgo and Halls Creek, communities ravaged by alcohol and violence. Booze is not a big issue in Mulan, he explains. People go into Halls Creek about once a fortnight to drink but they generally don't bring grog back into the community and there is no alcohol for sale in Mulan. There is no police officer here and no real need for one. This is a strong tribe with links to the land.

As we are sitting in Lockie's kitchen sipping tea, one of his workers wanders in. Stanley is 21. He spent five years at boarding school in Darwin before returning to Mulan last year. He wants to become a builder and Lockie says that of all the men he's worked with over the years Stanley is the most likely to succeed.

I tell Stanley that I am writing a book and ask if I can interview him. He says he would be happy to talk.

'My goal is to get a building ticket,' he tells me. 'I might have to go to Darwin or Broome to get it and then one day I want to come back here and be involved in building.'

He has worked as a builder's labourer in Broome and says the work he is doing with Lockie is developing his skills.

Stanley has a young child and a partner and he wants to do something constructive with his life, he says. It is hard sometimes, living in a traditional Aboriginal community and trying to achieve these goals. 'A lot of people here, they don't have a goal for themselves,' he says. 'They don't look long-term and they can't see beyond the horizon. They don't like it when others get ahead either.'

He recently bought himself a 2002 Commodore and if one of his uncles demanded the keys, it would be hard for him not to hand them over.

'It depends on the situation,' he says. 'My aunty was sick and she needed to go to Halls Creek the other day so I took her 'cause it was a state of emergency. But if one of my uncles was going in to get on the booze I reckon I might be able to resist – but it would be hard.'

He would risk having his vehicle smashed and there would be little he could do about it.

Sometimes, he says, he would like to move away for good but there is a strong pull back to Mulan. 'It's about the country and family; your family defines your spiritual being. It makes you feel more comfortable and accepted and it's something that sometimes you can't overrun, no matter how far you go, you always tend to come back.'

We spend a pleasant half hour chatting about Stanley's life.

When we walk outside an elderly lady by the name of Anna approaches Lockie and asks him to fix her broken door, which he does. Anna and I chat briefly.

Somehow Wade finds out I have talked to Stanley and Anna. He bails Lockie up and says that we have 'stolen' Stanley's story and 'haven't even paid him'. Lockie tells him to calm down and says that Stanley has a right to talk to us if he chooses. Wade accuses us of taking advantage of Stanley and the community. He tells Lockie that any journalists who come into the community need to be 'controlled'.

Lisa is furious this time. She says she feels like she's back in Pakistan where she spent three years working with local journalists and lobbying for media freedom so that ordinary people could be given a voice. She didn't think she would find this sort of Orwellian censorship in her own country. 'I thought freedom of speech was a right enjoyed by black and white Australians. The suggestion that Stanley can't speak to us without somebody else's permission, I find patronising in the extreme,' she says. Wade sees himself as the good old leftie from Central Casting but he seems to have no concept of freedom of expression or freedom of the press. He and Kim would argue that in an Aboriginal community there can be severe consequences for anyone who speaks out without permission.

Kim is frosty when she next sees us. She says she is going to Balgo, the nearby community, for a smoking ceremony. We are not allowed to attend the ceremony but we can go to the arts centre, she says.

We have become pariahs. The situation is a farce and all we can do about it now is joke with each other as we bump along behind Kim on the 44-kilometre trip to Balgo. 'They've decided the only safe place for us is in another community looking at dot paintings,' Lisa says, laughing. 'Not that we will be able to talk to the artists.'

The arts centre is closed.

We go to have a look at the store.

Balgo is one of those problem towns that flares up every now and again. The community of 500 contains several different tribes that were forced together during the mission days and the schisms remain.

Outside the store the petrol pumps are completely encased in steel mesh and a hard-looking Caucasian man stands next to the bowsers with a money belt and a heavy stick resting by his side.

School has just ended and dozens of kids and their parents are filling up with big boxes of hot chips. Inside the store anything of any real value – motor oil, toys, electrical goods – is locked behind a steel cage. I need a pen but a woman at the cash register says they don't stock pens. She goes into the office and sells me a secondhand one for a dollar. A town of 500 people and they don't stock pens.

The woman in front of me has two little kids and is doing her daily shopping. In her basket she has two large bottles of Coke, two large packets of chips, two boxes of Coco Pops and two large frozen pizzas.

'Balgo is a difficult place,' Kim Mahood wrote in her book *Craft for a Dry Lake*, 'one of those places where one feels something volatile and even inimical in the landscape itself.' She describes the petrol sniffing youths and the whites who live here in a state of 'quasi-siege' behind steel mesh verandahs.

I am outside jotting down some of my own observations about Balgo when she fronts me. 'Greg, the same thing applies for Balgo as it does for Mulan,' she says, curtly. 'You really shouldn't be reporting about this. I don't want to be the gatekeeper, but ...'

I walk away rather than telling her to fuck off.

Lisa steps in to clear the air. 'Look, Kim, our presence here seems to have created a lot of tension, but we're not really sure why ...'

Kim tells her there are a lot of issues. She says until now 'she's managed to fly under the radar' and to work without creating problems. Her uncertain relationship with the new administrators is only 'part of the problem'. She's also dealing with an Aboriginal friend who is deeply offended by something Kim has written recently about Mulan. And she's concerned about what we might write and how it might compromise her position.

Lisa calmly tells Kim how we feel, particularly how upset we are about the incident with Stanley.

'I understand,' says Kim. 'I don't want to be the gatekeeper. But things are different in Aboriginal communities and people don't have the same right to speak as they do in the white community. If Stanley has said something he shouldn't have, he'll be in big trouble. There are people, within Aboriginal culture, who don't have the same right to speak as we do in the white community.'

The conversation doesn't lead anywhere but it clears the air, for the moment.

The next morning Kim takes our letter to the council. Unfortunately the council meeting has been cancelled because the chairman and a couple of the other councillors are on a piss-up in Halls Creek and won't be back for a couple of days.

As an alternative Kim organises a meeting with some of the senior women from the community. That afternoon we sit down with four Aboriginal women, and Kim.

The women tell us that until 1979 they had been living on the mission at Balgo when an Aboriginal man by the name of Rex Johns led the Walmajarri people back to their homeland on the edge of Lake Gregory. Rex's wife, Anna, is one of the four women.

'We heard the government was giving land out to the people so my husband thought we'd try and get Lake Gregory,' Anna explains. The first few years in Mulan were very difficult and everybody lived in tin humpies. But they made the right decision, she says, returning to their lands.

'There's a lot of alcoholics in Balgo,' she says. 'Lotta fights.'

One of the other women, Bessie Doonday, tells me how her mother gave birth to her under the stars. 'There was a fire to make heat for giving birth. They make a fire to make the baby come out, that's how I was born.' It seems incredible to me to be sitting here, digital recorder in hand, with a woman who was born in a time that may as well have been the stone age. Bessie's daughter May Stunda is another of the women. May has a different name from her mother because when she first went to school her teacher misunderstood the pronunciation; she's been Stunda rather than Doonday all her life.

May went to boarding school in Broome and of the four women her English is the best. We organise to meet her the following day to talk.

Finally it seems we are getting somewhere.

We arrive at May's house at the appointed time. She is a large 42-year-old woman with skin as black as night, stubble on her chin and a mop of dark hair. She is wearing a brightly coloured floral dress. Joe jumps up into her arms and May gives him a big hug. We sit on plastic chairs in the shade of one of Mulan's few trees and for a little while May's daughter Valerie joins us.

May tells us she's much happier living in Mulan than in Broome. Here the pace of life is slow and she is connected to the land and her family. But, she says, it is important that black and white people interact and learn from each other. 'We need to learn the white ways to run our farm and for the tourism and for the books.'

White people can learn from Aboriginal people too, she says, to slow down, look at the land and contemplate things. 'You white fellas always rushing,' she says. 'No time to think.'

There are kids playing outside May's house and Joe follows them inside. I go in to check that he is okay. Inside there are three or four adults and five or six kids sitting on the floor. The room is filthy and there is no furniture apart from a large television. A person is playing a video game with a creature that looks like a cartoon version of the Tasmanian devil. Everyone is sitting transfixed except Joe and another little boy who are sizing each other up.

In the old days, a lot of time was spent hunting and gathering food in this harsh environment. It seems that's been replaced by television and video games.

Back outside, May tells us religion plays an important part in her life. She was a Catholic but converted to the Assembly of God. The church for her is a mix of traditional beliefs blended with Christianity.

'Aboriginal people can see God in creation, in everything, in the beauty of the land and in the children when they're laughing and playing and having fun. That for us is God.'

Lisa asks her what she would like the rest of Australia to know about the people of Mulan.

She says Aboriginal people are just the same as any other race, but they are still learning the ways of the modern world. She says she appreciates the people who come to Mulan to help out. 'We can do little things, but not big things right away, but little things.'

She has a grandson and hopes that he gets a good education. 'I'd like to see him go to school to get an education so he'll have skills, learning things both ways, the white people way and the Aboriginal way.'

The conversation is easy and warm and we feel as though we've made a real connection. May says the following afternoon she is going out hunting for bush tucker: goanna, some snakes, witchetty grubs, frogs. She invites us along and we jump at the opportunity.

We check with Lockie and then invite May and her family for a barbecue after the hunt. That afternoon we go to the store to buy food for the barbecue. It is in the centre of the community and is the only place to shop. Most people don't have fridges, so they buy what they need each day. It is owned by the community but run by a white husband and wife team. None of the groceries have prices marked on them so it's not until we get to the counter that we realise the exorbitant cost. Lisa asks for a receipt. The potatoes are $1.50 *each*, half a pumpkin costs $14.42, 1.4 kilos of mutton chops are $33.92. The bill comes to almost 150 bucks, about three times what we would pay in Sydney. The cost of freight to these communities is horrendous.

We walk out of the store in shock. 'There's no way we could live on welfare and feed our family a balanced diet here,' I say to Lisa.

Not long afterwards we run into Kim and start chatting to her about the high cost of food. 'Yes,' she says, 'Bessie [May's mother] came to borrow money from me recently because she said the food was so expensive and that she was going hungry.' We talk about how outrageous it is and Lisa mentions shooting the story for SBS TV. Kim says that would cause her lots of problems with the white people in the community, so Lisa says she'll leave it.

But within a few hours we have both changed our minds. 'We are pathetic if we don't tell this story,' Lisa says after we've talked it through. 'If people are going hungry because they can't afford to eat then the rest of the country should know about it.'

We talk some more with other people in the community. One of the nurses tells me the high cost of fresh food is causing all sorts of health problems. Many people in the community are malnourished, the nurse explains. Lockie too encourages us. He says it is the elderly who are worst affected because they go without food to ensure children don't go hungry.

We decide to do the story and for maximum impact aim to pitch it to *The Sydney Morning Herald*, *Melbourne Age* and *The West Australian*.

Lisa and I then set about conducting interviews. We are driving over to meet someone when we see Kim. I stop the car and say to her, 'Look, there is something we need to tell you. Lisa and I have talked about this and ethically we think we need to write the story about the cost of food.'

She is not happy. She says she's working with others on an open letter to send to governments and to newspapers signed by the elders. I tell her it's a hit-and-miss strategy. It may land in the in-tray of a chief of staff with 150 other press releases and nothing will ever come of it.

'Well, you know, I am the one who got you in here. You don't have permits. I fly under the radar here. You have seen what's happened to Lockie. It can be virtually impossible to work out here if white people start giving you a hard time.'

She makes it clear that she doesn't want us to write the story. 'You have to make your own ethical choices.' And then she walks off. Later in the day she tells Lisa that 'if people end up getting better or cheaper food then I suppose that's more important than me coming back here.'

The next afternoon we go over to May's house to go hunting. We knock on the door and there is no answer. I knock again. No answer.

May's mother, Bessie, comes out of the house next door.

'May's gone to Ringer Soak for a funeral,' says Bessie.

'How long has she known about it?'

'A few days.'

Only a day ago she had been so keen to show us her culture. She said she wanted us to have a good impression of Aboriginal culture, but now she's gone without a word.

We tell Lockie. 'Now you've had the genuine Mulan experience,' he says, grinning.

It's time to leave. It's been an exhausting, fascinating and confusing week. We had left Tennant Creek with the Aboriginal leader Noel Pearson's words ringing in our ears. The only way forward, he argues, is to break the dependence on welfare. But what do you do in a place like Mulan? It's unlikely there will ever be many jobs but does that mean the people should be forced to leave? As Lockie pointed out, the alternative might be far worse. People would move to the fringes of Balgo and Halls Creek, violent places drowning in alcohol. Mulan has made us less certain about our opinions, more aware of the complexities. The only thing we know for sure is that no one solution will fix the problems.

Our story about Mulan, under the heading 'Forced to Live in Hunger', is today on the front page of *The Sydney Morning Herald* with a big picture I took of the local Assembly of God pastor sitting cross-legged in the red dust outside the Mulan Community Store. Next to our story is an article by the paper's medical editor, Julie Robotham, about a study on the cost of fresh food in remote communities. The study found that high prices are encouraging people to eat a diet rich in carbohydrates putting them at greater risk of cancer, diabetes and heart failure and severely compromising the development of children. Fruit accounted for just 1 per cent of energy consumption in one Aboriginal community.

Our article also appears on page three of *The West Australian* and is followed up by various other media, including ABC radio's *The World Today*.

The story explodes like a grenade in Mulan's white community. The local storekeeper bans Lockie from the shop for talking to us and sends a letter of complaint to the *Herald*. We hear through Lockie that Wade is claiming the story has given ammunition to those who want to close down Mulan because it portrays it as being unviable. Kim, apparently, isn't pleased either. The community administrators, we are told, are insulted that we didn't talk to them. They have plans to build a community garden.

And the Aborigines?

'They all loved it,' Lockie says. 'They all reckon they've been paying too much for food for years and they'd like something done about it.'

34

A frigid wind is blowing across the desert and the only place we can find shelter in Balgo, this desolate Aboriginal community of wary dogs and wrecked cars, is behind the local arts centre. Most Fridays since we've been on the road, Lisa and I have done a live radio interview with the ABC in Sydney, talking about the trip. And each week we have faced the same dilemma – what to do with Joe while we are on air. Some weeks we shove him in the van with lots of toys or hand him over to kindly grey nomads camped next to us. Today our only option is to leave him in the warmth of the four-wheel drive with a handful of biscuits.

We left Mulan early and hurtled across the rough bush track to Balgo where we can get mobile phone coverage. The interview is scheduled for 9.50 am Sydney time, that's 7.50 am Balgo time. And here we are, a man and woman crouching beside a wall in beanies, trying to find a position of minimum wind interference while a little boy peers through the window of the four-wheel drive, dribbling biscuit.

A gardiya woman arrives at the arts centre and asks what we are doing. Lisa explains. The woman invites us in out of the cold and volunteers to mind Joe while we do the interview. We plan to talk about the high cost of fresh food in these outback settlements and how it's affecting people's health.

We wait and wait. Finally the call comes through from Sydney. There's a baby humpback whale called Colin — who turns out to be a Colleen — stranded in Sydney harbour. Apparently the entire city is captivated by its fate. Journalists are at the scene doing live crosses. We've been bumped until next week; starving baby whale trumps starving blackfellas.

We drive out of Balgo onto the Tanami Track, bemused. City life now seems very foreign. Mid morning we come across a broken-down Toyota with seven or eight Aborigines sitting beside it drinking beer. 'Gardiya, gardiya,' they yell, hailing us down. They've been in Halls Creek on the booze and have run out of petrol on the way home. We only have diesel. I offer to call somebody when we get to Halls Creek but nobody seems to hear me.

After four hours on the Tanami Track we reach Halls Creek. I manage to find some good wine at the bottle-o — the town's shop of misery — and, in my mind, plan a romantic evening watching the stars by the warmth of the campfire. We're planning to spend the night at the Purnululu National Park with its magnificent bee-hive hills, the Bungle Bungles, before heading back to Kununurra tomorrow.

North of Halls Creek, we turn off towards the national park. The road is so bad that we are forced to bump along at 20 kilometres an hour. There are corrugations, deep creeks to cross, steep climbs, tight corners. It takes us more than two hours to drive about 50 kilometres and it's almost five o'clock by the time we arrive at our campsite.

Lisa and I are both exhausted and Joe has had enough of the car. Beside a dry creek bed, we erect the three-man tent that we hired with the four-wheel drive. Joe's portable cot takes up most of the room and our sleeping mats are wedged in either side. Joe will be comfortable, but Lisa and I have about as much room as bread in a toaster. It should have been a signal that my hopes of romance were doomed.

I boil some water and Lisa and I settle down with cups of tea in our camp chairs to enjoy the serenity while Joe fights off crows or wallabies, or whatever is in his imagination, with a set of barbecue tongs. It is then that I look up. The tent is beneath a big old gnarled river gum and directly above us a large dead branch has broken off and is resting precariously on another branch – if it fell during the night it would probably kill us.

We get up from our comfy chairs and move the tent and all our gear 10 metres away. Lisa feeds Joe baked beans and puts him into his portable cot where he talks himself to sleep. I put pasta on to boil and pour two glasses of wine into our plastic wine glasses.

It is then that the tension of the past week erupts over nothing. Lisa snaps at me. I snap back. The fight takes on a life of its own, like a summer bushfire, and escalates into a fury of 'I can't stand the sight of you,' and 'Well, I can't stand the sight of you either,' followed by an indignant 'I can't believe you just spoke to me like that.' After a few minutes Lisa storms off into the tent with graphic suggestions as to what I should do with our nice bottle of chardonnay.

I sit outside by myself, fuming, eating my bowl of pasta in the dark and gulping wine. I am determined not to budge and be the first to say sorry. In silence I reach into the tent and drag out my mat and sleeping bag. This fight, I convince myself, is definitely *her* fault. She can say sorry and until she does I am not talking to her. She, unimaginatively, has adopted an identical strategy.

I spend the night outside in my sleeping bag shivering but determined to make a point while she is warm inside the tent, making the same point.

In the morning I have a dreadful cold. We pack up and communicate with monosyllabic grunts. We drive quietly over to the Bungle Bungle range nearby.

The Bungles are probably the most spectacular natural landform I have ever seen. We stop the four-wheel drive when the beehive-like domes come into full view and a truce is called as we get out and allow ourselves to be overcome by their beauty. Joe stays in the front seat, pretending to drive the car – his favourite game.

Lisa reaches over and grabs my hand giving it a little squeeze – victory! Hostilities have officially ceased. Remarkably, fights like this have been rare. We put Joe in a backpack and wander through Cathedral Gorge with me a bundle of snot, ill but content.

35

The Kimberley is a land of epic proportions. We have driven 700 kilometres west of Kununurra, where we picked up our new Volvo, and are only halfway across the region. Everything here is on a vast scale and the property we have come to visit, Fossil Downs, half an hour out of Fitzroy Crossing, is colossal.

Its story begins with the most remarkable of journeys. In March 1883 an expedition headed by two brothers, Charles and William MacDonald, set off with a mob of 670 cattle, 70 horses and 26 bullocks hauling two drays packed with supplies from a property near Goulburn in NSW. It is believed they purchased another 500 head of cattle along the way, in northern NSW. They were inspired by reports of rich grazing land in the Kimberley by the explorer, Alexander Forrest, who surveyed the area in 1879.

The MacDonald's expedition was just a couple of decades after Burke and Wills had come to grief. The route they were to undertake was even more difficult, and, in addition, they were droving cattle. The brothers made their way north to Bourke in north-west NSW, then up through the Queensland channel country, almost to the Gulf of Carpentaria, past where Ludwig Leichhardt is thought to have perished. Then they headed west across the Northern Territory to Katherine. They battled droughts, crocodiles, ticks, severe illness and attacks from tribes of Aborigines.

Finally, in June 1886, they arrived at the junction of the Fitzroy and Margaret Rivers. Only 300 cattle made it and the brothers too were lucky to be alive. One of the drays was lost in a river in the Territory, but the one that made it was the first wheeled vehicle to cross the continent. The MacDonalds's trek is believed to be the world's longest and most difficult droving expedition ever undertaken. By the time they had finished, they had walked their cattle a distance further than Paris to Cairo.

Little is known about the details of this great droving expedition. No journals or diaries have survived and the two brothers appear to have been so traumatised by the experience that they never liked to talk about it. 'It took us three and half years to get here,' old Willy MacDonald used to say, 'and a lifetime to forget.'

While his two brothers were droving, another brother, Donald, who must have drawn the long straw when old MacDonald handed out the jobs, sailed to Derby and organised a grazing lease. A million acres was waiting for the cattle when they finally arrived.

Donald's granddaughter is now sitting with me on the wide verandah of the magnificent homestead of Fossil Downs, a property which has been in the family for 125 years.

Annette Henwood, nee MacDonald, 66, is a well-groomed woman with pearl earrings and a fresh frangipani tucked above her ear. Apart from her time away at boarding school in Perth, from the age of seven, and a stint helping to manage another property when she and her husband, John, were first married, she has lived on Fossil Downs all her life. It was named so because a couple of German archaeologists found fossils here a few years before the MacDonalds arrived.

The homestead has the look of those grand mansions from the deep south of the United States. It sits at the head of a large U-shaped drive, with a couple of elegant cottages, storehouses, a mess, stockmen's quarters, the governess's residence, workshops, stables and machinery sheds fanning out down either side of the drive. Everything is immaculate, well maintained and freshly painted. The homestead is white and the other buildings a soft pink. The stables are swept clean and saddles and bridles organised neatly on hooks and rails. In the workshop there's not a spanner out of place or a drop of oil on the floor.

The lawns, several hectares, are irrigated year-round and planted with poinciana, African tulip trees, mahogany, mangoes, frangipani, banana trees, palms and the strange-looking boab. They are tended to by a full-time gardener. An Australian flag flutters on a pole in the drive.

The double-storied homestead, built by Annette's father in 1936, has hosted Princess Margaret. The large bricks used to construct the house, 10,000 of them, were handmade with sand shovelled from the nearby Margaret River. The house is spotless and visitors are asked to remove their shoes so as not to damage the painted and polished cement floors. It is kept almost as a museum piece and John and Annette live in one of the large, handsome cottages next door.

Our caravan is parked in the shade, next to the homestead.

John's job, Annette tells me, is to run the property while hers is to oversee maintenance of the grounds and the buildings. 'It's been my life's work,' she explains.

They run 15,000 head of cattle and sell off about 4000 each year. It is one of the last remaining great cattle runs still in pioneer hands and certainly the last in the East Kimberley. Most have been sold to large corporations. If Fossil Downs is ever sold much of what we see would be pulled down simply because of the cost of maintenance.

'We inherited it this way and we intend to keep it this way,' Annette says with the drive sweeping out before us. 'You've got to have good accommodation for your staff and you've got to have comforts for your staff and we pride ourselves on treating everybody the same way we would like to be treated. We treat them all as family. Rightly or wrongly, foolishly or otherwise, we have poured all our resources back into the place.'

A cook, a cleaner, a gardener and a general station hand all have their own quarters. The bookkeeper flies in from Perth every few months to stay a week or two.

The Henwoods now employ contractors to do all their mustering by helicopter. When she was a child, Annette's family employed about 15 white people and a further 70 Aborigines who lived in a camp behind the homestead. 'About 20 were stockmen, 10 or 12 were house girls, and the rest would be oldies and tiny tots. We really believed that those days were good days because they [Aborigines] were cared for and they belonged and they had pride. They genuinely had pride.'

Her husband, John, comes to join us on the balcony and the conversation moves, for a time, away from their relationship with the local Aborigines, who have all moved off the station and now live in a settlement across the river called Mudludja, or into Fitzroy Crossing.

John is a tall, fit-looking man of 68 who is wearing a cotton shirt, short denim shorts with his socks pulled up and his hair neatly parted. The top part of one ear is missing, presumably from some farm accident.

His father was the manager of a property 70 kilometres away and Annette says she'd had a crush on him since she was about 15. 'He kept running away with all the different governesses that came out to the country and I had to run him down. I eventually gave up, to tell you the truth. My father died when I was 21 and the year he died, my mother told me to go away and do something. So a girlfriend and myself drove around Australia. We took our swags, and took about five and a half months to do 27,500 miles. Unbeknown to me, my letters home got forwarded on to John. He eventually saw the light and so it was rather good. We were married in 1965.'

John smiles.

When Annette's father built the current homestead he consulted his elderly Aboriginal employees about the safest place to build it. The old corrugated tin homestead, 15 kilometres from the present one, had been 'washed askew from it stumps' by a flood in 1914. 'My father decided that if this was going to be his life's work he wanted to move and build something beautiful.'

A big flood in 1956 didn't reach the homestead and everybody assumed the Aborigines' advice had been right. But in 1983 everything changed. 'We hadn't had much rain here at all, we were pretty dry but we'd heard there had been big rains up the top. The water started to rise on all fronts. It came up from both directions and it just kept coming and coming. Since I was the only one who'd been here forever, everyone said, "When will it stop Annette?" and I said, "Oh, soon," and when it got up to near the front steps we literally watched it come and didn't move because we had no concept of what was going to happen. Suddenly the water started to rush around the buildings and meet up with the water that was rising this way. It was then that I said, "My god, something really untoward is happening here . . ."'

She pauses for a moment and almost cries, but catches herself before continuing. 'But it was already too late, because whilst we were trying to save one thing another thing was going. We made the mistake of assuming it couldn't happen. For example, in the billiard room we put all the books from the bookshelf on the table, never in our wildest dreams thinking the table would go under. Where we're sitting here now, it was up to my chin and the water was flowing so fast and so fiercely that you couldn't stand on your feet without being swept away.'

It is like a tale from the Old Testament. All their machinery, their furniture, their clothes – everything was washed away. Five thousand cattle perished along with 87 of their 120 horses. One hundred and sixty kilometres of fencing, tanks and troughs were all washed away. The insurance covered things at the homestead, but not on the cattle run. Annette says they were diddled by the insurance company and after that no one would insure them again.

It was supposed to be a one in 100 year flood. But then the water came again in 1986, 1991 and twice in 1993, two weeks apart.

'All our resources have been gobbled up each time trying to put it back together again, and then with the two floods in 1993, well, John and I don't mind admitting we were going through a pretty rocky stage by then in our marriage. I suppose it was the fact that I represented problems – Fossil and problems. If he was going to trade me in, it was then.'

After the 1986 flood they realised they would either have to move the homestead or learn to live with it. Annette says she could never move and so they live with it. Now, every year before the start of the wet season, the cattle and horses are moved to higher ground, along with all the machinery. Everything else is moved upstairs.

'Before everyone goes on holidays, we have a period where we say, "Every day of this week, we'll do one floor of one building," and we move it. It takes about a week with everyone working. Since those floods, gradually we've moved every power point about flood level, every door has a hook behind it so it can be held open for the current to go through so you don't have the smashed glass effect. All the leadlight in the hall was smashed and I had to walk Perth trying to match glass because it was all old-type glass. We've done a lot to try and help ourselves. We've now got pulleys that take the billiard table up and the pianola as well. We only did that after we'd restored the billiard table twice and lost two pianolas. We couldn't afford to buy another one.'

After every flood each building needs to be thoroughly cleaned of the stinking mud. There are about 20 buildings in the house paddock, including the meat house, stables, sheds and dwellings and all of them need to be scrubbed, spotless.

While we are talking about floods, a bell is struck and the ring indicates it's time for lunch. Each day Annette and John eat lunch and dinner with the staff. We make our way over to the building that houses the kitchen.

Annette plays with Joe while she waits for the food to be served. She has a daughter Amber, 36, who lives with her partner Stuart and they manage a property together in Queensland – she hopes they'll return to Fossil Downs one day. She doesn't approve of them not being married but would very much like a grandchild. 'I just want to be Nanette,' she says, jiggling Joe on her lap.

We all gather around the table for lunch. I put my hat at the end of the table and John gently admonishes me for it, out of earshot of the others. 'We have been trying to teach the staff not to bring their hats inside.'

The food is good old-fashioned fare, corned meat and chicken and salad with iceberg lettuce. 'There's only one rule around here,' Annette informs us during the lunch. 'No garlic. John just can't stand the smell of it.'

'Just one rule?' Lisa jokes with me later.

It feels as though we've been transported back to a time long before garlic.

After lunch Annette and John have to leave for a few hours. An Aboriginal man called Arthur has died and they are off to pay their respects. Arthur is the son of Butcher Cherel, 'One of Dad's best men.' Butcher is still alive and is a 'dear old family friend'.

'In the old days we used to have sports days on Christmas Day, running races and high-jumps, and they all loved it,' Annette recalls. 'Butcher was a natural athlete, always won everything, magnificent physique, the whole works, good looking.'

When he left the pastoral industry Butcher took up painting and is now one of the best known artists in the East Kimberley. His work hangs in galleries all over the world. 'He's been to London to meet the Queen,' Annette says proudly. 'I've got one of his etchings, that's all I can afford.'

While John and Annette are away paying their respects to Butcher's family, Lisa, Joe and I go for a swim in the pool. It is a big water tank on a hill behind the homestead that doubles as the irrigation tank for the lawns. Afterwards, we chat with the bookkeeper. She's been with the Henwoods for almost 30 years and says they're terrific people. John, she says, manages the farm but Annette in many ways runs the business. 'She's a tough one, that one,' she emphasises. 'Smart.'

After they've returned Annette says that it was wonderful to see her old Aboriginal friends, many of whom came up to give her a hug and to reminisce about the good old days. She and John still get along well with some of the older Aborigines, she says, but things are not like they were on those Christmas sports days, back in the old days.

'The government of the day decided that stations would pay equal pay for all their Aboriginal employees and I feel, looking back, that this was a terrible decision. There was no way one could afford to pay equal pay because each Aboriginal person that you employed had aunts, uncles, grandparents – all sorts of rellies that you actually looked after. What governments didn't realise was that it cost us a lot to look after entire Aboriginal groups that lived on each station. Everybody had their role to play on the station. Somebody just held a hose and did some watering, somebody else did some raking up, somebody else was a housegirl, somebody else was a horse tailor, someone was in the bush camp, but they all had a job. Some were little jobs, some were big jobs but it made everybody feel that they were part of the place and that they belonged. That is what they lost.'

Black and white people in northern Australia look back with fondness on the days when Aborigines worked in the pastoral industry – the pastoralists point to the push for equal wages as bringing about the demise. The truth is, however, the days were numbered for all stockmen – black and white. Fossil Downs once had 25 to 30 permanent stockmen. Now all the mustering is done by a handful of men with helicopters and motorbikes who come in for a few months and then leave.

What is undeniable is that the drift of Aboriginal tribes into urban settlements and the subsequent access to grog and welfare has been devastating. Annette says she's watched this all unfold with great sadness.

'I'd love to be able to help them now because they are wallowing in a sea of inactivity and feel victimised,' she says. 'It doesn't help anybody. It's a very tough one.'

In the old days both she and John were given Aboriginal names which Aboriginal people used to call them. 'Now, the young, when they see you coming they say, "Gardiya, gardiya". It means white man, but it's said in a nasty way like people used to say "nigger". This has been fostered by so many well-meaning people telling them that they were here first and that maybe they were part of the stolen generation, or they should have this or they should have that, and it has rubbed off on the young ones.'

They don't believe the million acres their family has occupied for the past 125 years may have belonged to someone else beforehand. 'I feel we should stop calling them traditional owners, it is just perpetuating a sense of you owe us,' Annette insists.

John chips in and says that they provide free 'killers' – beef – for the nearby Aboriginal community, Mudludja, for funerals and other big events and allow people access to his property to fish and go camping. 'But invariably they leave the gates open and we have tried everything, leaving notes on the gate, even padlocking them. Because it is such an inaccessible area we have to get helicopters in to muster the cattle at great expense.'

John wrote a letter to the Kimberley Land Council suggesting the Mudludja community should be liable for some of the costs when gates are left open. The deputy of the council wrote back and said 'basically they could do what they liked because they were the traditional owners'.

That night we are invited to the weekly Saturday barbecue. The staff had spent the day canoeing in a remote gorge and show us pictures of some incredible Aboriginal rock art. The gardener and the cleaner are cuddling up with each other and it's obvious they are an item. John tells me later he is very happy for them. 'They are both happier people for it,' he says.

The next morning John takes me over to the airstrip. His Toyota Landcruiser has done many thousands of kilometres but looks as though it's just been driven off the showroom floor. There are canvas seat covers to protect the upholstery and at each fence we stop for a moment to let the dust settle before I get out to open the gate.

The homestead from the air is a patch of green in a sea of brown. It is late in the dry season and the land is parched. The river has stopped flowing but there are still great stretches with plenty of water. Below we spot a crocodile sunning itself on the riverbank and giant jabirus take off below us. In the wet the river may spread to be many kilometres wide – an enormous amount of water flows down here every year and John wants to show me the ranges at the back of his property. He has a grand scheme that he's been pushing for years, without much luck, to build a hydro dam on this river.

We fly for 20 minutes or more before we reach the range and then John manoeuvres the plane up though a deep gorge to show me where the dam wall would be built. 'The water here would be 350 feet deep,' he shouts. 'I have flown 20 miles up this gorge and my gauges tell me it would still be 150 feet deep up there.'

He's raised the matter with state and federal politicians but has so far been unable to get any traction. Recently he's been discussing it with some of the local Aboriginal elders to try to get them on board.

'It would provide jobs and a future for the Aboriginal people here,' he claims. 'We could provide electricity for industry and irrigation.' I listen and nod. I don't tell him I think it's unlikely to happen. Living out here in isolation, John hasn't realised that such grand engineering projects, altering the flow of rivers, are now out of vogue.

It takes us a good 45 minutes to fly to the far side of the place and back.

On the ground back at the homestead, we all have a cup of tea together before we leave. I ask Annette what it is she loves about the Kimberley.

'I have had such a fortunate life to have lived here. For every season there's a different lot of birds. You hear the brolgas, particularly in the winter time. In the wet season you get all the storm birds and the cuckoo pheasants, those sorts of birds, and for every season there are different sounds. And for all the different seasons there are the different smells, whether it's the bloodwoods coming into blossom or the smell of the first rain on dust, or the smell of the stockyards. And then there's the country itself. The ruggedness of it, sometimes the harshness, sometimes the sheer beauty of it at sunrise or sunset – it's all a bit romantic. I can look at some country down south which might be worth a phenomenal amount of money per acre and it's very rich and it produces wonderful sheep or wonderful cattle and it just doesn't do anything for me. And yet you can look at some stony ridge or some piece of the Kimberley and your heart rolls over.'

Joe hugs everyone, from the gardener to the cook, and we drive off to Broome, out into that landscape that makes our hearts roll over too.

36

The east coast of Australia is entirely different from the west. Over east, the coast announces itself long before you see it, usually somewhere down the slopes of the Great Divide. You have about 100 kilometres in which to acclimatise as you pass through rainforest, cane fields and dairy farms before you hit the ocean. On the drive from Fossil Downs, the rugged Kimberley landscape stays with us almost to the water's edge.

Here in the West, you can be surrounded by savannah, Brahman cattle and anthills one moment and then, with no adequate warning, be on the beach with pink Englishmen in bad shorts frolicking in a turquoise sea. Because of this, Broome is a delight – it's a fusion of the Kimberley outback and the coast. It's where red desert meets café chic.

The people too are fused. The pearling industry, which began in the 1880s, relied on Asian divers: Japanese, Malays, Chinese, Indonesians, Filipinos and Islanders. They came by the boatload to work on the pearls, even when the country's White Australia Policy restricted immigration to mostly white Europeans. In Broome, the policy didn't apply. Asian divers were indispensable and many of them bred with local Aboriginal women.

As a result Broome has the best looking shop assistants anywhere in Australia – possibly the world. The women are so striking that Lisa is perving too, which grants me full immunity. One day in the supermarket she says to me, 'Did you see that woman serving at counter eight? She is one of one of the most amazing women I have ever seen.'

'Yes,' I reply, thinking the ones at counters two, six, nine and 11 are pretty amazing too.

For a few days we wander around the shops of old Chinatown, lamenting how much better looking we may have been were it not for the White Australia Policy. We also try to dodge the heat. The build-up to the wet season has begun and the airconditioner in the caravan has broken down. The mining boom has soaked up almost every available tradesman and we beg a man called Bob Kiss to come and fix ours. He might get around to it, he says, and orders us to be at the van at four o'clock. When he doesn't turn up, we wait for two hours and then call to meekly ask his whereabouts. He gets annoyed and grunts he'll come tomorrow, maybe. In a mining boom, the man with a spanner is king.

We spend our days cooling off at the beach, drinking good coffee and waiting for Mr Kiss. We think about investigating stories on Broome's multicultural history, but don't do much to achieve it. In this place of so many bold colours – pink bougainvillea, deep red soils, luscious green plants and stunning turquoise seas – it is very easy to lie back and do nothing.

Broome may make us feel languid, but for others this place is inspirational. The town has spawned a vibrant arts scene with lots of good galleries. Mercifully, they are airconditioned. There is one particular sculpture that takes Lisa's eye in the Monsoon Gallery. It looks like a throne from China or Tibet and is inscribed with symbols from various religions and cultures. The sculpture was made by a local artist called Marilyn Tabatznik, we learn from the piece of paper stuck to the wall next to it. It is made from thousands of pulped police reports. 'I wanted to take something problematic and make it beautiful,' the artist wrote. We can't afford to buy it – the price tag says $25,000 – but we decide to try to meet the woman who made it.

In the city this may take some time to organise, but not here. I ask for Marilyn's number and the woman at the gallery gives it to me. I call the artist and she says, 'Come on over.' This was what the world was like before the pandemic of public relations.

That afternoon, after Mr Kiss finally fixes our airconditioner, we meet Marilyn in her studio. Lisa and I are both instantly drawn to her.

She reminds me immediately of my elder sister Megan who makes hats for a living – very beautiful hats – and is now the head milliner for the London Opera. While the style and grace of Megan's artistry is undeniable her own dress sense is a little more questionable. Megan has adopted a particular fashion that mixes lots of pinks, lime greens and purples together all at the same time. It is a look that only someone who works in wardrobe at the theatre can get away with, and then only just – a sort of slightly upmarket bag lady look. My sister once held a party where her friends were asked to come as *if dressed by Megan*. 'To have asked people to come dressed *as* me may have been too cruel,' she told me.

Marilyn has come dressed as Megan. She is a woman in her mid fifties with a mop of white hair and over her loud dress, like Joseph's coat in an Aztec design, she is wearing a floral cowgirl shirt with tassels. Around her neck is a brightly coloured necklace that's been fashioned from plastic bottle tops and other bits of rubbish, made by African village children for a poverty alleviation project. Somehow she pulls it all together.

Marilyn Tabatznik is warm and intelligent and within half an hour she invites us to stay at her house. This has happened to us time and again on our trip around Australia – outside the city people are so much friendlier. We receive dinner invitations from people we've only just met, and even offers to camp in their backyards.

My reversing skills have improved over the months and the next morning I back the van through a narrow gate and into Marilyn's life for a few days.

Marilyn was born into a working class white family in South Africa in 1951. Her father ran a small shop and served in the army. Like the rest of white South Africa, she grew up with black servants. From a very young age, Marilyn had a strong sense there was something deeply wrong with her society. 'When I was four something happened that affected me,' she reveals as we sit in the shade of her courtyard, surrounded by her sculptures. 'My nanny had nine children of her own who lived in the bush but she looked after me. One of her children was badly burned and she asked my mother if she could return to look after him. My mother said no, because her job was to look after me. The boy died. Up until quite recently, I believed I had killed that boy. My whole world altered from that time on.'

To the embarrassment of their parents, Marilyn and her sister became heavily involved in the anti-apartheid movement. They taught in the townships and were arrested several times at university in Johannesburg. It was the early 1970s and the regime was becoming particularly violent towards activists. Marilyn and her boyfriend, fearing for their lives, fled the country for London. He became a barrister while she became an academic, lecturing in comparative religion. 'We stayed together for 18 years,' she says, 'a lot longer than we should have, but that's what happens when you hold each other's history.'

A little further along the way she ditched her bloke and academia and took up art. She lived in New York, Denmark, Israel and the Sinai desert. She wandered the world and for a while worked with Mother Theresa's order in Delhi. 'Fuck knows what they got out of it, but it helped me.' She had a lover in New Zealand and when that relationship ended she wound up in Australia.

People had told her she wouldn't like Australia and when she travelled up the east coast she found that to be the case. 'It was bland,' she recalls. 'The east coast was a pastiche of America in the 1970s – there was just suburbia. It was white, really white, everything was white, no black people, and I thought, "There's got to be someone else who lives here." It didn't have any spirit for me.'

She crossed the Nullarbor to Western Australia, headed north to Monkey Mia and then decided to leave for Japan. She was planning to take a bus to Perth but when she arrived at the bus stop, 'something said, you're going the wrong direction'. Instead, she got on a bus to Broome. It was 1991.

'I arrived in Broome. It was very late at night and there was this overwhelming smell of frangipani. I'd never smelt frangipani before. It was pitch dark and they dropped me off at this backpackers in the middle of nowhere. Fuck! The smell! I couldn't identify it but it was beautiful, overwhelming.'

For the first time since she had fled South Africa all those years ago, she felt at home. She didn't meet the requirements for residency but tried anyway. 'I wrote a letter apologising for not being a 24-year-old aircraft engineer but, I said, I've just spent eight months in your country and I really believe we've got a lot to offer each other.' Within three months her application had been approved.

Marilyn has a broad perspective and we are interested to hear her views about our country. Apart from the Aborigines, she says, our history has been reasonably peaceful. 'If you look at Africa or Britain or Europe the soil has been stained for generations with blood – if you go to Israel or Russia it's stained to the earth's core. But in Australia, apart from the Aborigines, that hasn't happened. I feel sometimes like a child here. It's got an innocence that touches its people. No great horror has befallen it, except for the Aboriginal people – no wars, no great disease, no great disasters – so historically it's been that way and that's continuing. It creates a sweetness in the people.'

For Marilyn, that sweetness and innocence also has its drawbacks. Australians, she reckons, have a general aversion to plumbing intellectual and emotional depths. 'It kind of hit me after a while that it's actually a profoundly different culture from others I have encountered,' she says. 'In the general culture in Australia nobody really has had to have a depth of thinking because nothing really phenomenal has taken hold and shaken the country, so there's no reason to go to those dark depths. On an intellectual and emotional level I was quite lonely for a while until I found a group of people who were prepared to push the boundaries a little bit.'

She adds, with a laugh, 'I'm a hunter and gatherer now. I've obviously learned from the Aboriginal way – you take what's available.'

Marilyn's house is full of her sculptures. In her lounge room there is a complex steel object that spins like a carousel. She says it is an interpretation of dreams and memories. Lisa is particularly taken with a small and serene sandstone piece which Marilyn says is an interpretation of a character from *Ubu Roi*, an early French surrealist play. Out in her courtyard is a steel sculpture that contains the figure of a child within it. It is from a series she did called Silent Witness about the things children see adults do. Several times Joe, who is still mastering his scooter, almost turns Silent Witness into Road Kill. Marilyn doesn't seem to mind. 'Let him go,' she says when we try to contain him.

And so, while Joe explores, we sit, sip tea and talk about why artists find so much inspiration in Broome and the rest of the Kimberley.

Marilyn believes it's because of the extremes. 'There is a tremendous pull of the tides which affects emotion, so there's lots of emotion. The colours are dramatic, the weather's dramatic, it's quite harsh in a way too, so there's no hiding behind prissiness or pretension. It kind of peels a few layers off the onion in spite of oneself. I noticed years ago that people would come for five minutes and three months later they were sitting here changing dramatically. It's a place that changes the course of people's lives.'

Her most productive periods are during the wet season, a time that 'needs to be endured' rather than enjoyed.

'It's very intense and when the wind is blowing, the sound of the wind is deafening. The tides are much bigger in the wet season. The lightning is huge. The thunder is huge. Seven billion frogs croak when it rains, and then the crickets start. So the noise of nature is incessant. The nature here just becomes overwhelming and the air is so thick that you are cocooned by it.'

It is a wonderful town, she says, but she's concerned about the changes taking place, particularly proposals to start mining ventures. There are several projects on the drawing board, including a massive Liquid Natural Gas processing plant.

'They can fuck this place too you know,' Marilyn warns. 'They've had their way with the Pilbara and they are coming here next. I don't want to leave this place, but if there are going to be 700 helicopter flights a day taking people out to a gas rig and there are traffic jams and all my mates have to move away because they can't afford it, then who am I going to talk to?'

Even without the influence of the mining companies, Marilyn says Broome is changing. Its popularity means it is becoming expensive and that's driving people away, particularly creative types. She says a couple of good artists have recently left and she has other friends who've packed up too.

Marilyn hopes to stay — after all, she 'migrated to Broome, not to Australia'. She's comfortable with change, she says, as long as it doesn't involve big bulldozers. 'I kind of like the influx of people, it's like the tidal thing, it brings in lots of dross and lots of jewels.'

We are on the tide going out. It's getting too hot for thin-skinned southerners like us. And we want to explore the Pilbara. We bid farewell to Marilyn and turn south to a part of the country where a man in a hard hat has always been king.

37

Port Hedland is the ugliest town in Australia. And the landscape we travel through to get there is pretty ugly too.

Not far out of Broome the country becomes desolate and flat and doesn't change much for the next 600 kilometres. The hot season hasn't officially arrived but it's 42 degrees at the Sandfire Roadhouse when we stop for fuel. The journey south offers few redeeming features and is an appropriate gateway for what lies ahead.

On the outskirts of Port Hedland there are mudflats and vast salt mines on one side of the road and a railway track and a sorry slab of grazing dirt on the other. The railway tracks, which bring iron ore from the mines on trains many kilometres long, run through the old part of town and a film of ore dust coats everything. The original town centre, which contains a few decent old buildings, consists almost entirely of banks and government departments, with a couple of greasy takeaways and a pub. There's hardly a shop. On the wall of the pub are the photographs of a couple of dozen people who've been banned – from six months to life. About three or four kilometres away, there is a 1980s mall and then, at South Hedland, 18 kilometres away, another new shopping centre has been built. The town centre has been split three ways, like a watermelon with the back of an axe.

This is a large rural town of 14,000 residents. A further 4000 workers fly in and out of Port Hedland on a regular basis. And yet the town has no restaurants. Proprietors simply can't get chefs or waiters, and backpackers tend not to linger here. There's a chronic housing shortage and rents, for the most basic houses, are $1500 to $1800 *a week*. Workers who aren't on mining wages simply cannot afford to live here.

Port Hedland has been a major mining port for 40 years and yet there is no real sense of permanency. There's none of that confidence you see on display in so many rural NSW, Victorian and Queensland towns which delivered their citizens fine civic buildings designed to last a couple of hundred years. No one sets out to live forever in Port Hedland.

A good slice of Australia's export wealth has been generated from this one port. Billions and billions of dollars worth of minerals have come down the railway tracks from mines owned by BHP and others and been shipped off to become steel in the mills of Japan and China, but this place hasn't much to show for it.

Port Hedland is just the arse-end of the production line.

We get one of the last spots left in the caravan park which is brimming with mine workers. The place is hot and buzzing with mosquitoes and sandflies and there's not a tree in sight. There used to be lovely trees here a few years ago, we are told, but they were all blown over in the last cyclone.

The mayor of Port Hedland, Stan Martin, is a retired builder with a tattoo on his forearm. I meet him in his office the day after we arrive. Stan tells me the growth has simply been too rapid and the town has been unable to keep up. 'We've just completed a very interesting document called LUMP – Land Use Master Plan – which is our vision for the town for the next eight to 12 years,' he tells me, in council speak.

But the mining companies don't look like slowing down to let the town catch up. Over the next decade they plan to increase the amount of ore shipped from this port *eightfold* – from

100 million tonnes a year to 800 million tonnes a year. As I sit listening to all this, I wonder if some of that ore might belong to future generations. Just because we can dig it up eight times faster, does it mean we should? Are we going to end up like Nauru when the phosphate ran out? Why isn't our country having a debate about this?

Stan has obviously been having some doubts of his own. After giving me the mayoral blurb, he tells me he misses the old Port Hedland and is not entirely sure how good all this rampant growth is for the town and its people. He was born in Balmain, Sydney, and he his wife decided to settle here after discovering it on a trip around Australia in 1974, when it was just a little country town. They moved here to get away from the hustle and bustle of city life.

Now his own daughter and her husband have had to move away from Port Hedland. They had wanted to stay but realised they could never afford a home in a place where entry level houses start at $800,000.

'On a personal basis there's not a lot of point to it all,' the mayor tells me. 'But we have to look at the future of the country, I suppose.'

People in Port Hedland are getting rich, but at what cost? Their house prices have skyrocketed but they've lost their sense of community and their kids can't afford to buy in. The mine workers might be able to afford a Harley and a new boat but shiftwork means no one can commit to train the junior soccer team. The fly-in, fly-out workers are disconnected from their families and the rate of family breakdown among them is alarming.

And then there is the gender imbalance. Port Hedland is a town overwhelmingly of men – lonely men with plenty of cash. Wherever that occurs, prostitution follows.

I had heard that brothels in towns like this employ fly-in, fly-out workers, just like the mines. What is it like for these women, I wonder, flying home to Perth or Sydney on the same plane as the men they've seen as clients? What is their take on the mining boom? What is life like for a hooker in a mining town? I figure finding out will be more interesting than talking to blokes in hard hats about iron ore. I decide to go brothel creeping.

On the day I plan to visit one, it is stiflingly hot and the airconditioner in the caravan is struggling to keep it cool. Lisa insists on coming along with Joe to escape the heat. And so our little family of three heads off for an outing to the brothel.

After a bit of searching we find it located in an industrial estate called Wedgefield, halfway between Port Hedland and the satellite town of South Hedland. We drive down streets of welding shops, bulldozer yards and smash repairers to JEMS.

I pull the car up out the front and ring the bell. A young guy comes out and says the brothel doesn't open until 6 pm. I explain what I want and he invites us all in. 'I'll get the madam,' he says, a little bemused. 'She's actually my mother. She doesn't usually talk to journalists.'

The madam, Jo Woodward, emerges from a corridor – she is a large woman with blonde hair and a friendly face. She looks us up and down, chats for a bit and then laughs, 'You're the first bloke who's ever brought his whole family to the brothel.'

We talk for half an hour and she shows us around. We photograph Joe in the African-themed room, complete with the head of a lion. Madam Jo might not usually talk to journalists but, perhaps because our little boy beams so brightly, she invites me to come back that night so I can interview some of the workers.

'They grow up so quickly,' I say to Lisa on the way back to the van. 'Joe's first visit to a whorehouse, and he's not even two.' Our little boy is spent and snoozes contentedly in the back seat.

Jo Woodward came to Port Hedland from Sydney four years ago. The 54-year-old and her boyfriend were going to set up a business taking tourists into Karijini National Park. The business never got off the ground and the relationship ended. Jo, a registered nurse, also had some experience managing brothels back in Sydney.

'A friend rang me up and told me this place was for lease and I thought I'd give it a go.' She called her business JEMS – Jo's Escort and Massage Service. I suggest Boom and Bust would be a great name for a brothel in a mining town. 'I like it. I might use it next time,' she giggles as we sit sipping Bintang in the kitchen of a four-bedroom house behind the brothel. The girls live in this house while they are here, each has her own room. The accommodation is basic, but neat and tidy and good by Port Hedland standards. Each girl flies in for two weeks to a month and then flies out again. In that time she can earn a lot of money. It is so lucrative that one of the girls working tonight flies over a few times each year from New Zealand.

'The girls come up here to make big money and then go home to do whatever it is they have to do – pay school fees, pay off a debt, buy a bigger house,' she explains. 'All my girls have had previous experience. I don't take on any newcomers.'

Jo is a member of the Chamber of Commerce and sees herself as providing an essential service. She says all the girls have an ABN and pay tax. 'If they don't pay tax they can't save money and they just waste it all.'

I chat to the girls in between jobs and towards the end of the night Jo says, 'Do you think Lisa would like to work on reception for a few nights, to see what it's really like?'

I tell Jo that I'll ask her, but I already know the answer.

38

(by Lisa Upton)

'You know everyone's going to think you're a hooker,' whispers Greg. We have just walked into the mess hall of the single men's quarters for dinner with Madam Jo and her sex workers. I am already feeling self-conscious but now I start to blush. This is a fishing expedition and I am part of the bait – I can feel every eye upon me. I glance at the other women. It's no secret they're sex workers and yet they seem perfectly comfortable to be here, advertising themselves as they wait in line for corned meat and white sauce. And what better place to reel in clients: this is home to 1000 men in the mining game, many of them lonely, bored and cashed up. 'Modern-day prospectors without prospects,' quips Greg.

The buffet offers classic RSL fare. There are creamy potato salads, pasta bakes drowning in cheese, overcooked vegetables and a lot of meat. As I make my selection, Madam Jo leans towards me, chicken leg in hand, and announces smugly, 'Got my first client for the evening.' By the time we've made our way 20 metres across the dining hall to our table, she's hooked her second. 'Can you guess who they are?' she asks, once we're seated.

'I wouldn't have a clue,' I say. I haven't dared look at anybody.

I wouldn't feel so conspicuous if I had Joe in my arms, but he's attached himself to a woman whose working name is Nikki. While he sits on her lap and digs his fingers into her roast beef, Nikki tells me she enjoys working in Port Hedland 'because the men aren't too fussy'. They're obviously not very fussy about their food either, I think, as I pick at the plate in front of me.

For the next half hour, Madam Jo talks me through my new job. For two nights I will be a trainee receptionist, working alongside a woman called Tracy. I will be provided with a uniform and I will greet clients and answer the phone. 'It's important that you don't speak for too long,' instructs Jo. 'Sometimes the men will want to keep you on the line while they're . . . you know what . . .'

Then she adds, 'I'll fill you in on how to answer questions about anal sex back at the office.'

Three hours later with Greg and Joe tucked up in bed, I walk into the brothel. Four men are on their way out, including a Greek captain and three young Asian men from a ship that docked earlier in the day. The Asian men's eyes are all possum-wide – they seem as surprised to be here as I am.

The reception is a spacious room with a large L-shaped lounge and a big fish tank. The yellow walls are adorned with cheap prints of Monet masterpieces and scantily clad women. On the desk there's a showgirl lampshade with beads dangling from it. The base of the lamp is a woman's legs clad in black high heels and fishnet stockings. It emits a soft red glow. Next to the lampshade sits a small wooden penis made in Bali.

Madam Jo greets me and tells me the receptionist, Tracy, will be along shortly. She then escorts me through a hallway to a small room where the sex workers are gathered. I am not familiar with the social hierarchy in a brothel and am not exactly sure how I should interact with them. I find myself sounding deferential.

While I fumble through the small talk, Anna, Ava and Nikki touch up their makeup. Anna is the most reserved of all the women. She is wearing a cute little number, like the one Marilyn Monroe wore in the famous shot of her trying to stop the wind blowing up her dress. Marilyn wore white, Anna is wearing midnight blue. She is petite with shoulder-length brown hair pulled up in a ponytail. If makeup is a mask, she's well disguised.

Ava looks like a sex worker. She's wearing a tight little black dress that clings to her voluptuous figure. She has long blonde hair, sultry lips and solid legs that are still solid at her ankles. I would have guessed she just stepped off a plane from Eastern Europe except she speaks with an Australian accent.

And then there's Nikki from New Zealand who is warm and vivacious and the kind of woman I would expect to meet on a netball court. She would play centre or wing attack. She's wearing a black boob tube and a short pink cotton skirt with a ruffle. Around her neck is a striking blue stone that she tells me is a 'replica of an opal'.

Jo hands me a shirt that looks like a Retravision uniform from 1990. It is electric blue with a collar and buttons and slightly puffed sleeves. JEMS is embroidered above the left breast. It is the antithesis of sexy. I wear it with black pants.

Jo and I do a quick inspection of the various themed rooms: the Asian room, the Blue room, the Monroe room and, my personal favourite, the African room. The queen-sized bed is covered in zebra-striped cushions and a faux leopard skin rug while the maroon walls feature two enormous lions' heads, like those you can win at the show if you have a talent for shooting little yellow ducks.

'Now,' says Jo, after she's checked that each ensuite contains soap, deodorant and mouthwash. 'If a man asks you about anal sex just tell him it has to be negotiated with the particular lady. It's the same with kissing. The women don't kiss. Any extras have to be personally negotiated and all the money goes straight to the lady.'

'How much will men pay for anal sex?' I ask.

'Could be anywhere between $200 and $400.'

She takes me through the price list. $250 an hour ($130 goes to the woman); $190 for half an hour ($100 for the woman). Then there's the 20-minute option, popular with young blokes who don't have much money and don't take too long. It sets them back $160. The women will also visit men in their homes. An escort, as it is known, is the most expensive option at $280 an hour.

Back in reception, Tracy is on the phone. She's running through the list of women available tonight. 'There's Nikki. She's a brunette, she has blue eyes, she's curvy, she's 24 and she's a size 10. Then there's Anna ...'

When she's finished, Jo introduces me. Tracy is 27 years old, a big woman with long black wavy hair, pale skin and stunning cornflower blue eyes, courtesy of the coloured contact lenses she's wearing. At first glance she looks a bit like a Goth but when she smiles her face is transformed. I see something beautiful – a combination of compassion and vulnerability.

Tracy shows me how to use the database. And then she warns, 'Men will hit on you. It happens to me all the time. Lots of guys who come here ask me out on dates but there's no way I'd go out with any of them.' The problem is, she explains, there simply aren't enough women around. 'Every woman in Port Hedland has a boyfriend no matter how fat she is or how ugly.'

There is a knock at the door. Two men walk in. One is a big, scary bikie dude covered in tattoos who looks about 45. Beside him is a smaller, younger man with a black eye. They have been drinking.

Because there are no other clients, the men can choose which sex worker they want.

'The girls will come out to introduce themselves one at a time,' says Tracy. She explains they're not allowed to hustle for business or to seek an unfair advantage. 'If you don't watch closely some of them might offer to give extras, like kissing, for free.' To ensure this doesn't happen, Tracy beckons me to stand beside her in the middle of the room where we can catch every word. Like a pair of overzealous school mistresses, we're ready to pounce on any prostitute who makes a promise she shouldn't.

Anna is the first to walk out. She is very formal, she offers the men a quick hello and a limp handshake and then turns on her heel and prances back up the hall. Ava's handshake is a little more firm. She is followed by Nikki who collapses onto the lounge between the two men and puts her arms behind their shoulders. 'Hello there,' she says with gusto. 'I'm Nikki. I hope you men are having a lovely evening.'

The bikie opts to spend 30 minutes with Nikki. The smaller man with the black eye says he will wait for his mate.

Tracy and I sit back behind the desk and she starts to tell me about herself. She's lived most of her life in Port Hedland but has also spent some time in the Northern Territory. Tracy and her mother worked as cleaners in a Darwin brothel but she makes it clear she has never been a working girl. 'These girls have sex with more men in one night than I've been with in my whole life.'

Tracy used to work at the local Shell service station, on an isolated block, not far from the brothel. One day Madam Jo asked if she knew anyone who wanted to be a receptionist. Tracy said she'd like to give it a go. For a while she juggled both jobs, but before long she started feeling safer at the brothel than she did working overnight at the servo. At Shell she worked alone and there was no grate separating her from the customers. 'One night I accidentally hit my emergency buzzer and it didn't even work. I called the police to tell them I was okay and they didn't know what I was talking about.'

And then she got sick and was admitted to hospital. Jo rang her and asked whether she needed any help. Somebody from Shell also called, demanding to know when she'd be back at work. Tracy quit the job at the service station and came to work at JEMS full time.

Over the next few nights I will come to appreciate Tracy's many skills. She is savvy and a survivor and her cunning brings in extra money for the business. She is a wealth of information because both the sex workers and the clients confide in her. She knows which women are offering extras for free, which clients can't get it up and who gets turned away with the clap. She will tell little lies to cajole men into the place and then to lure them back. She is friendly but she never flirts. She is also discreet. When she sees a client in the supermarket with his family she will turn in the other direction to avoid an awkward moment. She worries about the wellbeing of the workers and has no hesitation throwing a man out if she feels he has acted inappropriately. Any kind of violence, including sex she deems too rough, and she will ban a man for life.

She tells me about a particular incident that took place in the African room one night recently. The woman had agreed to have anal sex but before long Tracy became concerned about the noises coming from the room.

'What kind of noises?' I ask.

'Rough noises. I could hear him thumping into her. I kept banging on the door asking if everything was alright.' The woman said she was okay but Tracy says the noises suggested otherwise. When it was over the sex worker was in tears. Tracy told the man never to come back. 'It's the quiet ones you've got to watch,' she confides.

Tracy is a woman who knows a thing or two about violence. Her former partner, and the father of her two young children, used to sometimes treat her as a punching bag until she finally decided to leave him. As a parting gesture, he beat her until her skin shone purple.

Now she is having a relationship with Tim, an American in South Carolina with whom she connected on the internet. They have never met but speak on the phone for a couple of hours each day. She calls him in the early hours of the morning when she gets home from work, before her children are up. They had a bit of misunderstanding at first. 'He saw a photo of me and said I looked a bit thick. I thought he meant dumb but they use the word thick in America to mean carrying a bit of weight.' Tim apparently likes 'thick' women. Tracy tells me she has recently lost 27 kilos.

Tim is with the US marines, 'He fought in Iraq and he killed people, even babies.' Tracy says that Tim talks a lot about God and, because of his influence, she is thinking of joining the Catholic Church. 'He knows he's going to heaven but sometimes he jokes that he's going to hell because of all the bad things he's done.'

Nikki, who has spent 30 minutes with the bikie, joins us in reception where the conversation about religion continues. Nikki says she was a member of a non-denominational church in New

Zealand for many years. 'I had a big trauma when I was about 12 years old and the church was a good place to be because nobody was looking at me sexually.'

Later, I ask Tracy whether all the sex workers have had a traumatic experience that has led them to do this kind of work. 'I really don't think so,' she says. 'They earn very good money and a lot of the women do it for that reason. Anna told me she used to dream of being a hooker when she was a little girl. She's a make-up artist from Queensland. She's passing herself off as 25 but she's actually 39. Her boyfriend has no idea that she does this.'

Over the next few hours we answer the phone and greet a handful of men, but it isn't until my second night, a Thursday, that I see the place in full swing.

When I arrive at 10 pm, the reception is packed. The place has the feel of a doctor's waiting room except the men aren't staring at their feet or reading magazines five years out of date. They are actually talking to each other. In groups of two and three they wander outside to smoke cigarettes. There are all sorts here: well-spoken geologists, pimply-faced teenagers, middle managers, working class miners, single men who are lonely and married men with their list of excuses.

It takes me a while to register why this feels so strange. And then I pinpoint what's bugging me: it's the sense of normality. Nobody seems self-conscious or uncomfortable. In this context, what they are doing is not only legitimate, it is mundane. It's as ordinary as their monthly haircut or their yearly dental checkup.

Anna, Ava and Nikki are all working again tonight, along with an attractive woman called Toni, who is of Pacific Islander heritage. When Tracy is on the phone talking a potential client through the list of available women, she also mentions a mature-aged woman called Jazz.

'Is Jazz working tonight?' I ask when she gets off the phone.

'No, she's not back until tomorrow. I thought I'd just tell him that in case he's interested in older redheads. Might get him in the door.'

Over the next few hours, Tracy and I are busy answering phones, meeting men and ushering the women from one client to the next. I get confused about how long each woman has been with a man and forget occasionally to knock on a door when the time is nearly up. Tracy doesn't miss a beat.

I keep wondering how the women cope, going from man to man with just a quick shower and a change of sheets in between. Physically it must be exhausting, I think. Nikki tells me at one point, 'You've got to manage your time in the room. You can't let them pump you the entire time.' There's talk, there's massage, there's oral sex and then, at the end, intercourse. Pacing yourself, she tells me, is essential.

At midnight two young men, probably still in their teens, walk in the door. They tell us their names are Matthew and Jason. Matthew has brown scraggly hair and bad skin. Jason is tall and skinny and bald. Matthew does the talking. He speaks in monosyllabic grunts, like a few of the dimmer boys I knew in high school. He looks at me as though he hates me. I know before he tells me that he and his mate will be taking the 20-minute option. But there's a hiccup – their credit cards don't work. Matthew says they will go down to the service station, withdraw some cash using another card and be back as soon as possible. Tracy guides them out the door.

'Will you hold the girls for us when it's our turn?' Matthew asks her.

'Yes, I will,' she says.

'Will you really?' I ask when they've gone.

'No, but I want to make sure they come back.'

They return before long and are asked to wait. Matthew is eventually ushered into the Asian room, but his friend is forced to sit even longer. When Jason's turn comes he is sent to the Blue Room with Toni, but he isn't there for long. Toni conducts a routine inspection of his penis and discovers it is covered in sores. Jason tries to tell her he burned it as a joke to impress his friends. Try getting a story like that past a sex worker. Jason has genital herpes.

Tracy is informed and she takes charge. She doesn't want to see Jason embarrassed in front of the other men so she picks up the phone and, with a ring tone in her ear, walks through the reception area speaking loudly into the mouthpiece.

'I am so sorry,' she says in front of all the men in the waiting room. 'I completely forgot that you booked Toni for two hours. Look, if she hasn't started I'll pull her out of the room. Can you just hold on a moment?' She disappears into the Blue Room. Her little soliloquy, designed to save face for Jason, is entirely convincing.

Tracy gives him a refund and then says her challenge is to get Toni another client as soon as possible so that she doesn't lose any money. She can't bring Toni back into the reception area, but somebody calls a few moments later wanting a woman to visit his house. The brothel's driver, 60-year-old Ian, takes Toni to the appointment.

As they leave, a fit, 40-something man with a moustache and a receding hairline comes out of a room after an hour with Ava. He is keen for more. He walks over to the desk, looks me straight in the eye and says, deadpan, 'I'm just soooo horny.'

'Well I guess you're in the right place then,' I mutter.

'I want to go again.'

'I'm sorry,' I say. 'I'm pretty sure Ava is going out on an escort.'

'That's fine. Is Nikki available?'

Nikki will be available shortly and this man, Andrew, is happy to wait. Tracy whispers that he's new in town and has been spending every second night here. One evening, he stayed for seven hours and had sex with every woman in the place. He didn't want to leave but after spending $1750 his credit card was maxed out.

Nikki, when she emerges, is only too happy to see Andrew. 'If he's got the money then I've got the time,' she whispers to me before disappearing into the African room.

In the early hours of the morning, a sweet man called Lachlan arrives. He's wearing an orange miner's uniform and has some sort of mild intellectual disability. He pays to have sex with Toni, who's returned from the earlier escort job. When she greets him, Lachlan looks at her as if she is the great love of his life. 'It's great to see you,' he says tenderly. 'How are you?'

'I'm fine,' she says breezily, trying to lighten the tone. While, it's only fleeting, I'm sure I catch her squirming as she leads him away. I wonder if it is his disability that offends her or whether she simply doesn't like emotion attached to a business transaction.

Finally, things slow down a little. The sex workers are still with clients but the waiting room is now empty. Tracy and I sit and chat for a few minutes until there's another knock at the door. Three men wearing singlets and covered in tattoos walk in. Each of them is carrying a can of Jim Beam and Cola. 'I'm a member of the Frequent Fuckers' Club,' one of them announces loudly. 'Does that mean I get a discount?'

'I want to watch porn while we wait,' demands another.

Tracy is polite but firm. She tells them they can't have a discount and they can't look at porn. They can, however, watch any of the DVDs available including *Collateral* which is currently on the screen. I glance up at the TV and see a blood-splattered Tom Cruise sitting on a train.

'Okay, then, are you girls going to come out and talk to us or are you going to sit behind that desk like a pair of snobs?' asks one of the men.

Tracy obliges but I can't bring myself to follow her. From behind the computer I listen to them talk. The men demand to know just how pretty the girls are and which one is the slimmest. They all want to have sex with a size 10, a size 8 would be even better. Tracy says that a couple of the women are size 10.

'Well what does that mean? Are we talking 60 kilos?'

'What about a virgin? I want to fuck a virgin.'

Tracy walks back to the desk and I ask her if these men are going to be trouble. 'No, they're fine. They're just showing off.'

I find them disgusting. I know it's time to leave. I thank Tracy for being such a generous host and then say goodbye to Jo, who's playing cards with her son and a couple of friends. She gives me a big hug, takes my photo and insists I keep the uniform.

I collect my bag, hop into the Volvo and check the rear vision mirror three or four times. And then I drive, faster than I should, out of Port Hedland's industrial area. It is a 13-kilometre journey back to the cocoon of the caravan and my secure little world – a place where kisses aren't negotiated extras.

I burst in the van and all my toxic thoughts come tumbling out. 'Disgusting, undignified, revolting,' I bellow. Greg lifts himself slowly onto his elbows and looks at me, groggy with sleep. 'Darling,' he says, softly, 'surely you didn't expect to find anything glamorous in a country brothel?'

39

One of the most recognisable beats in Australian rock'n'roll is the fast-knocking thump in Midnight Oil's 'Dead Heart'.

> *We don't serve your country,*
> *Don't serve your king.*
> *Know your custom, don't speak your tongue.*
> *White man came took everything.*
> *Da, do, do, do, do, do, do, do.*
> *Da, do, do, do, do, do, do.*

The *do, do, do,* was inspired, says the band's drummer, Rob Hirst, by the knock of an axle on an old Toyota four-wheel drive hammering across a gun-barrel track in central Australia.

We have plenty of time to contemplate such things as we leave the hookers of Hedland and head south to escape the heat. Radio National is our saviour and we've been inspired by a program about the influence of the landscape on Australian music.

We stop at Coral Bay and plan to do some snorkelling on Ningaloo Reef but are blown off the beach by a constant wind howling in from the Indian Ocean, day and night. It follows us south to Kalbarri, where we persist for a couple days before giving in and scurrying south to Perth, where one of Lisa's best friends from university, Kirsti, lives in a big house with a big backyard. There's a spare bedroom and a couple of playmates for Joe. Luxury!

We let Joe run free, drink good wine, eat out at restaurants, sleep in a real bed and talk to our mates about the things in WA that have piqued our interest: music and mining. Kirsti and Jamie and their kids moved from Annandale in Sydney to Leederville in Perth three years ago in the hope of buying their own home, but the mining boom hit and prices soon matched those in Sydney.

At the kids' school, a large proportion of the parents, particularly the men, work in the mining industry or in jobs that service the industry: engineering, public relations and information technology. Kirsti, who works for the ABC, says when she first arrived she was shocked by the lack of criticism or debate.

'People I spend time with are well educated. They're concerned about the environment, they recycle and they worry about climate change. But they don't talk about the mining that's currently taking place. To be fair, though, I've never brought it up. I can hardly ask them how they reconcile their concern for the environment with the fact that their family makes its money from mining.'

But Kirsti isn't standing on the sidelines looking down her nose at her friends. She's confesses she's actually considered applying for a job in the industry. 'Every week I look at the employment section of the newspaper and see if there's a job I could do, some sort of community relations role. I can't believe I'm actually considering it.

'You just get swept up in it. You start looking at what you're doing, what you're earning and you think, if I just did this for a couple of years I could go from renting to actually buying a house.'

From mining, the conversation moves to music. They tell us about WA's vibrant music scene — it's a state that's consistently produced great acts, from Rolf Harris to The Waifs.

Kirsti suggests we try to contact John Butler, the head of the John Butler Trio and one of the most successful musicians to come from WA in the past few years. She has a bit of a crush on him — he's a pin-up boy for the mulching and recycling set.

Butler honed his amazing guitar skills as a busker on the streets of Fremantle and is now one of Australia's biggest-selling artists. He is also a generous philanthropist, supporting young and indigenous musicians with scholarships and donating to environmental causes. He has worn dreadlocks for about a decade and has been referred to as the Million Dollar Hippie since appearing on the *BRW* list of highest earning Australian entertainers.

But how to contact him?

I have a friend called Max who also has dreadlocks and who has worked in the music industry, managing band tours. I ring Max and ask him if he knows John Butler. He does. (There's a secret society of dreaded people around Australia – they are like the Masons without combs.) Max is, in fact, good friends with Butler's sister and knows John. The problem, he says, is that John tours for 10 or 11 months of the year and is not often home in Fremantle. Max puts in a couple of calls.

We are in luck.

The next day my phone rings. It's John Butler. He's at home and invites us over.

Lisa, Joe and I head off to his house with a bag full of juicy lemons from the garden. 'Don't forget to tell him they're from Kirsti,' says Kirsti, adding that they're organic.

We arrive at the house, a cute and modest wooden cottage in one of Fremantle's charming narrow streets. There's nothing rock'n'roll star about it.

I knock on the door and there's no one home so we wait, with our bag of lemons and our son.

John Butler arrives about five minutes later in a green Subaru and apologises for being late – he's just dropped the kids off somewhere. He is smaller than I had expected and he has recently chopped off his trademark dreadlocks. He's dressed neatly in a pair of trousers held up with an old Scouts belt – more mod than hippie. There's a touch of Johnny Depp about him.

John invites us inside and Joe immediately takes off into the garden out the back, after spotting some toys. We sit at a table in the backyard to talk. John's wife, Danielle Caruana, has her own band and is away on tour while he's at home minding his daughter Banjo and son Jahli, aged five and two.

John speaks with a slight American accent, the result of having spent the first years of his life in California with an American mother and an Australian father. He offers Lisa and me a small bottle of Chinotto and explains that his American accent was not appreciated when he moved to the country town of Pinjarra, an hour south of here, at the age of 11 in 1986.

'Pinjarra was pretty much a segregated town in those days,' he recalls. 'The Aborigines lived on one side of the tracks and everyone else on the other. I came into town thinking I'd just blend in but I had this enormously strong American accent and had to deal with xenophobia for a very long time.'

People tend to romanticise what it's like to grow up in rural Australia, but if you don't conform it can be a difficult experience. 'There's a brutality there that people don't want to talk about,' he says, tapping his bottle of Chinotto. 'I have come to terms with it and with those people, but it was hard for me for many years.'

He hung out with other outsiders, sometimes with the Aboriginal kids, and spent a lot of time out in the bush, camping. 'Me and my friends would pack up the station wagon and go out bush, play guitar, smoke pot and go swimming. I was just trying to find a culture apart from barbecues and sport. You could escape the yobbos, you could escape the cops and you could head out and make your own world.'

That childhood bullying is something that's obviously inflicted deep wounds and later in our conversation he says he's thinking about taking up martial arts. 'I still struggle with the notion of peace,' says the 33-year-old. 'I'm thinking about doing martial arts and hope that learning how to protect myself will make me believe in peace a lot more.'

How?

To understand peace, he says, he has to overcome fear and to overcome that deep fear he needs to know that he can protect himself – possibly from those yobbos who once held him up by the throat at a party, just because he had an American accent.

In those sometimes lonely teen years his guitar, he says, became his therapy.

'I played as a hobby and it was there as an outlet for all that stuff I was going through, as a way to make sense of the racism and the segregation or the girlfriend dropping you and cheating on you with some other guy. The guitar was a great diary entry. It helped me get through. It wasn't like something I was going to do. I was going to be an art teacher or a skateboarder.'

After school in Pinjarra he moved to another world, to university in Fremantle, where he enrolled to become an art teacher. Fremantle was full of freaks, just like him. There were wogs, punks, hippies, Goths and buskers. There were also coffee shops, cobblestoned streets, history, venues and to some extent anonymity. He loved it from the moment he arrived.

He relished just wandering the streets of the old city and soaking it up. It's something he still enjoys. 'I walk through the old town at least once or twice a week when I am home. I do nothing but just feel it. My wife laughs at me all the time. She says, "So you're going to the Round House again to stare at the buildings." And that's what I do. I just feel the place. I walk and I just feel it.'

It was on these streets that he first began busking and realised that people liked what they heard. They started buying his self-produced tapes for $10 each and after a year of university he dropped out to pursue a career as a busker. He built a following from his tapes, was soon playing gigs and then started touring.

It was here too, on the streets of Freo, that he found love. One day he wandered out to get some breakfast and came across this 'gorgeous girl' who asked him for directions to a café. The next day, while he was out busking, he saw her again, riding a bike. Something stirred in the shy guy and he plucked up the courage to shout out to her. 'Yesterday you asked me for directions and now you're riding through town like you're a Freo local. Who do you think you are?'

They shared a cigarette a few nights later at a gig and then he went off on tour, supporting The Waifs. He travelled with them to Sydney and then went on tour alone up through the middle of Queensland to Mount Isa, Darwin, Katherine and across to Broome. After this massive trek he stopped his van in Broome, got out, and there sitting on the ground was the same girl he had seen cycling in Freo.

'Hello, Mr Butler,' she said. 'What are you doing in Broome?'

It is a long, romantic tale, and he loves telling it. We get the short version and that lasts for 15 minutes. He is still very much in love and he somehow manages to get away with the soppiest of love songs about her, 'Daniella (be my Cinderella)'.

> *You light me up, little girl, like the 4th of July.*
> *I love you more than every single star man in the sky.*
> *You are the best damn thing that ever happened to me.*
> *Want to take you home start making family.*
> *You are a damn fine lady like no other,*
> *Want to introduce you to my father and my mother.*
> *I am damn happy you want to be my lover,*
> *Can't wait to get you home and get you under the covers.*

He says that meeting Danielle gave him confidence as a person, and pushed him, musically. 'I rose to her occasion. I was quite happy being a bit of a stoner, I guess, and she gave me something to stand for. I think good women do that. You see a lot of boys who don't want to become men and they get these great women and they realise if they want to keep them they need to take life to the next level.'

We spend about an hour chatting while Joe plays in the garden until John has to pick up one of the kids. We organise to come back the following day.

He thanks us for Kirsti's lemons.

We tell her he said they were the juiciest bag of lemons he'd ever seen.

★

The next day we sit in the living room, a space that could belong to any lefty from Fitzroy to Surry Hills. There are some musical instruments, a little bit of art and a couple 'No Uranium' posters. They even have a flatmate, a chiropractic student, who looks after things while the family is on tour.

John is uncomfortable with being described as the Million Dollar Hippie. Most of the money he makes goes back into the business, he says. He's spent almost $2 million breaking into the US market and says he pays himself only a modest wage.

But he has a dilemma few hippies ever have to face – what to do with a lot of money. He has set up a scholarship program for young and Aboriginal musicians called the JB Seed. Other artists, such as Paul Kelly, The Waifs and Missy Higgins contribute but John and Danielle are the backbone. This year the project will hand out more than $400,000 in scholarships.

He also gives generously to organisations like the Wilderness Society and the Australian Conservation Foundation.

Those groups, he says, need all the help they can get because the 'pirates' are just having their way in Western Australia. 'Every mining company comes in and says that they will do things differently, but I don't think any of them have a great track record,' he claims.

There's no proper debate, he says. The mining companies have convinced everyone that unless they have unfettered access to everything the state will be in turmoil. His views put him at odds with many in the mining state, including some old friends.

'People can make choices about what they do,' he says. 'They can go to Kalgoorlie so they can afford to buy a new flat screen TV, but I am hardly going to endorse it.'

These people, he says, are 'hardly in touch with their own spirit so how are they going to feel the spirit of what they're doing'.

Lisa and I both like him but he sometimes sounds like a first-year university student when he talks about the 'implications that come with colonisation and imperialistic economic regimes'.

★

Still, he loves the west and while he was born in the United States he says he feels Australian and he has a great connection to the land. 'When I am away I dream about this place. I dream about the smell of the eucalypts and about the places that I've camped all up and down this coast.'

About seven years ago, John and Danielle moved to Melbourne, where her family is based, but he couldn't stand the weather and they moved north to Byron Bay where their daughter was born.

'We came back here for Christmas and it just hit me like a rush – the big sky country. On the east coast it's a different sky, having the sun set over land. Here, as the sun approaches the ocean each evening I get a very deep lovely feeling.'

Perth and WA have developed an interesting music scene, he reckons, being so far from other major cities. 'We have access to music from around the world but the isolation here produces something unique,' he says. 'If you isolate something in a Petri dish something interesting usually comes out of it.'

He has other appointments now so we thank him for his time. Before we go, though, he shows us something he's just bought. It's a tagine, a Moroccan cooking pot. He wants to impress Danielle and asks if we know how to use it and what to cook.

Tagine, I tell him, is just a flash word for stew. Chop it up and chuck it in, is my advice. A day later I email him one of my favourite recipes for a lamb and date tagine.

He sends back his thanks and signs off 'Peace, John'.

The next day we pack up to leave Perth. We are 5000 kilometres from Sydney and yet it feels like we are almost home.

But first we have to find the keys. We search through Kirsti and Jamie's house for an hour without any luck and then we do it again. In desperation we bribe the kids, Daisy and Jesse, to join in the hunt. After 15 minutes in the garden, Jesse returns triumphant with the Volvo key. He found it in a garden bed in the backyard. We pay him his $2. Joe, it seems, is not too keen to resume life on the road.

40

Joe now has about 20 words. One is beer and another is wine. He's just learned cheese and he gets plenty of practice using all three because we are in Margaret River, visiting vineyards and sampling the local goodies.

The Margaret River region is undoubtedly one of the prettiest parts of Australia. The tall jarrah forests are grand and impressive, the surf rolls onto pristine beaches, the fields are green, the cattle plump and the people pleasant. But after six months in the north it all seems a little too prissy – great for a weekend away, but not the place to linger on an adventure around Australia. Too yuppie, we tell each other. So, after three or four days, we pack up our Persian fetta, quince paste, chilli olives, sesame seed crackers and bottles of Margaret River reds and whites and head east until we come to Albany.

I love it the moment we arrive. Albany is more than five hours' drive from Perth – too far for city weekenders. The old port city is yet to be gentrified and still has a gritty feel.

The town is stretched out around a magnificent deep-water harbour. It is protected from winds that roar up from the Southern Ocean by two bald-faced cliffs, like a pair of whales, at the harbour's entrance. A military base was first established here by the British in 1826, the first white colony in the West, and until the construction of a port at Fremantle in 1900 this was Western Australia's major port.

On a hill, overlooking Princess Royal Harbour, grand sandstone and timber houses sit alongside humble fibro and tumbledown workers cottages, all within walking distance of the port. Rich and poor share the same view. Albany is a regional hub of 25,000 people and yet it's the sort of place where people still run a sheep or two on the spare block next door to keep themselves in mutton.

The caravan park is right on the beach and 20 bucks a night.

We are deep in Tim Winton country. He moved here from Perth when he was 12. Winton says that Albany is Australia's second great harbour town, after Sydney. But it has a dark past.

'That whole whaling thing was so grim,' the writer said in a recent interview. 'We used to go out and watch whales get chopped up for something to do ...

'The stench was just unbelievable. I mean, I can still smell it. Every now and again I'll pick up an implement in some old bloke's back shed, like a shovel, and he's got whale oil on it and instantly I'm in Albany, bang, in 1973 and it never goes away. I think the sort of carnage and the strange kind of war on nature has a sort of a psychological effect on a place.'

From 1952 until 1978 more than 5000 humpback whales and 14,600 sperm whales were taken by Albany's whalers.

People now come in their droves to see live whales. And what was once the scene of the carnage, the Cheynes Bay Whaling Station, is now Whale World – one of the best regional museums in the country. Everything from the whaling days is still here: the flensing decks and the enormous boilers used to turn the blubber into oil. The giant steel tanks that once stored oil now house movie theatres that show visitors short videos from the whaling days. There's an excellent photographic display. Even one of the old whale chasers, *Cheynes IV*, is on display.

Lisa and I take turns to have a look around while Joe enjoys the play area. There's a big concrete whale with a slippery dip for a tongue that he slides down again and again.

'1978 is not such a long time ago,' I say to Lisa, when Joe finally gets bored with the whale and its tongue and we drive back into town. 'There must be people still living here who worked in the industry. I wonder what they think now about those days?'

After a few phone calls, I track down Mick Stubbs, a man with a place in Australian history.

Whaling was one of the first industries in Australia. The whalers arrived not long after the First Fleet. Over the next two centuries thousands were taken. It all ended on the afternoon of 21 November 1978, when a whale chaser called *Cheynes III* came in through the bald heads at Albany to the safety of Princess Royal Harbour. Mick Stubbs was standing on the bridge of the *Cheynes III* that day with a beer in his hand, 'which would have been a Swan Lager in them days'. Public disgust at the slaughter, rising costs and the development of synthetic oils consigned these men and their occupation to history.

Mick's wife, Dawn, died 12 years ago and he lives alone in the same fibro cottage he occupied in 1978. It has a million-dollar view out across the bay. He invites me in and we sit at the kitchen table where the condiments – Worcestershire sauce, Saxa salt, McKenzie's white pepper, soy sauce, Vegemite, coffee and a packet of Arnott's Ginger Nut biscuits – have a permanent home on the table. The place is bachelor tidy – neat, but in need of a good scrub.

Mick, who's 67, is wearing a faded orange towelling hat. The nicotine from countless boxes of Stradbroke 50s has stained his grey, seaman's beard. He's a stocky man with a melancholy face.

He was born in Albany, he tells me over a cup of coffee. His father was the captain of a whale chaser. Mick followed him into the trade. He worked for a few seasons on whalers up north, out of Carnarvon, chasing humpbacks, but returned to Albany in 1963 when the humpback whaling was banned.

The whalers here then switched to hunting sperm whales. The continental shelf is only a few nautical miles off the coast of Albany and the whalers would steam out to the shelf to pick off the sperm whales as they rounded the corner of Australia to head north.

'They were off the shelf, feeding on big squid,' Mick says. 'They'd come up from the south and follow the continental shelf west.' Three whale chasers from Albany would head out to the shelf and a spotter plane would take to the skies to direct them to the whales.

The boats would steam up beside the whales and the skipper would come down from the bridge and man the harpoon. It was always the skipper's job to deliver the blow. The harpoon was fitted with a grenade which would explode inside the whale.

'Would you aim for the head?'

'Nah. You wouldn't get a harpoon into a sperm whale's head, they're that hard. Nah, you'd aim behind the flipper and hope to hit some vital organ and once the grenade head exploded they were gone. Sometimes the harpoon would just go straight through him and you'd just have a hole. It was cruel at times . . .'

The whales knew they were being chased and would try to get away, but from 1970 onwards, with the fitting of sonar, there was just no escape. The whales would dive, sometimes for an hour, and when they rose for air they would be harpooned.

In Albany, whaling was a big employer. Whalers were well paid and well respected, even when the tide of opinion was starting to change around the world. Mick rose to be first mate on the *Cheynes III*, second in command, and was paid a wage of $25,000, a big sum for the time.

He remembers the protestors coming into town and the animosity he felt towards them. 'That bloody Jim Cairns and his trollop, what's-her-name Gina Morosi, they came here. They had a protest out at the whaling station and the cops tried to run them out of town. We hated them. They even sooled a local bikie gang onto them at one stage. They were trying to steal our jobs.'

But deep down, he says, they all knew what they were doing was unsustainable and that whale numbers were declining.

On the morning of 21 November 1978, Mick walked down to the wharf at 6 am. Normally the crew would have been out on the water before dawn but they had a union meeting that day to discuss their severance pay.

'We buzzed off at about 7.30 am and steamed out to the shelf,' he tells me. There were 13 blokes on board: the skipper, the first mate, a sonar operator, four deckies, a cook, a couple of firemen and three engineers. The mood was sombre but occasionally broken by someone telling a funny yarn.

They hit the continental shelf three nautical miles off the coast and turned east while the spotter plane buzzed overhead. They searched the seas until early afternoon and then word came from the pilot that there were no whales. 'Any whales that he found, further east, would be tomorrow's whales and there was no tomorrow.'

And so they headed back for shore.

There were a couple of dozen live shells that had to be let off, for safety. The captain let everyone have a go, firing the live rounds into a vast ocean. Then they cracked the Swan Lager and 200 years of whaling in Australian waters came to an end.

'It was a good life,' Mick says as he gets up to boil the jug again, 'an adventurous life.'

Things were never the same after that. 'When it closed down, the government wanted to whack us up in the coal mines. Well, you been at sea you don't want to be underground, do ya?' He was too old for the prawn trawlers so he tried his hand at tuna and other types of fishing, but nothing was ever quite as exciting.

Mick shows me the front room of his cottage. It is a shrine to whaling and packed with memorabilia he's collected over the years. There are harpoons on the wall along with flensing sticks and two enormous whale penises, a metre and a half long. In the middle of the room is the wooden wheel from an old whale chaser. There are barometers and lifebuoys and pictures of Mick as a young man with a sparkle in his eyes. There are beautifully carved whale teeth. And there, on the floor, in three old wine flagons is the gold they sought – whale oil.

I ask Mick to take off the lid to have a sniff. It smells a bit like pungent vegetable oil. It doesn't conjure up the same scenes of carnage for me that it does for Tim Winton.

I ask Mick if he had his time again, would he go out on the boats.

'No,' he says, without hesitation. 'I have had a lot of time to reflect upon the cruelty of it all. It was very cruel. I remember once chasing a pregnant humpback cow off Carnarvon, when I had just started out. It was heavily pregnant and about to give birth. Anyway, we chased it in towards some rocks but it couldn't stay in there and when it came out we knocked it off.'

He hesitates for a bit, lights a smoke and says. 'I thought it was bloody cruel. I can still see that cow now.'

I meet Mick twice over two days and we talk for a couple of hours each time. When he talks of whaling he uses the language of an old soldier – they did what they had to do. It was acceptable at the time.

But that doesn't mean it hasn't affected him.

Like Tim Winton suggests, the 'war on nature' has had a lasting impact.

41

Australia is the sixth largest country on the planet, behind Russia, Canada, China, the United States and Brazil. It takes up a fair percentage of the bits of the earth that are not water. So it is with more than a little surprise that I open the door of our caravan in Esperance to find Tim Smead and one of his kids standing in front of us.

This is the same Tim Smead we first met six months ago in Cairns travelling with his wife Kate and their four kids. Since then we've driven about 20,000 kilometres – half the circumference of earth. We met the Smeads again briefly, in Alice Springs after we'd been robbed and they'd trashed their caravan on a treacherous track. And here they are again, in Esperance, at the bottom of Australia. What are the chances?

'G'day journos,' says Tim, forgetting our names. We reintroduce ourselves. We are staying in an enormous park and the Smeads are camped just 10 metres away. Had they been staying in another part of the park we may have missed them. There are another two or three caravan parks in town.

There are only two choices, I figure: invite them for dinner or call the police and get an order, stopping them from stalking us. It's cold and blowy and Joe needs someone to play with – dinner wins out.

The blustery wind continues into the night and once they've put their kids to bed the four of us squeeze in around our kitchen bench. Over dinner – a seafood chowder – we exchange stories of our adventures. They too are heading east across the Nullarbor, but unlike us, they have actually planned how they are going to do it.

Many days we have driven out of a town in the morning, only to drive back again after 20 kilometres, having forgotten fuel. We never know where we are going to stay. We only planned one thing on the entire trip, our visit to Mulan, and look where that got us. The Smeads have booked ahead. They know where there's fuel, they've got emergency supplies, they've got videos to keep the kids occupied and they've even bought enough small chocolates to give each child one every half an hour across the Nullarbor. Tim is an engineer and can fix things – I reckon he used to be a Scout and is carrying a mirror. If he breaks down he will be able to alert passing pilots with a glint of reflected sunshine.

We decide to drive in convoy. After travelling by ourselves for so long it is lovely to have the company of another family.

The Nullarbor is not what I expect. I had a vision of it being desolate and arid – a place of unending boredom. But much of the vast plane supports spindly eucalypts or small shrubs and there's been rain. Occasionally we see flowers. The Nullarbor is spruced.

Maybe we have changed too and we can now appreciate such a landscape.

Much of the Nullarbor was deemed too inhospitable for wheat, sheep or cattle and yet, ironically, it is in far better shape than the agricultural land either side of it. Much of that land is degraded after having been cleared for crops or for grazing on soils too light and too dry to support either.

The days of driving are meditative and relaxing – there's nothing to do but look at the scenery. I read somewhere that Greenland has a thousand words for snow. I reckon Australia should have a thousand words for green, I tell Lisa.

'There should be words to cover the whole spectrum, from the vivid tones of the rainforest to the dull olives of the mulga scrub. There should be at least 20 words for shades of dull olive.'

'There probably are,' says Lisa. 'On a paint chart.'

At Eucla, near the South Australian border, we stay in a park high up on an escarpment overlooking the Great Australian Bight – it's as if we're looking out at the end of the world.

There's a tiny settlement here at Eucla and I can't imagine the lives of those who live here. There are a couple of policemen whose months of boredom, booking speeding motorists and truckies must be punctuated by moments of horror – pulling the ones who've fallen asleep from their mangled vehicles. But what do they do the rest of the time, 500 kilometres from the nearest town, here on the edge of the earth?

We chat at night with the Smeads. Travelling around Australia is something they have wanted to do for many years and they haven't been disappointed. Their trip has been a very different one from ours. Kate said she wanted to show the kids the 'icons' of Australia – Uluru, the reef – and that it has lived up to all their expectations.

They have been shocked, they tell us, by the conditions they've witnessed in some of the Aboriginal towns. They hadn't really expected things to be as bad as they are. Both of them are committed Christians – Kate's dad is an Anglican minister. Tim says they would like to do something practical to help through their church when they get home. But just what, he's not sure. 'Maybe it could be as simple as spending a couple of weeks in one of the communities helping to fix blocked toilets and broken windows. I just feel that we should be doing something.'

The Smeads have only encountered Aboriginal Australia from afar. Tim tells me the only conversation they have had with an Aborigine was with a person in the mall at Alice Springs who had tried to sell them some art.

There are racists in Australia – and we've come across plenty – but I reckon they are vastly outnumbered by people like the Smeads who would like to help, who would like to see things change but are not sure what they can do. I am not sure anyone does.

Tim and Kate have been married for more than 10 years and say they have always had a strong relationship. But Kate says she saw this trip as a chance to strengthen the bond between them and the children. It has been great, she says, for Tim just to hang out with the kids. But there have been challenges too.

'Our van is terrible for intimacy, although we haven't entirely missed out,' she says, cheekily. 'One night eight-year-old Annabelle woke and yelled at us to stop rocking the van!' They need a panel van sticker.

The next day we stop to look at the whales that come to calve at the head of the Great Australian Bight. We've missed them by two days, the ranger says. Further on we come to a section of scrub that has been burned out by a bushfire. The new leaves are bursting into life while the charred remains of the old scrub look on, like portraits of long-dead ancestors hanging on the wall.

After a massive drive we cross the last of the Nullarbor and arrive at a little place called Streaky Bay, at the top of the Eyre Peninsula. Here, golden wheat fields run right down to the ocean. It must be one of the more pleasant places in the world to plough a paddock. It's an old town right on the bay and most of the houses are built facing the street, indifferent to the view.

One afternoon, Joe and I go for a walk on the jetty. There is a fisherman on the end of it. He's an Irishman with a strong northern accent. He reckons Streaky Bay is paradise on earth and he's been coming here for years, for holidays.

'How long have you been in Australia?'

'Twenty-five years. I came from Belfast.'

Jokingly I say, 'Ah, still on the witness protection program from The Troubles, even after all these years.'

The man packs up his things and without a word walks off the jetty.

We push on a couple of days later, with the Smeads, to Port Lincoln.

SOUTH AUSTRALIA

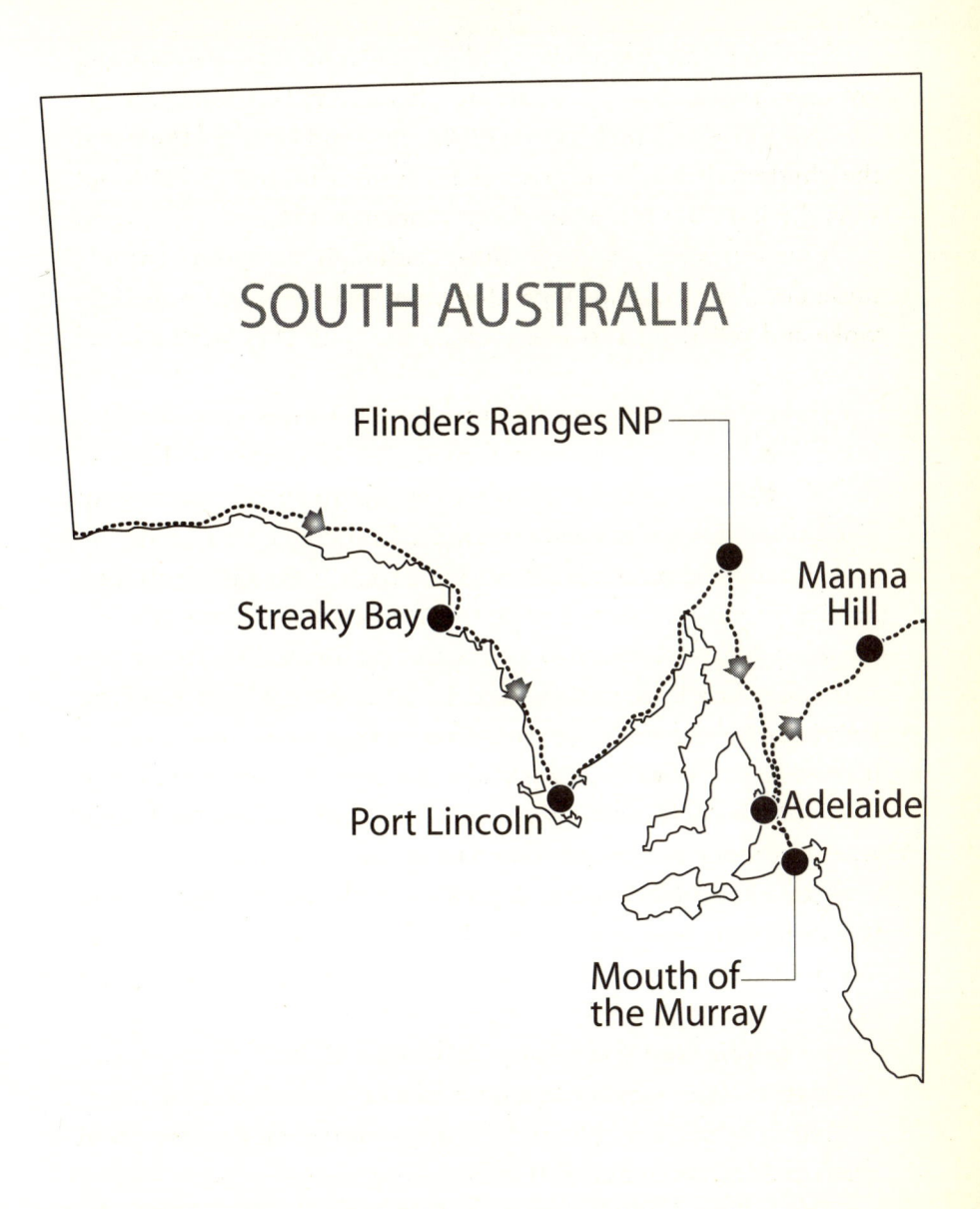

- Flinders Ranges NP
- Streaky Bay
- Manna Hill
- Port Lincoln
- Adelaide
- Mouth of the Murray

42

Port Lincoln is a town with a swagger.

It sits inside the western lip of the Spencer Gulf, 650 kilometres from Adelaide, on an enormous sweeping bay protected from the ravages of the Southern Ocean by Cape Catastrophe. From the main street you look out through a line of Norfolk pines, over a park and onto the calm waters of Boston Bay.

In this park there's a life-sized bronze statue of a horse. It's a representation of the champion mare, Makybe Diva, who is owned by a local fisherman called Tony Santic. When he first bought the horse, Santic couldn't think of a name for his nag so he left the decision to the women who worked in his business, Tony's Tuna. The women, Maureen, Kylie, Belinda, Dianne and Vanessa, used the first two letters of each of their names and the horse went on to win a record three successive Melbourne Cups.

In one corner of Boston Bay, there are giant grain silos and a jetty that juts out into the water for several hundred metres. The opposite end of the bay is dominated by a building – a seven-storey 111-room luxury hotel. There's nothing like it in a town of this size anywhere else in Australia.

It is owned by another local tuna fisherman called Sam Sarin. The story goes that Sam didn't think the accommodation or the restaurants in Port Lincoln were up to scratch. He wanted somewhere he could entertain the Japanese tuna buyers who came to town each year to buy his fish. So Sam built himself a hotel and has a seat at the best table in the best restaurant in town any time he wants. It just cost him $55 million to build the hotel.

He also refurbished the local cinema, which was about to close, and when he heard the town's indoor swimming pool was going bust he bought it and kept it open. The pool has a giant water slide and Joe and I spend an afternoon sliding down it again and again. The tuna boat owners also chipped in to help refurbish the lovely theatre in the civic centre, which now has retractable seating for 500 patrons.

In the past few decades billions of dollars have been generated from fishing in Port Lincoln, a town of 14,000 people. But, unlike mining towns such as Port Hedland, where the wealth ends up in Melbourne or London, the money generated in Port Lincoln has stayed largely in the town.

And it is not just a little bit of money. Sam Sarin, the richest of the tuna men, appeared on the 2008 *BRW* rich list with an estimated wealth of $500 million. In this provincial town there are said to be more than 50 people who are, on paper at least, worth more than $10 million from tuna, prawns, abalone and lobster. Port Lincoln can lay claim to being the richest town in Australia.

And most of those who've made their fortunes here were migrants who came to Australia with nothing.

When they arrived, in the 1960s, it seemed the resources of the sea were endless. But by the late 1980s over-fishing here and elsewhere, particularly by the Japanese, almost led to the collapse of the tuna industry. In 1985, a quota of 14,500 tonnes was enforced for Australian fishermen with similar restrictions on the Japanese and New Zealanders. But the stocks had been so depleted that it was not enough. In 1989, the fishermen had their quotas – and their incomes – cut by two-thirds to 5265 tonnes.

Just about every tuna fisherman in Port Lincoln was in receivership and the place was 'like a ghost town'. But a local fisherman, a Croatian migrant called Dinko Lukin, saved them all. Dinko is the father of Dean Lukin, who won a gold medal for lifting the equivalent of a couple of fridges above his head at the 1984 Olympics. Dinko devised an ingenious method of catching wild tuna at sea and towing them back to Port Lincoln in big cages, fattening them along the way.

The industry changed completely in one season. Fish that was worth $1 a kilo at the cannery was now worth upwards of $40 as fresh sashimi in Japan. The tuna quotas were suddenly more valuable than gold and unbelievable wealth rained down on those who possessed them. It was the same for those who held abalone, lobster and prawns quotas.

'It was,' says Hagen Stehr, one of those migrant fishermen who faced bankruptcy in 1989 with $20 million worth of debt, 'like manna from heaven. It was as though the skies opened up and it started to rain money.'

Hagen Stehr and his wife Anna live in a mansion overlooking Boston Bay, up the hill from Sam Sarin's hotel. At the front of their house is an enormous stainless steel gate that slides back to let me in. The gate has been copied from Tiffany & Co in London.

Sixty-six-year-old Hagen meets me at the gate. He is a big, powerful man with short-cropped silver hair and a head on him like a Hereford cow – his friends call him Box Head, The Hun, or worse.

It must have been hard being German, I suggest, coming out here not long after the war. 'It was hard, but I am fucking arrogant you know. The Bible says you should love yourself first before you love any other bastard. People always tell me what an arrogant prick I am. At first, it was fairly raw, but I could handle myself pretty well.

'Anyway, I always tell people that not only am I German, I am Aryan – I am super white.'

He leads me down into the house, which is light and open and airy. He and Anna have owned it for many years and have recently had it completely renovated. The living area opens out to a pool and beyond that is an uninterrupted view of Boston Bay.

Hagen proudly shows me his art collection and his wife joins us. The first major work they bought was a portrait from Pro Hart's Monday Morning Miner series. It is a picture of a miner, despondent after a weekend on the booze. Hagen paid for it with 1000 pounds of prawns 25 years ago. The Stehrs's taste has become more sophisticated over the years – also adorning the walls are pictures by Hans Heysen and Clifford Possum.

Anna tells me she buys art that is beautiful while Hagen buys art that he thinks will appreciate in value. 'He won't buy anything unless he has first seen it in a book,' she explains, and he always bargains hard. Recently, she says, they were evicted from a gallery in Tasmania because Hagen 'hassled and hassled' and when they'd finally agreed on a price, he said he didn't like the frame and wanted a discount, or a new frame. The owner threw him out, Anna giggles, because he just went one step too far.

In the dining room there's a massive jarrah dining table that seats 12 people and on the walls are pictures of Hagen with famous people. The photograph of Hagen and the former Prime Minister, John Howard, taken at the Lodge, has been removed and sits on a sideboard, ready for storage. 'I sat next to him at dinner,' Anna says. 'He's a nice guy.'

Hagen describes himself as a 'fairly right-wing lunatic' but he has friends on both sides of politics. Labor's Federal Minister for Trade, Simon Crean, is a good mate, he says, as is the former Liberal Finance Minister, Nick Minchin. He hates nobody, except if they're from the Greens or Democrats.

'I am what you call an industry leader,' he says.

'What gets you access?'

'Money. Donations.'

Then he adds, 'It is not just the donations – we can make it easy for those guys or we can make it hard for those guys.' They always take his phone calls and they bestowed an Order of Australia on him, which he shows me proudly.

The South Australian government recently put forward a plan to turn 45 per cent of the South Australian coast into a marine park, which would make it difficult for the tuna men to farm their fish.

'This week I rang the minister. I said, 'Minister, what the fuck is going on?' I got a place in North Adelaide so he came to my place. We talked and talked and talked and we got somewhere. But that takes years and years of experience.'

Hagen Stehr came to Port Lincoln in 1960 as an illegal immigrant. He was 20 years old when he jumped from a Swedish ship that had come from Nauru with a load of phosphate. He had been in the French Foreign Legion, he tells me, in North Africa, before joining the Swedish ship.

When the vessel docked in Port Lincoln, he and some of the crew went to a party in town and got pissed. Everyone was so friendly that seven of them just decided to stay.

They went down to the police station and the sergeant told them to get a room at the pub until the immigration official arrived from Adelaide. If they got drunk, they would be deported, the policeman warned. The immigration official flew in a fortnight later, gave Hagen some papers and told him to behave himself. There was no Baxter Detention Centre then. The next day Hagen started work with the council digging ditches for the town's new sewerage scheme.

He didn't last long. Men with strong backs and seagoing experience were in demand on the tuna boats. It was back in the days when tuna were still polled. It was tough physical labour. Hagen worked his way up, got an abalone licence followed by some lobster pots. Then he bought his own tuna boat. He never looked back.

Of the 12 richest tuna fishing families in Port Lincoln one is an Italian immigrant, 10 are Croatian and then there's Hagen. 'Why didn't any Anglo-Australian's make it as tuna men?' I ask.

'Because where we had come from was bloody tough. The Aussies had this laissez-faire attitude to things – they don't work Saturday. They get pissed, go to the footy. These immigrants came from nothing and they were highly competitive and they bloody work hard. From the middle of December until the middle of

January, the middle of the tuna season, no Aussie bastard would be out there. They would all take a holiday. I would be out there working right through Christmas, along with all those mad Croats, and would come back in the middle of January. People would say to be me, "You greedy bastard," but I would say to our crew, "Now you go home and now you have party. Buy your wife a nice dress and this and that." The moral of the story is that we just took that extra yard — it is nothing to do with superior intelligence.'

Anna says that her husband is driven to succeed, over and over again, to prove himself to his mother, a dour Prussian woman who said her son would never amount to anything. Hagen's parents, whom he describes as 'both fucking Nazis — literally,' divorced when he was 12.

By 1972 he was making good money and wanted to show off to his family. He bought a brand new Holden Monaro with an enormous bull bar on the front, and had it shipped to Italy. 'Everyone in Europe has a Mercedes. But I wanted to show them the Australian Mercedes.'

He and Anna and their two young children flew to Naples where they picked up the Monaro. It had Northern Territory number plates. Hagen drove triumphantly to Germany to the 'shit-box ugly industrial town' where he grew up. He parked the car out the front of the family home and walked in. His mother and all his uncles were waiting. He had a bag full of money and he tipped it all out onto the table. 'There's plenty more where that came from,' he said.

Anna laughs, revealing that they were actually quite broke at the time. 'By the end of the trip he was ringing his bank manager up saying, "I'm out of money, can you send me some money," and the bank manager told him he needed to come home.'

Hagen flew his elderly mother out recently, first class, and she stayed with them in their big house. 'I have 220 people employed. I earn a lot of money. My mother looked at me and asked when I was going to get a proper job. I got so pissed off. I said, "Mum, what do you want me to be? A foreman in a Volkswagen factory?" And she looked at me and told me I could do a lot worse.'

We speak for an hour or two, then Hagen has to go back to the office. He is in the middle of a big project that he calls the Holy Grail. Apart from his tuna fishing business he has invested heavily in aquaculture and his company has perfected a technique to breed and farm yellowtail kingfish – a world first. His scientists are now working on breeding tuna. If they can crack it, the industry will be revolutionised, he says.

'It's a completely new horizon... Some people said it is equally as important as when Armstrong took his first step on the moon. I'm not saying that but other people have said it.'

He goes off to his meeting about the tuna moon landing, and we arrange to meet the next day. I leave the mansion for our little caravan by the sea.

Our travelling companions, the Smeads, decide it's time to move on. We say goodbye and for a while I lose Lisa to that scoundrel, Barack Obama. She has become obsessed, quoting passages from both his books and oohing and aahing over everything from the 'elegant way he crosses his legs' to his vision for Middle East peace. In between talking to tuna men, we sit in our caravan glued to the internet and the US Presidential race. We watch Obama's beautiful acceptance speech and John McCain's gracious concession.

Joe makes friends with some other kids and plays contentedly in the nearby playground as parents take turns to supervise. As Lisa and I sit alone in the van, I reach over and squeeze her hand. I stare into her eyes and give her *The Audacity of Hope* look. Today, she's saving herself for Barack.

I leave her to her new love and return to the Stehr's house that afternoon. Hagen is not home, so Anna and I sit at the giant jarrah dining room table and chat.

Anna shows me some photos of their wedding. She was an incredible almond-eyed beauty. At 62, she is remarkably well preserved.

Hagen and Anna met when she was 17. Her Greek father owned a drycleaning/fruit and vegetable business where Anna worked. One day, Hagen came in to pick up some clothes, started chatting her up and insisted she come to the movies with him. Anna said she didn't go out with boys but he refused to take no for an answer. She snuck out. Her father was waiting on the verandah for both of them at the end of the night. It was a rocky relationship between the two men from the start.

Initially Anna's father didn't want his daughter marrying a German. But things changed when she became pregnant and had a little boy called Marcus.

Marcus now works in the family business. Anna says Hagen and Marcus have a feisty relationship and that she is often called in to mediate. Anna believes Hagen is too hard on their son and attributes it to her husband's own upbringing.

She says her own relationship with Hagen is wonderful but she has to work hard to keep things fresh. 'You've got to try to keep yourself neat. Take pride in how you dress and what you cook. We still have candles and I keep the romance going. When he walks in the door I race up and give him a kiss and still flirt with him. That's the secret to a happy marriage.'

But living with Hagen, she says, is like 'living with a volcano. When he walks through the door you don't know if he will be sleeping or erupting.

'Hagen is actually very insecure. That's why he loves accolades, he loves praise, he loves uniforms. It confirms he has achieved and that he is a success. Every day you've got to reassure him that he is a success. I often feel sad for Hagen because I think he hasn't got true peace or contentment in his heart. He's always striving, searching, wishing. He doesn't have the ability to sit back, relax and say, "Hey, I've done well, I'm a success."'

She pulls out three enormous leather-bound journals. They contain every newspaper article that's ever been written about Hagen.

Hagen comes down the stairs and into the house as we are looking at the journals. He points me to the significant stories and says he'll have his staff photocopy them for me. He's in a good mood, a sleeping volcano today.

We sit down and he tells me what a wonderful country Australia is and how it has given him so many wonderful opportunities.

'Best country in the world. Without a fucking doubt.'

He tells me about being invited to a dinner at the Australian Embassy in Paris a few years back – him, a bum fisherman from Port Lincoln.

'Anyway they sat me next to this guy and he introduces himself. He said, "I am George Clooney." I didn't know who the fuck he was – the penny didn't drop. I thought he must be the ambassador for Luxemburg or something. I said, "I am Hagen Stehr from Port Lincoln," and we talked about fishing. I am just yap, yap, yap. He seemed interested. I then asked him what he did, what country he represented. He said something about making movies. I said, "Oh yeah, I been on *60 Minutes*," and this and that.'

Finally the ambassador said, 'Hagen, it's George Clooney, the movie star.'

'I said to him, "Shit mate, why didn't you say so?" I mean, I didn't think he was all that big or exceptionally good looking. If I was a woman I would not want to make love to him.

'Anyway, he was making some movie and they were using the embassy in the shoot. The movie was called *Beach 11* or *Beach 12*, or something like that. You know what? The guy's a fucking communist. We sat and argued for three hours. I like George Bush. I like the war. I said to the ambassador the next day, "I don't care who you invite, don't sit me next to any fucking communists." But it was a lot of fun.

'I have since found out that a lot of people from Hollywood are left wing, or what you say, liberal, in their approach.'

Lisa and Joe arrive to pick me up. Anna insists on giving us three bottles of Shiraz from her own organic vineyard. Hagen orders me to come with him while he loads me up with two big boxes of tinned tuna.

We walk up the stairs, wave, and the gates of Tiffany & Co, Port Lincoln, close behind us.

43

Fatigue has set in and the nomadic life is getting to both Lisa and me. We limp on around the Spencer Gulf to Adelaide, stopping off at the Flinders Ranges. We camp near Wilpena Pound, pop Joe in his backpack and go walking in the national park. It is beautiful but I am bored. We've been living this gypsy life for almost 10 months now and the comforts of home are beckoning. We yearn for our king-sized bed, our friends, some fresh sushi and an oven. I've tried cooking a roast in a pot but it's just not the same.

Then there's the constant mess. We attempt to keep things tidy but it seems we are not natural-born campers. There are people who have compartments for everything and we watch them enviously as they pull up next to us, unfurl their caravan annexes or tents and then settle down with a cup of tea. Each time we move it takes more than an hour to pack up and when we arrive at our destination it takes another hour to park, let down the 'bedrooms' which fold out at either end of the van, erect Joe's cot, put down the stabilizers, pop the top, hook up the hoses and power, then think about what we'll have for dinner. Within a few hours of setting up, our camp resembles a housing commission estate, strewn with toys and eskies and upturned chairs. We wait hopefully for DOCS case workers but they never arrive.

And what about poor Joe? I remember being in Year 6 at Guyra Central School and getting excited about the annual school camp to Bonny Hills at the coast. One day my mother announced that Dad had something very important to tell us. When Dad arrived home from work, he sat my little sister Jenny and me down and said, 'Kids, this year I am coming to school camp to help out.' I'm not sure if I cried, but I wanted to. My dad at school camp! How embarrassing! I had hopes of pashing Jenny Pickering – or her sister, Lindy!

Sometimes parents can be *too* involved in their children's lives and I wonder if this is the case with Joe. I know all the literature says that contact in the first two years is vitally important, but can you overdo it? We spend 24 hours a day seven days a week with him. Is he bored with us?

Luckily, Granna Joan flies into Adelaide and the poor kid has some relief.

44

South Australia is known for Don Dunstan, bizarre murders, great food and a dying river. Dunstan, the former premier who famously wore a pink safari suit into parliament, is now dead. While we are in Adelaide there's a double-page spread in *The Advertiser* where a senior police officer reassures us that South Australia has no more murders than anywhere else in the nation. The disappearance every few years of entire extended families and a host of weird murders, like the bodies-in-the-barrels at Snowtown, were all just run-of-the-mill occurrences that could have happened anywhere, he claims. With assurances like that, we are left with good food and bad water.

We have been conducting a competition to find the worst meal in Australia and so far the Chinese restaurant at the Gloucester Bowling Club is running equal first with the Italian restaurant at the Kuranda caravan park. In Gloucester one night we thought we would treat ourselves to takeaway. I arrived back with a meal so foul that each dish was inedible – even the steamed rice. 'But the cook,' I said to Lisa, 'he was Chinese. I saw him.' 'Yes,' she replied, 'probably a very good diesel mechanic in Guangzhou before this.' In Kuranda we ordered a vegetarian pizza and beneath a rubbery mound of processed cheese we discovered chunky pieces of raw celery and carrot. When I took it back the man at the counter handed me my money without a mumble, as if it was part of the job description.

And so it is a joy to be in Adelaide – a city of good food. I am enthralled by the Adelaide Central Market. I usually hate markets – all that potpourri, ridiculously large cakes of expensive soap, purple velveteen dresses for hippies and Goths and wooden toys that grandparents buy for grandkids, thinking they can compete with a PlayStation. Adelaide's market, by contrast, is bliss. There are stalls that sell 20 types of mushrooms while others specialise in salami. You can get a strong, smooth cup of coffee and there are escalators for Joe that go up and down, all day. You can even buy vanilla bean and elderflower ice-cream. It's my idea of heaven.

We visit the galleries and then the Adelaide Hills and see those grandfatherly gums that inspired the artist Hans Heysen. All the while Granna Joan dotes on her grandson – he's just happy to have someone other than Lisa or me to play with.

One night I meet up with my friend Max. Max is, allegedly, the World's Most Handsome Man. He's a scientist who studies birds in the Simpson Desert. Women say that he is extraordinarily beautiful. Gay men say the same thing. I can't see what the fuss is about. Anyway, in between his desert jaunts he manages touring rock bands and is in Adelaide with a British group I'd never heard of called Bloc Party.

Max and I go out to a good Chinese restaurant for a meal of duck. As we are eating dinner, deep in an earnest discussion about saving the world, four young women at the next table are falling in love. As they leave one of them slides a note onto the table and walks out the door. I pick up the note and laugh. Max is embarrassed. 'Dear Sir,' it reads. 'I don't normally do this but I am quite taken by you. Could we meet up later for champagne, coffee . . . whatever. Amanda 0423 798 . . .'

This sort of thing only happens in the movies to people like that communist, George Clooney. And Max. I am not sure what those Hollywood pinkos would do in such a situation, but Max is a gentleman.

He texts the woman to say he is flattered but he has a girlfriend. 'She's a lucky woman,' beeps the reply.

In the morning I tell Lisa about the woman and the note.

'How did Max know it was for him?' she asks, grinning. 'Did she place it on Max's side of the table? Are you sure? It could have been for you. Isn't it a bit presumptuous of Max to think it was for him?'

We both giggle. It was for Max.

We're inclined to linger in Adelaide, eat more good food and let Joe work on his new moves in the caravan park playground; sliding down the slippery dip head first. But we also feel obliged to visit the mouth of the Murray River. It's not something we're desperate to do. It feels more like an obligation, like paying our respects to an ailing aunt.

The drive south-west of Adelaide takes us through undulating wheat fields, irrigated vineyards and some dairy country. But the closer we get to the mouth of the Murray the drier it becomes. This was once a major dairy area but most of the milk men have sold up and moved on. The water is now simply too salty to be used for irrigation or to water cattle. The river system is on dialysis.

The mouth of the Murray River has become a sombre tourist attraction, like a cemetery on a battlefield. It's a place to lament and reflect. A steady stream of vehicles makes the pilgrimage to the end of what was once one of the world's great river systems. People get out of their cars, grim faced, hands in pockets, to be confronted by a sign saying 'Murray River Sand Pumping Project'. Beyond the sign there are barges and pumps working day and night to keep the water flowing into the ocean. The water in the lagoons and lakes at the bottom end of the system are actually below sea level. The seawater is held back by weirs.

Millions of tonnes of salt, sediment and refuse have been washed down the river to end up here. The pumps are, literally, pushing shit uphill and into the ocean.

We wander down over a sandhill to watch the barges and pumps at work. Recently I'd watched a *Four Corners* program which revealed the Queensland government was still allowing irrigators to extract even *more* water. 'I think it's unfortunate that southern commentators, ill-informed southern academics, concentrate on Queensland,' said the Queensland Water Minister, Craig Wallace. His words are ringing in my ears. There's nothing academic about this.

In the great battle for water the river simply lost out.

The Murray–Darling is Australia's food bowl and in the past 50 years countless giant dams have been built in its upper reaches and on the plains. Millions of hectares have been levelled to grow irrigated crops and this is the end result.

The wetland closest to the ocean, the Coorong, is now largely dead. This was once one of the country's most important fish and bird breeding grounds and it is now a watery desert the same consistency as the Dead Sea.

The pumps are running day and night to try to save the lakes just upstream – Lake Alexandrina, Australia's largest freshwater lake, and Lake Albert – from going the same way as the Coorong.

I talk to a few people about what is happening and someone gives me a phone number for Henry Jones, a man who has been fishing on Lake Alexandrina all his life.

I make contact and one morning I rise before dawn to go fishing with Henry on the lake. Henry's grandfather was a fisherman on the lakes and now his grandson has followed him into the game. I want to hear his take on the water debate – he's not an academic or a commentator, just a fisherman.

There's a chill in the air when I arrive at his house at first light. Henry is waiting and issues me a pair of gumboots and a weatherproof fisherman's jacket. He is a short, stocky man in his sixties with his hair combed to the back of his head, like a country butcher.

The lake is only a few hundred metres from his house. We drive his car, loaded with plastic tubs, down to the water's edge where the boat is moored. Henry first began fishing here in 1961, he tells me on the drive down, and in those days the morning sky would be filled with birds. There's none to be seen this morning.

The cement ramp that used to lead into the water stops 100 metres shy of its destination. We drive across to where the water has retreated and then wade out through thick mud to get to the boat, carrying the plastic tubs with us. 'The lake has never been this low before, not for thousands of years,' says Henry. 'The mouth of the river is the kidneys of the whole Murray–Darling basin, the only place we can get unwanted nutrients and salt out to the ocean. It's been happening for millions of years, but when it closes or when there's not the flow, the kidneys aren't working and everything slowly dies.'

We push out into the water and power out to where he has his nets set. Hundreds of fisherman used to make a living, right up and down the Murray–Darling system; this is the last commercial fishery left. Here 34 small-time fishermen make a living from the lower lakes. They operate under strict, self-imposed conditions, covering the length and number of nets, number of boats and employees. There is no trawling. They don't use electronic winches and when they dig for cockles it's all done by hand. The fishermen have voted to do things the old-fashioned way to save their fishery.

The problem for Henry and the other fishermen is not a lack of fish, but a lack of water.

In 1981, for the first time in living memory, and possibly for thousands of years, the water coming down the Murray stopped flowing into the ocean. It was the boom years for cotton irrigators further upstream. That was the year the Murray cod, a fish that had inhabited these estuaries for hundreds of thousands of years, disappeared from Lake Alexandrina.

Today, three times more water is being extracted than it was in 1981. In the past year, thanks to over-extraction and drought, the level of water in Lake Alexandrina has dropped more than a metre.

It breaks Henry's heart to watch his lake disappearing. 'I've fished it for nearly 50 years so I know every channel, every rock, everything in the lake. At certain times of year there are certain places where the fish will run and so, yeah, that's where I set my traps.' He has no sonar or electronic fish finder.

'My grandson works with me two days a week and with his father three days a week. I'm teaching him and I'm really enjoying that. I'm getting up in the years and it's really nice to be able to pass something on. I guess that's one of the reasons I've worked so hard to keep the Murray in a reasonable condition.'

We reach the first of Henry's nets after 15 minutes on the water. He cuts the motor and puts on a pair of pink rubber kitchen gloves. He reaches into the water, picks up a float and slowly drags the net up until he comes to a fish. It's a European carp, an introduced species which has now infested the entire inland system. The carp is the rabbit of the river system.

Carp, he says, have a bad name but they're still edible. 'I'm not saying it's the best. But it's good protein and we'd be really silly to throw it out. The way we eat it is simple. I cut the bones out of it, powder it with flour, put salt and pepper on it, olive oil, heat the pan, put oregano in the olive oil, cook it two minutes either side ... it's good.'

There's a demand for carp at the Sydney fish markets. It's popular with Asian customers and Polish people traditionally eat it at Christmas, as we do turkey, he says as he untangles one from the net and tosses it into a tub.

He soon pulls up a good-sized bream, some more carp and then a couple of golden perch. The perch are the prized fish and last week he was getting $25 a kilo for them at the market. Carp and bream fetch $4.50. Redfin, another introduced species, sells for $13.

'The prices are pretty good so you can make a good living fishing this way. We don't need to fish it out. It is a lovely lifestyle, being out here on the water.'

But for how much longer?

There has been talk about putting a weir across the bottom part of Lake Alexandrina and letting the salt water flow in. It is a plan that horrifies Henry Jones.

'It would be the ecological equivalent of letting off a nuclear bomb. The system has operated like this for hundreds of thousands of years and there is a push by some people down the bottom because they want to float their boats.'

We motor on to his next net.

The only answer, Henry says, is to allow more water to come down through the river system. The ecology and the lower lakes need to be on at least the same footing as the irrigators upstream.

'It can be saved, all we've got to do is get more water. I could see all this in 1981 but in those days no one would listen to me. The mouth closed for the first time in at least 8000 years, probably longer, and since then it's got progressively worse.'

A flock of a dozen pelicans floats on the water as Henry pulls the net in.

'Those poor buggers are in strife,' he says, motioning towards the birds. 'I look after them as much as I can, keep a fair sort of colony going but they're in real trouble because the stocks are down and the species that they eat are in real trouble, so I feed them some of my bream.'

For another few hours Henry works his way around his nets until the tubs in his boat are loaded with fish. On the way back to his house he gets me to take the wheel while he starts filleting fish, ready for market.

Back at his house, he invites me in for a cup of coffee. We sit at a table which is laminated with a poster of Fish of the Murray River. 'There are 46 species of fish in the Murray–Darling,' he says, pointing to the poster. 'Twenty-seven are in danger.'

Now when Henry Jones speaks about the need for more water, people listen. They know he's right, they know more water needs to come down the system. How this can be achieved is the difficult question.

Before I leave, Henry takes me out into his shed. He's filleted a couple of good-sized golden perch and he wraps them up for me and issues cooking instructions: olive oil, garlic, and dust them with flour. Cook them for a minute or two each side and then serve with a squeeze of lemon.

I drive off wondering what the future holds for Henry's grandson and the perch of Lake Alexandrina.

45

Manna Hill, a dot on the highway with a pub and a police station and not much else, sits on a barren stretch of the Barrier Highway, 350 kilometres from Adelaide and 150 kilometres out of Broken Hill. Our map indicates it has a petrol station, which is fortunate because we are almost out of fuel.

I drive up and down Manna Hill's main street, the only street, but can't find a petrol station. There are some old bowsers outside the pub with bits of hessian strung over them. I figure it's my only hope. The bar is dank and smelly and there are two old women inside, one behind the bar and one on a stool, the type of people who inhabit a bar in the middle of nowhere at 11.30 am on a Tuesday. They are sipping schooners.

'We don't sell fuel no more,' the barmaid says, as if I'd asked for credit.

'It says on the map you can get fuel here.'

'Well I don't sell fuel no more. I've taken down the signs. Yous'll have to go back to Yunta.'

'Is there anywhere else in town where I might be able to get some?'

'Dunno. Ask the copper.'

The police station appears to be locked up. I knock on the door and there is a little commotion inside, as if I have interrupted something.

A dog starts growling from behind the door and after a short delay a policeman appears.

He's a tall man in a khaki South Australian police uniform.

'Mate, you wouldn't have any fuel would you?'

'Why didn't you fill up in Yunta?' he growls.

'Our son was asleep and we didn't want to wake him. And the map says you can buy fuel here.'

'You've got to think,' he says, tapping his head. 'Don't believe what you see on the maps. You should have filled up when you had the chance. You could die out here you know.'

He then gives me a long spiel about being prepared in the outback. I don't point out that we are standing beside the main highway between Adelaide and Sydney.

Finally he reveals he has 20 litres of diesel that I can have for $35. I say I'll take it.

He returns with the fuel and says bluntly, 'I'll hold the funnel. You pour, slowly.'

I follow his instructions and attempt some small talk. 'How long have you been here?'

'All day.'

There is a long silence before he speaks again. 'Been here a few years. I like it.'

'What are the major crime problems out here in Manna Hill?'

'People who run out of petrol,' he says, deadpan.

I pay him $35 and we drive on towards Broken Hill.

As we cross the border into New South Wales we beep the horn and let out a cheer – we're a mere 1200 kilometres from Sydney but that doesn't seem so far. We are almost home.

Broken Hill has one of the best regional art galleries in the country, located in a magnificent double-storeyed stone and wood building. While we are in town, the Country Energy Prize, Australia's richest landscape prize, is being exhibited.

One of the finalists is Amanda Penrose Hart. She paints landscapes which often feature old caravans. I like her work. I make a few phone calls, discover she has a studio in Sofala, near Bathurst, and organise to meet her.

We motor on to Cobar, the only town we have visited twice. When we were here eight months ago, it was booming. My friend Roger Jackson, who owns a mining services business, had 240 employees on the books and was looking to employ even more. Now, he is down to 100 people and is fighting to save his business. The bust that nobody saw coming has arrived and houses that were commanding Sydney prices now struggle to get buyers, at any price.

After a few days listening to tales of mining gloom, we press on to Sofala.

Sofala sits on the Turon River and bills itself as 'Australia's oldest surviving gold town'. It once had 40 pubs. Only one remains and it is in danger of toppling over. There are a couple of cafés, a school and a lolly shop run by some gay guys. The place survives on local welfare cheques and tourists who pop in on Sundays.

The area surrounding the village is a poor person's paradise. During the mining boom, a hundred years ago, much of the land up and down the Turon River was gazetted. Those small half-acre blocks remain. People escaping the city, or escaping something, have managed to scrape enough money together from a divorce settlement or a compo payout to buy one of these rural retreats. Many of them live in old caravans.

We set up camp on a pretty patch of the Turon River, shaded by spindly river oaks, a few kilometres upstream from Sofala.

Amanda Penrose Hart owns a steep wooded 20-hectare block just outside Sofala. She's built a large corrugated shed high on a hill that serves as a both a studio and a bush retreat. Her paintings sit at one end of the shed lit by floodlights when she's working. A few single beds sit at the other end for her and her eight-year-old daughter, Teah, and anyone else who comes to stay. A makeshift kitchen has been built along one wall. Amanda and Teah divide their time between Sofala and Sydney.

The afternoon we arrive, Amanda is wearing bright red lipstick, Blundstone boots and paint-splattered trackie dacks. She has pale skin and dark hair and looks younger than her 46 years. She is a polite host. We're taken on a tour of her property and then offered brewed coffee and fancy orange chocolates. But her generous welcome doesn't conceal a certain social awkwardness. She readily admits she's more comfortable in front of a canvas than she is in conversation. 'It is a great excuse to be antisocial,' she says. 'You start painting and people just leave you alone. You can be as selfish as you like.'

Fortunately, our mutual interest in caravans gives us plenty to natter about. As we sit drinking coffee, we ask Amanda about her upcoming exhibition. In front of us are five or six paintings in various stages of development. The first thing I notice is how much paint she uses, layer upon layer that gives her work an almost 3-D feel. The paint must cost a bomb. 'They take months to dry,' she says.

The paintings all feature caravans; in some they're a tiny dot in a predominantly brown landscape, in others the vans dominate the picture. There are no fancy new Jaycos or Coromals, though. Amanda prefers Millards and Viscounts – worn out caravans that are an intrinsic part of Sofala's landscape; vans that were a dominant feature of her youth.

Amanda grew up in Brisbane. Her father was a merchant seaman who worked on a huge dredge, which was sent all over Queensland to pump sand from silted rivers. When he wasn't on the water, he liked to be in a caravan. 'When he came home he enjoyed the seclusion and womb-like structure of his caravan. It was as small as you could get, 12 or 14 foot compared to his enormous ship.'

Family holidays were always in the caravan, Mum, Dad and five kids. They would drive for days, from Brisbane to Cape Tribulation on one occasion, from Brisbane to Portsea in Victoria on another. On those holidays they would fish and read and draw and sleep, and drive and drive and drive. 'Dad was addicted to long drives.

'There were so many of us that we'd have to take an annexe and a tent as well. It must have been hell for my mum cooking for seven people in a tiny caravan.'

Weekends had a familiar routine. Each Sunday the family would go to church. Afterwards, the five kids would squeeze into the back of a white Holden station wagon and they would drive to nearby caravan parks to perve on other people's paraphernalia. 'Dad would drive around at about 2 kilometres an hour looking at people's ropes and eskies and annexes. We'd be all in the back rolling our eyes, bored witless. Now, I'm 46 years old and doing exactly the same thing — dragging my daughter around making her look at caravans.'

It's late in the afternoon and that daughter, Teah, has to be picked up from horse riding lessons. We arrange to catch up in a few hours' time for dinner at our campsite by the river.

We're very happy to do the food but advise Amanda that at our place it's a bring-your-own-chair arrangement.

Amanda and Teah arrive at the appointed hour, chairs under their arms. Joe plays with Teah, whose job it is to keep him away from stinging nettles, while Amanda, Lisa and I sit around a campfire with a bottle of wine. The caravan conversation continues.

Like many artists before her — John Olsen, Brett Whiteley and Russell Drysdale — Amanda Penrose Hart was drawn to Sofala and nearby Hill End. 'Others painted the old buildings, the scarred landscape or the dogs, but no one seemed to have noticed the caravans.' That might be a good thing; we could have had a Millard hanging in the National Gallery, shaped like Wendy Whiteley's backside.

Amanda began painting caravans about six years ago. 'It was a break from just straight landscape painting. I like caravans as structural objects. I like their monolithic shape. They have an unusual palette, quite discordant. They are not colours that you see anymore.'

Her caravan paintings became more popular than her regular landscape paintings.

In her first caravan exhibition, a doctor who lives in the upmarket Horizon building in Sydney bought one of her paintings.

He told Amanda he had grown up in a caravan park and his mother had struggled to put him through university. 'He said the painting made him feel very emotional.'

There's a certain irony about wealthy people with homes overlooking Sydney Harbour who are willing to pay thousands of dollars for a picture of a daggy old Millard caravan.

'They see the caravan, they don't see the landscape at all. It might be a great big painting, the van might be only a centimetre big and then they tell you a big, long story about their holidays in vans.'

'Perhaps your paintings represent a simpler life,' I suggest.

'I think they're the complete antithesis of what everyone's working toward: the big house, the industrial-sized fridge, the flat screen television. The caravan says: let's see if we can manage with tinned soup and the world's smallest fridge, as opposed to the fridge we have at home with an ice maker and a computer.'

Is that why so many Australians – thousands of us – get in a caravan every year and circumnavigate the country? Is stepping out of a linear life in the suburbs to drive a very big loop an attempt to return to a simpler life; to connect, somehow, with the land? Perhaps. It has certainly made Lisa and me think about the way we live and what we want for our son. We don't have all the answers, but sitting under the stars in Sofala one thing is clear; we're not after a bigger house in a better suburb.

There are obviously other reasons Australians pack up the caravan and do this trip. It has something to do with identity; with knowing who we are and where we come from. White Australia doesn't have the history, the architecture, the languages or the culture with which so many Europeans identify. Instead, we have the land and the space and the light; light that ruins our skin and makes us squint but is so spectacularly beautiful that artists like Amanda spend their lives trying to capture it. We have extraordinary scenery; those advertising executives at Qantas have been milking it for years. Their ads are soppy, they're unapologetically nationalistic, but they're what a lot of us see when we're in some dodgy backpackers in Asia with a bad belly and pining for home.

Perhaps some of the Aboriginal ways have rubbed off on us whitefellas; we feel the need to go walkabout, to take in the land, to move along those Aboriginal tracks-turned-droving routes-turned-dirt roads-turned-highways.

Our conversation with Amanda takes in all this and more, as we sit staring at the fire and pondering the place of the caravan in Australian culture. It gets late, we put Joe to bed and Teah grumbles that she wants to go home. But before leaving, Amanda shares with us a very personal story about the last time she and her father went looking at caravans, two years ago.

She was preparing for a new exhibition and needed ideas for a show. She and her father went on a tour of the caravan parks around Maroochydore. Forty years ago, he'd been the driver and she'd been the reluctant passenger. This time she was behind the wheel. 'We drove slowly up and down and he would point out things and I would take pictures of them. "Look at those gnomes," he'd say, or, "I can't believe they've spent that much on an annexe for an old van." He had a big beaming smile, he loved every minute of it. We drove around for ages. It was a lovely day and I had no sense that it would be his last outing.'

Amanda's father was suffering from bone cancer. That drive was the last one he would ever take.

'The last thing he saw of the outside world was a bloody caravan park.'

46

Our trip is almost over. We are less than a day's drive from home. In 11 months we have driven almost 50,000 kilometres and circumnavigated the continent. We've spent $11,000 on fuel. In that time we've killed a car, but not each other, and lost our son, but only once. I can now reverse a caravan, a skill that Lisa never quite mastered.

Our last stop is Mudgee. A group of Sydney mates joins us at the Mudgee Tourist and Van Resort to experience a slice of caravan life — some urbane gays, a few singles and a couple with two kids. They stay in three cabins next to our van. For them, this is slumming it. They're so soft.

Over wine and dinner we talk about our trip. 'What are the great themes of your book?' demands one of our literary friends.

I am not really sure. We set off to escape suburbia, avoid childcare and have an adventure. We've achieved those things and, in addition, we've discovered much about our country. It's as beautiful as those Qantas ads.

I still don't feel qualified to make any grand pronouncements on the nation and its people. I do, however, feel a new connection to the country. The Kimberley, the Tanami Desert and the Queensland channel country are no longer just places on a weather map.

A few weeks back we called Angus Emmott, after the big rains in Queensland. Nature Boy enthused about the floodwaters that had swept down through the channel country to 'Noonbah' and the immense flourishing of life he was witnessing. We've also been in touch with Chris and Brenda Garstone, our Aboriginal mates from Kununurra, who are coming to stay with their kids. They are on a big trip, over east, to see Brenda's showman father, Gary Miller, and his wife Nita Bell for the Bells' Christmas Carnival at Batemans Bay. We've spoken to Peter Lockyer, our generous host in Mulan, who was banned from the local shop for granting us an interview. He's not going back to the Tanami next year. He's been hustled out, he said, by the new administrators. Jo Woodward, the madam of Port Hedland, has also called – she's planning to open a new brothel with 10 rooms and then retire to be a full-time grandmother.

These people, and others, have linked us to the land. They've helped us see Australia.

The global financial crisis is starting to bite but I can't help thinking it's all just a sideshow. The two great issues facing Australia are the environment and the plight of Aborigines and neither gets the attention they deserve. These issues will still be with us long after commodity prices have recovered and Kevin Rudd's deficit is repaid.

One of the best things about the trip has been spending time with my family. Lisa and I have grown even closer. She is the world's most wonderful woman. And I've had the chance to watch Joe grow from a baby into a little boy. Surely there's a Slim Dusty ballad about a little boy who takes his first steps in a Longreach caravan park. Joe may not know the Wiggles but he can name more than a dozen native species. How is he going to fit in with other kids at daycare, we wonder, when his favourite pastime is looking at *The Slater Field Guide to Australian Birds*? 'Ark, Ark. Daddy,' we hear him chatter as he drifts off to sleep. 'Ark, Ark. Crow. Crow. Ark.'

Our journey into Caravanastan has been the adventure we had hoped for, although, it will be a while – possibly years – before we step foot inside another van. We can't wait to have a separate kitchen, bedroom and bathroom: a place to pee in peace.

In Tasmania, we heard an Aboriginal woman on the radio who said that life was about 'stories, family and country'. And so it is for us. Our little family has travelled around Oz and returned with a Volvo full of yarns.

As we make our way back to Sydney, we think not only about what we've done, but about what awaits us in our spectacular city. I recall the cheeky words of the former Prime Minister, Paul Keating, who once said: 'If you're not living in Sydney you're camping out.'

Lisa turns to me, grinning, and says, 'PK just didn't understand the value of camping out.'

Acknowledgments

Many thanks to the following people: Mike Ward – who showed me the seedy side of Tassie and then nursed me afterwards; Guy Fitzhardinge – a wily old fox who knows this land; Ashley Hay – the adorer of flora; Deborah Callaghan – in any blue in any situation at any time, I bags her on my side; Nick Coakley and Lucian Pearce – 'Help! I'm rooted. My computer won't start'; Richard Coleman – the legal beagle; Peter Lockyer – our saviour in Mulan; Frank Robson and Leisa Scott – sailing and sun in the Whitsundays; Roger Jackson and Robyn Aldermann – for the boom and the bust; Jeff and Michelle Ticehurst – for a night in Venice; Beck and Damien Hepburn – who thought we'd never leave; Judith Whelan – who thought I'd never come back; Nikki Christer – who thought I'd never finish; Brandon VanOver – who knows his way around a non-defining clause; Desney King – who knows how to spell Nullarbor; Angus and Karen Emmott – for helping us to appreciate boring stuff; Odette Odisho – for maps at short notice; Michael Fitzjames – for some class in a sea of crass; Ray Leggott and Chris Kirby – for a cottage by a stream; Kirsti Melville and Jamie Nelson – for juicy lemons, good wine and a real bed; Joe and Bev Dennis – for little Joe's introduction to shearing; Nicolette Bearup – for a barrister's eye at mates rates; Helen and David Bearup – for unending support and for taking my side over my little sister in the tussle for the holiday house (sucked in Jenny); Marilyn Tabatznik – for pulling us in as the tide went out; Terry Ryan – for fixing lights, drilling holes and moving furniture, again, and for generally being calm.

Special thanks to Granna Joan Dennis, who arrived when all seemed doomed, like Supergran, to save the day and then, later, for morphing into Grammar Joan. And to Steve Offner, for the many hours he spent massaging words and ideas.

And finally, of course, to Lisa. As my father said, there are two reasons this book happened and they are both Lisa Upton.